THE LAST TRIAL OF
T. BOONE PICKENS

THE LAST TRIAL OF
T. BOONE PICKENS

CHRYSTA CASTAÑEDA
& LOREN C. STEFFY

STONEY CREEK PUBLISHING
www.stoneycreekpublishing.com

 Published by
Stoney Creek Publishing
stoneycreekpublishing.com

Copyright © 2020 Chrysta Castañeda and Loren C. Steffy
Distributed by Texas A&M University Press

ISBN: 978-1-7340822-0-3
ISBN (ebook): 978-1-7340822-1-0
Library of Congress: 2019919052

Cover & interior design by Monica Thomas for
TLC Book Design, *TLCBookDesign.com*

Cover image of T. Boone Pickens by Melissa Phillip/©Houston Chronicle.
Used with permission. Images from AdobeStock.com: Oil Extraction © Prussia Art; Gavel and Scales of Justice © Andrey Popov; Star of Texas © Melanie

Printed in the United States

"Most people, both in business and in life, surrender. As a result, they fall short of their dreams, opportunities, and potential. I learned that if you never give up, if you push through the resistance and keep driving for what you want, you will ultimately achieve rewards beyond any you had hoped for. Because down deep, just beyond the hard, tough spot we all have found ourselves in, there awaits the opportunity to become stronger, more successful, and more fulfilled than you have imagined. Never, never, never give up."

T. Boone Pickens,
The First Billion Is the Hardest

CONTENTS

PART ONE   **The Red Bull** 1

    CHAPTER 1   "Don't Pay Her" 3

    CHAPTER 2   The Legend of T. Boone Pickens 17

    CHAPTER 3   "The Chainsaw" 37

    CHAPTER 4   The Red Bull Prospect 52

    CHAPTER 5   The Lawsuit 60

    CHAPTER 6   "The Wrong Guy to Eliminate" 69

    CHAPTER 7   Lingering Doubts 83

PART TWO   **The Trial Begins** 95

    CHAPTER 8   Morning in Monahans 97

    CHAPTER 9   Prepping Pickens 105

    CHAPTER 10   Day One 116

    CHAPTER 11   The "Guidances" 124

    CHAPTER 12   Picking the Jury 128

    CHAPTER 13   A Tough Act to Follow 136

    CHAPTER 14   My Turn 145

    CHAPTER 15   Growing Frustration 153

    CHAPTER 16   "We Are Zombies" 164

PART THREE   **Pickens Takes the Stand**................................**169**

CHAPTER 17   "The Biggest Prospect Ever" 171

CHAPTER 18   From Hell to Breakfast................................186

CHAPTER 19   Pickens Versus the Defense........................193

CHAPTER 20   "Don't Rush the Monkey"............................202

CHAPTER 21   "You're Going to Get Yours!".......................208

CHAPTER 22   "Blinders On" 212

CHAPTER 23   "Your Client Is Not Well" 223

CHAPTER 24   The Power of a Penny 229

CHAPTER 25   "No Amendments Required" 242

CHAPTER 26   Closing Arguments......................................249

CHAPTER 27   All or Nothing..270

CHAPTER 28   "Show Up Early. Work Hard. Stay Late."....279

Epilogue...289

Acknowledgments.....................................294

A Note on Sources.....................................297

Index...299

Part One

THE RED BULL

Chapter 1

"DON'T PAY HER"

I took a deep breath as the elevator doors rolled open to reveal the lobby of the Best Western Swiss Chalet. I'd long since gotten over the irony of the name. The Swiss Chalet was located in the most un-Switzerland-like spot on earth. Pecos, Texas, is so far west that even people in places such as Lubbock and Odessa refer to it as "way out there." Sitting on the eastern edge of the Chihuahuan Desert, tucked under the arm of New Mexico, its barren vistas, tumbleweeds, and blazing heat reinforce almost every Hollywood stereotype of Texas.

The lobby décor, with its Alpine photos and display cases jammed with beer steins, provided a jarring contrast to the hardscrabble prairie and trucks carrying massive drilling equipment zipping by on the freeway just outside the front door. Pecos, long known mostly as a stop for weary travelers making their way along Interstate 20, was enjoying an unprecedented oil boom. And the Swiss Chalet offered the best lodging in town. Dozens of other mid-range hotels—Holiday Inn Express, LaQuinta, Hampton Inn—had sprung up to house an expanding workforce that grew daily as hydraulic fracturing unlocked new oil deposits in shale rock thousands of feet below the sun-baked West Texas dirt.

For decades, the Permian Basin—an oil-rich area that stretches from Midland to eastern New Mexico—has endured the economic undulations of boom and bust that define the energy economy. By the mid-2000s, however, many thought the Permian had finally petered out. Then, just a few years later, hydraulic fracturing—or fracking—combined with horizontal drilling techniques, broke open vast new underground reserves inside shale formations thousands of feet underground. By 2016, the Permian was on the verge of becoming the world's most prolific oil and gas field, rivaling the massive Ghawar Field of Saudi Arabia. Oil workers came from hundreds of miles away, drawn by the six-figure paychecks for drillers, truck drivers, and roughnecks, a vast nomadic workforce that tended to the thousands of new wells puncturing the Permian. Hotels couldn't be constructed fast enough, and even with the recent building boom, there still weren't enough beds in town. We'd booked our rooms at the Swiss Chalet, twenty in all, months in advance and were lucky to get them.

The scene was a far cry from my office in the West End of Dallas, a historic district adjacent to the downtown sky-scrapers. As a lawyer who specializes in fights over oil and gas rights, I'd spent my fair share of time in dusty little towns in the middle of nowhere. Some of them made Pecos look like a thriving metropolis. There's an old industry saying that oil isn't found in pretty places, and that's mostly true. It's relegated to deserts and badlands and seabeds deep below the surface of the unrelenting oceans. And when drilling deals in those remote areas go bad, when the partners get into a dispute they can't resolve, they call me.

That's how I wound up in the Swiss Chalet. This, however, was no ordinary dispute. I was the lead trial lawyer representing T. Boone Pickens, an industry legend who had spent decades drilling for oil and gas around the world before becoming the dean of the corporate takeover game in the 1980s. He'd lost his first fortune in the 1990s, then built a new and much bigger one in the 2000s. He'd even become a social media sensation in his eighties. Now, he was suing a group of companies that he claimed had cut him out of a lucrative oil deal in the Permian.

The stakes, in other words, couldn't be higher. This realization set in anew as I stepped out of the elevator and braced for the conversation I was about to have with my famous client in the conference room just around the corner. It was early evening, and it had been a long slog at the courthouse. The trial was in its fourth day, and we'd experimented with an unusual tactic of calling a hostile defense witness to open our case. It was a risky move, and I still had another full day's worth of work waiting for me back in my room that I'd have to finish before bedtime. Such is the life of a trial lawyer. When you're in court, a typical trial day is wake up at 4:00 a.m., sleep at midnight, repeat.

Rarely does dramatic testimony in court energize the proceedings, like you see on television. Those moments are few and far between—if they happen at all. Even a crucial turning point in a trial might seem dull to those watching it, unless they are a lawyer or someone directly involved in the case. Most of the time is spent on more mundane matters, a daily tedium of preparation and review. It's vital for victory, but it's also exhausting.

We had been holed up at the Swiss Chalet for about a week— with several more weeks to go—and I was worried. Trying business cases before a jury is always challenging. You're dealing with complex topics that can be difficult to explain. Oil and gas cases typically involve a combination of arcane geological and engineering terms and convoluted financial analysis—fractional interests, overriding royalties, pay zones, decline curves, probabilistic modeling. It isn't easy stuff for me to get through, and I have degrees in law and engineering.

One of the routine but vitally important matters I had to deal with was keeping my client informed about how the trial was going while I simultaneously planned for the next day. In this case, it was even more crucial. Pickens may have been a billionaire, but he didn't believe in leaving details to others—especially not if they affected his fortune. He was absorbed in every aspect of the case and he had his own views on all of them. At eighty-eight, he was mentally sharp and didn't hesitate to share his opinions. He also didn't suffer fools.

Dozens of reporters over the years had learned the hard way about the perils of posing a stupid question to Pickens. Sometimes, he would mark up their stories and send them back. Other times, he would simply counter their questions with one of his own—especially if the exchange was on live television. He was quick on his feet and his mind was always three steps ahead of everyone else's.

He had sharpened his skills during the corporate takeover battles of the 1980s. He'd been on the cover of *Time* magazine, and for a while had been, if not a household name, at least a business celebrity. He knew his way around an interview. He'd had his share of legal disputes, of course, including a contentious divorce from his second wife in which they battled over, among other things, custody of their beloved Papillon dog. But most of his business battles were settled out of court. He'd never been involved in a trial like this one, although he was comfortable in the limelight. He impressed me with his poise in public forums, which made my job both easier and more difficult at the same time, because he had his own ideas about what to say and do.

He was a great resource in developing the case and he had a knack for saying what the jury would want to hear. He also let me know right off the bat that he intended to sit through the entire trial, glued to my side, offering observations and critiques when he felt they were due.

The problem was, his time and attention to the details of the trial came at the cost of my time, which already was in critically short supply. I had to prepare comprehensive outlines of questions and assemble the documents we needed to examine the witnesses who would take the stand the next day and every day until we were finished. Normally, for a case this size, the lead trial attorney would leave most of that work to other lawyers, but I am not typical. Like Pickens, I do things differently.

No one, not even Pickens, realized how big the Permian dispute was when it started. To be honest, that's the only reason he hired me to represent him. Pickens' right-hand man would tell me later that they would never have chosen a solo practitioner if they had known how much money was at stake in the matter. When they picked me, I didn't have a large staff or junior partners working for me like when I'd been a partner with a big law firm. While I did have other lawyers helping me with this trial, I had assembled them ad hoc after Pickens' in-house attorney and I realized we wouldn't reach a settlement and were headed for the courthouse.

All of which meant that I hadn't worked with most of the other members of my team for more than a few months leading up to the trial, and I had a lot riding on the outcome. I'd formed my own law firm a few years earlier, and this was the first major case I'd accepted. A victory for Pickens would cement my fledgling firm's credibility. I couldn't leave anything to chance, especially not the intensive preparation required to cross examine the defense witnesses effectively. The other lawyers on the team didn't have as much experience as I did with oil and gas issues, and at the moment, I was worried about how things were going.

I tried to put all these thoughts out of my head and focus on Pickens as I headed to the conference room where he and the rest of the team were waiting. We'd scheduled a meeting for the nearly twenty people on our trial team every day after court recessed so that we could review what had happened and discuss the plan for the next day. It was a large group to keep happy and engaged. That was part of being the lead lawyer, too—a little bit of cheerleading, motivational speaking, maybe even some impromptu therapy.

Entering the room, I braced myself for what I knew would be a longer conversation than I had time for. At the moment, our unconventional tactic of leading with a hostile witness was not succeeding. We needed to do better.

We had already presented our opening arguments that laid out the key points of the case. Pickens and his company, Mesa Petroleum Partners, had entered into an agreement in 2007 with other companies that gave Pickens a 15 percent stake in a drilling deal near Pecos known as the "Red Bull." The parties set out to acquire enough oil and gas leases to be able to drill wells in the geologic formation called the Delaware Basin, which is technically a "sub-basin" of the Permian. When the well results came in, the group hoped they would prove that the area was a good place to produce massive quantities of oil, driving up the value of the investment. Pickens agreed to help pay for the costs of acquiring the leases and drilling the wells, and in exchange, he would get a 15 percent ownership interest, as well as 15 percent of any profits. At the time the deal was signed, the Permian seemed to have played out. Its production was declining, and the Red Bull looked like it might be a sickly cow. But fracking reversed the region's fortunes, and more importantly for us, led to a key discovery in the Red Bull two years after the deal was signed. By the time of the trial in 2016, the Red Bull Prospect we were arguing over had become some of the most sought-after oil and gas acreage in the entire Permian, if not the country.

That's why, as we contended in our opening statements to the jury, the other partners decided to cut Pickens out of the deal. He'd refused to give up his stake unless they paid him, and they wouldn't pay what he was asking. When he refused to sell to them in 2009, they had simply decided that Pickens had "opted out" of future participation in the deal and claimed his share for themselves. He hadn't even known they'd taken it from him. The other side argued that Pickens had said he wanted out, and that he only changed his mind after the value of the deal soared. Pickens and I believed that they couldn't back up their claims. They certainly didn't have the only evidence that mattered in my mind: a written document signed by Pickens agreeing to sign over his ownership interest to them.

Typically, you want to start a case like this with friendly witnesses. That way you can set the scene and explain your side to the jury before the other side gets its say. But after several intense strategy sessions with Pickens and my legal team, we decided to call one of the defendants' top executives first. We had to be able to explain key events in the Red Bull deal, but Pickens and his deputies couldn't provide them because the details had been kept from them. The Red Bull contracts didn't give the defendants much wiggle room, and we believed they had no credible explanation for how they'd taken Pickens' share of the deal, so we hoped that first calling one of their executives to testify was a risk that would pay off.

It seemed like a good strategy, but it wasn't working at the moment. Every few minutes, the defense lawyers interrupted, objecting to a question from my co-counsel, Mike Lynn. We'd all trundle up to the bench for long conferences with the judge, hashing out whatever issue the defense raised, while the jurors sat silently, listening to the indecipherable murmuring coming from the huddle at the front of the court. When we returned to our respective sides of the room, Mike would try to pick up his questioning, only to be interrupted and pulled into another bench conference. The defense lawyers objected so many times that we lost all momentum. It was clear from looking at their faces that the jurors didn't understand what was going on and they were getting annoyed.

Few jurors are familiar with the legal process. If they have an expectation about trials, it comes from television shows, where events zip along, testimony is riveting, and telegenic actors resolve everything neatly in an hour. Reality is far more painstaking and far less pretty. It's important to keep jurors engaged and attentive. If they start to feel overwhelmed or confused by the proceedings, you can lose them. The trial was just getting underway, and I worried we already were missing the mark.

That evening, everybody in the Swiss Chalet conference room could feel that Mesa wasn't winning. The rest of my team was sitting in the black vinyl chairs surrounding a wooden table in the center of the windowless space. The front of the room was dominated by a large, flat-panel television that sat silent. Above it, an ornate clock ticked out minute-by-minute reminders of how time was slipping away while we all still had too much to do. For some reason, the conference room was the one place in the hotel that didn't follow the Alpine theme. The walls were lined with western prints, cheap renditions of originals by famous artists like Howard Terpning and Frederic

Remington. Some of the real ones adorned the walls of Pickens' house at his 65,000-acre Mesa Vista Ranch in the Texas Panhandle almost four hundred miles away.

Pickens was on the left side of the table, still wearing his dark gray suit from court. As always, he'd saved the seat next to him for me. He wanted me to sit close because his hearing was failing and he wanted to listen to what I had to say about our day in court. Pickens' hair was gray and thinning, and he had developed more pronounced jowls in recent years, but his eyes were still a piercing blue. A longtime fitness and health buff, he remained trim from working out six days a week. When Barack Obama was president, pictures of his workout leaked to the press. Pickens, a staunch Republican, declared the presidential routine "pitiful" and challenged Obama, who was more than thirty years his junior, to try his hour-long cardio regimen instead.

Pickens started calling the shots as soon as I sat down. A geologist by training, he had an innate understanding of this oil deal and knew how he wanted to establish key talking points with the jury. But he wasn't a lawyer, and he didn't know how to examine a witness. This, too, is something TV makes look easy. It isn't. As a trial lawyer, you devote years to learning how to approach witnesses and coax pertinent information out of them. You can spend your entire career refining and perfecting the skill.

Most importantly, you must set aside hundreds of hours to study the tiniest details of every document and each bit of data. You need all of the facts at your disposal to cross examine witnesses. Only by achieving such a high level of understanding can you weave the tapestry of the story and distill it into a handful of concepts that will persuade the jurors. Make no mistake: mastery of the subject matter is the sole way to win a trial of this magnitude.

We all knew Pickens was used to being the smartest guy in the room—in almost any room, for that matter—and he understood more about oil and gas than all of us combined, including his own geologists. But that wouldn't be enough to convince a jury that Pickens was right in claiming that he had been illicitly cut out of the Red Bull deal. Pickens had run his own companies since 1956. While he had a congenial side, and he encouraged his subordinates to challenge him, he was also used to having the last word. If he insisted on something, his employees ultimately acquiesced. Although he'd spent years battling public opinion against his persona as a "corporate raider," he could dismiss that bad press as simply uninformed, or he could conversely lash out at the reporter. But jurors had power that Pickens couldn't control. They wouldn't take his views on faith and they couldn't be bullied. In other words, the twelve people in the jury box were something alien to a successful businessman like T. Boone Pickens. They didn't have to listen to him, didn't have to believe him, and didn't have to do what he said just because he said it. He would need to persuade them, not through the force of his personality, but through the merits of his testimony and his lawyers' arguments. If the jurors disagreed, Pickens probably wouldn't get another try.

Pickens' main beef that evening in the conference room was that my co-counsel, Mike Lynn, should be asking different questions. He wanted Mike to zero in on the geology of the drilling prospect, while Mike's instincts were to focus on big concepts like greed, lying, and cheating. The geological arguments Pickens was running through were not Mike's area of expertise, and the executive on the stand wasn't the witness to use them on.

I'd recommended that Pickens hire Mike's firm to support me during the trial not because of its expertise with geology or oil and gas law, but because Mike had built a formidable team of trial lawyers. His firm, Lynn Pinker Cox & Hurst, had won a $500 million verdict for a pipeline company a couple of years before based on a novel legal theory. The firm also had a stable of trained attorneys and paralegals who could handle all of the tasks a big trial requires. I would supply the leadership, the detailed knowledge, and the overall vision, but my small staff and I certainly couldn't deliver all of the time and personnel the Red Bull case demanded.

Mike listened politely as Pickens repeated the same information about the geology and the oil reserves at the heart of the dispute. Mike was trying to understand what Pickens wanted to do, but Pickens was becoming frustrated, and Mike wasn't getting any more adept with the technical points Pickens wanted him to make. Even worse, those points weren't the ones we needed to emphasize with the defendant's CEO anyway. We were all wasting time and I had to get this train back on track.

I'd barely stepped into the room to start the meeting and already the conversation was spinning out of control. One other thing about Pickens: he wasn't used to being corralled. When he spoke, he was accustomed to dominating the room until he had decided he was done. I intervened gently at first, growing more insistent as Pickens kept pressing his points. We had a lot of work to do, and we needed to focus. I told Pickens I obviously was interested in any opinion he had about the case but that arguing about the geological details at this stage was senseless. We needed to concentrate on the terms of the deal because the defendant's CEO wasn't going to admit anything about the geological points Pickens wanted to score. When Mike managed to get a question out without the endless interruptions from the defense, the CEO simply claimed ignorance. "You'll need to talk to another witness about that," had been his stock answer of the day.

Clearly, the defense team believed claiming ignorance was better than having the CEO admit the company knowingly took Pickens' interest in the deal without his written consent. He certainly wasn't going to voluntarily admit responsibility for breaching the deal no matter how much Pickens wanted him to. And, he wasn't going to volunteer key evidence about the geology that would help us establish how much the deal was worth.

I tried to explain all this, but Pickens kept insisting that Mike should ask questions about geology. I shook my head vigorously, which didn't help the headache I could feel rising from the base of my neck. I stressed—again—that this wasn't the witness with whom we needed to make those points. We would state our case, I told him, but we would do it when the time was right. And that time was not now.

Pickens grew more agitated. The tension in the room was as thick as a blanket but I couldn't back down. I knew I was right. We had to let Mike focus on what he needed to accomplish— laying out key events in the Red Bull deal—and then move on.

As I pressed my argument with Pickens, the weight of the moment hit me. At fifty-three, I was thirty-five years younger than my big-name client. I was still in high school in Kansas when he commanded national headlines with his famous hostile takeover bid for Gulf Oil. He had brought corporate titans to their knees. He'd tried to shake up the entire structure of Japanese business. He'd met with presidents and governors. He was a king maker in Republican politics, especially in Texas. But none of that mattered. He was paying me to win this case, to be the general in this war, and he could either listen to me or fire me and find somebody else.

The more I told him no, the more frustrated he became. Finally, he'd had enough: "Stop shaking your head at me!" he shouted. "Don't argue with me! You don't know what you are talking about! I've been in the business for sixty years! You will listen to me and you will do what I say!"

I stopped talking and just looked at him. How do you avoid telling your billionaire client, the only one you have at the moment because his case takes your entire focus, to shove it? How do you tell him you aren't going to be talked to that way? How do you tell him that you, too, have decades of experience at your job, and you, too, know what you're doing? How do you tell him those things when you are a woman in what, even in 2016, remains firmly a man's world? I could feel my face flush. Trial pressures are one thing. Verbal attacks from a client are another. I knew that anything I might say could be disastrous. And I still wanted to win the damn thing, because no matter how petulant or condescending my client was being at the moment, I believed in him. I believed what he had trouble believing himself: that he, the billionaire energy tycoon, the master dealmaker, had been snookered in the biggest oil deal of his life. A victory for a high-profile plaintiff like Pickens could not only burnish his image and recoup the millions he was owed, but it could also send a message to those who might in the future try to take advantage of others who had far less expertise. Besides, despite the fact that he could be cantankerous and that our political views were polar opposites, I genuinely liked him, and I knew he liked me. I wanted to help him. We could win this case if he would just let me right the ship.

I said nothing. I think in that moment I literally bit my lip. Then, I stood up calmly and turned toward the door. Over my shoulder, I could hear Pickens still shouting: "Turn around and sit down! Don't you dare leave this room!" He didn't say "young lady," but he might as well have.

I was in the doorway, and I looked back over my shoulder. I was angry, but I managed to say, with only a slight quaver in my voice, "I'm going to get some water." Then, I walked out.

The hotel had a water dispenser at the far end of the lobby, beyond the tables and chairs where we ate our complimentary breakfast every morning. I filled a plastic tumbler and took a long drink, hoping it would extinguish my anger and help me focus. As I swallowed, I made a decision. I wasn't going to back down on my point, and I also wasn't going to quit the team. Pickens could fire me, but I wasn't walking away. We were in this together until the end as far as I was concerned. I walked straight across the lobby and into the conference room. We'd see, I thought, if Pickens felt the same way.

I was only gone for two or three minutes, but by walking out, I'd reset the tone. Everyone was calmer now, including Pickens. He even looked a little remorseful. "I'm sorry," he said as I sat down. I apologized too. He chuckled a bit. I reminded him of one of his daughters, he said. I knew he was referring to Lizzy. Of his five children, she was the only one who could speak her mind and have him listen. They, too, had had some heated exchanges, he said. "We're friends, right?" he asked me.

I assured him we were. We got back to the discussion at hand, and things went smoothly for the rest of the meeting.

Afterwards, as we were packing up and after Pickens had left the room, one of my jury researchers pulled me aside. Pickens had been livid that I walked out on him, she said. He'd turned to his accountant and barked: "Don't you pay her for a single minute that she is out of this room!"

Later, when we looked back on the incident, Pickens and I agreed that it may have been the best three minutes I've ever worked for free.

Chapter 2

THE LEGEND OF
T. BOONE PICKENS

Our Cadillac Escalade pulled up to a white clapboard house at 217 North Kelker—or at least that's what the signpost out front said. In reality, Kelker Street was more than 280 miles to the northeast, in Holdenville, Oklahoma. But T. Boone Pickens had picked up his childhood home and moved it here, in the middle of his hundred-square-mile Mesa Vista Ranch in the Texas Panhandle. And he'd plunked the street sign down in front of the place as if to punctuate the move.

Pickens stepped gingerly from the front seat of the Escalade and, with the help of a walker, began making his way across the sidewalk and up the steps that he had hopped over easily as a child. In front of the house, a slab of concrete, liberated from the sidewalk in Holdenville, marked where the nine-year-old Thomas Boone Pickens, Jr., had scrawled his name in the freshly poured cement in 1939. As a boy, he hated the name "Boone," because none of his classmates pronounced it right. He wanted to go by "Tom," but that was his father's name. "Tom's already gone," his mother, Grace, told him. "Boone's the only name left for you."

When he was in his eighties, Pickens had the home disassembled and moved, piece by piece, to the ranch, where he restored it to the way it looked when he was a boy growing up halfway between Oklahoma City and the Arkansas border. Now, it was a regular stop when he gave tours of the Mesa Vista. He settled into a red upholstered chair just inside the door and directed our attention to a plate rack in the kitchen. Centered amid the white dishes, a tiny yellow divided plate stands out. It's adorned with two ducks, a bib-wearing cat, and a dog holding a spoon. That, Pickens told us, was his first plate.

The two-bedroom house was built by Pickens' grandfather, William Molonson. Pickens' father had worked as a landman for Phillips Petroleum, getting property owners to sign leases that allowed the company to drill for oil. Pickens' parents moved to the home after they married in 1923. He was born five years later and would spend the first sixteen years of his life in the house. He liked to say that his birth was a medical miracle, because he was the first baby born by Cesarean section in Holdenville. "The doctor had never done one before," he said. He still seemed proud of that. Was it the thrill of being first, or the fact that he had survived against what were probably dangerous odds? I decided it may have been both. Pickens' competitive edge came from somewhere. Maybe it was indelibly ingrained at the moment of his first breath. But he was also a survivor, persevering over a long career of stunning successes and embarrassing failures.

Sitting in the chair in his boyhood living room, Pickens was relaxed, and the stories came easily to him. It was March 2018, just two months before his ninetieth birthday, and he'd had a series of strokes that made communicating difficult. But in that moment, as the childhood memories flooded back, he was as lucid as I'd remembered him during the Red Bull trial in Pecos two years earlier.

Despite mounting health issues, Pickens still made the flight from his Dallas home to the ranch most weekends—although his private jet had been sold and replaced by a rented turboprop—and he liked to bring people with him. He'd invited me to accompany him on this trip, along with my co-author, who was writing about Pickens for *Texas Monthly*. A couple of other men in Pickens' orbit joined us, including Jay Rosser, Pickens' public relations chief.

A few months earlier Pickens had put the whole property up for sale with an asking price of $250 million—the country's most expensive piece of real estate on the market that year. With his failing eyesight and declining mobility, he could no longer enjoy the property as he once did, and he decided to sell in part to help fund his philanthropic efforts.

The ranch, his refuge since he began assembling the parcels of land to amass it in the early 1970s, is staggering in its magnitude. It spans an area more than twice the size of San Francisco. Some two hundred miles of roads crisscross its scrubby plains. It has twenty-four full-time employees and its own fleet of five fire trucks. Eight employees and their families live there full time. Pickens paid for their children—many of whom were born on the ranch—to attend his alma mater, Oklahoma State University. Pickens and his well-heeled visitors can enjoy a private air strip, capable, as he liked to note, of landing Air Force One. (George W. Bush was one of many high-ranking guests over the years.) A two-hole golf course provides entertainment. To highlight it all, Pickens built twenty-four miles of water features by tapping into the Ogallala aquifer that runs underneath the property. Later that day during our tour, I stopped to take pictures of the spring-fed swimming pool and the Roman aqueduct nearby.

Pickens once proposed pumping the water out, sending it through a pipeline, and selling it to cities such as Dallas and San Antonio. His proposal prompted an outcry from surrounding landowners and would have required a billion dollars of capital. Pickens' dreams tended to come with nine zeroes. A later plan to build a wind farm on the ranch had the same price tag, and like the water deal, it never materialized.

The water creates a series of more than twenty lakes on the property. Overlooking one of them, Pickens built an 11,500-square-foot Tuscan-style house for his fourth wife, Madeleine, whom he married in 2005. In the mid-2000s, he was at the peak of his wealth, flush with trading profits from his hedge fund, BP Capital. He spent some of those gains on the mansion: the front door came from one of Bing Crosby's houses, and a spiral staircase inside is lined with imported French stone. After he and his wife divorced in 2013, he didn't spend much time at that house. He preferred the 25,000-square-foot lodge several miles away. It could comfortably accommodate dozens of guests and features a huge board room to host foreign dignitaries, fellow executives, and celebrities. The dining area alone has nearly as much square footage as my entire home. That weekend, I slept in the Reagan bedroom, where the former President and First Lady had stayed.

The water features on Mesa Vista serve a purpose beyond adding to the landscape's beauty. Pickens developed them to create what many sportsmen consider the world's best quail-hunting habitat. He spent years cultivating the native grasses to provide ground cover amid the open plains and sweeping vistas that line the horizon. I am not a hunter and we didn't do any quail hunting that weekend, but we did do a little skeet shooting. My co-author says I put the other male guests to shame even though I'd never fired a shotgun before. I simply followed the ranch foreman's instructions on how to shoot.

We left Pickens' transplanted boyhood home to rumble along the dirt roads. Pickens sat in the front passenger seat of the Escalade and I was in the back, behind the driver, his ranch foreman. Pickens loved giving tours, and he pointed out the ponds that hosted a variety of migrating ducks— canvasbacks, mallards, common mergansers. They were beautiful, abundant, and seemed to enjoy the habitat.

We stopped at the 4,500-square-foot kennel, where Pickens kept nearly four dozen hunting dogs. As we stepped out of the vehicle, he quipped, "Chrysta, you know you're rich when your dog kennel is bigger than most people's houses and has air conditioning." Despite his humor, I could see the sadness in his eyes that in almost ninety years had witnessed both lean times and tremendous fortune. "This ranch couldn't be more T. Boone Pickens," I said at one point. "It's everything you love." He nodded but didn't reply.

Mesa Vista embodied everything Pickens cherished, everything he could dream of, and everything he wanted. It was an integral part of him. As I looked at the elderly man staring out the window of the Escalade, I tried to reconcile the image with that of the fierce corporate raider I'd read about three decades earlier. In some circles, especially among employees who lost their jobs as companies cut costs to thwart his takeover bids, Pickens is still considered a heartless predator. Perhaps he'd mellowed in later years, or perhaps there was a side they couldn't see. I came to know Pickens late in his life, when he was well into his eighties, and by then, he had softer edges. In any case, I identified with his early life, because he and I both had a humble start in the mid-American prairielands. We shared a pragmatism, a faith that effort produces results, and a certain hardheadedness that I believe many Midwesterners share. Visiting his Holdenville house that day on the ranch reinforced my belief that we came from similar roots.

Pickens' father sold the house in the real Holdenville in 1944 and moved the family to Amarillo, in the Texas Panhandle. After high school, Pickens got a basketball scholarship to Texas A&M University. A&M didn't renew his $25 monthly scholarship after his first year, prompting him to transfer to Oklahoma State (then known as Oklahoma A&M). Decades later, after becoming a billionaire, he donated more than $600 million to the school and its football team. Texas A&M's short-sightedness has been called the costliest cut in NCAA history.

Leaving the Holdenville house and kennel complex behind, the Escalade drove eastward, toward the more barren sections of the ranch. The next stop was Pickens' oil wells. He'd started drilling them a few years earlier, and more than fifty dotted the property by the time of our visit. This was a new venture for him. Despite his sixty years in the business, he'd never participated in a drilling deal in which he was also the landowner. The rig supervisor told me Pickens made frequent visits, checking on the wells' progress. They aren't as successful as those in the Red Bull, but as Pickens saw it, it was something of a return to his roots. "I'm back now to what I always did," he said, as we stopped at one of the rigs. "I've gone clean back around the corner."

As we drove, my mind drifted to years past. When had I first heard of Pickens? As an avid newspaper reader since my teens, I'd followed his exploits back when he was making headlines. I remembered that he came up in business classes I took in college some thirty years earlier, when the corporate raider paradigm was new.

Our paths had crossed several times over the ensuing decades. Soon after earning a degree in industrial engineering in 1985, I'd been hired by Arthur Andersen Consulting (which is now Accenture) to help design software systems for oil and gas companies. In my first deployment for them, Andersen sent me to Mesa Petroleum, the company Pickens founded in 1956. I was assigned to develop computer systems that would manage the complex partnership structure that Mesa had adopted.

I didn't meet Pickens; I worked in a different office in downtown Dallas. But the excitement of being even remotely connected with such a famous businessman was heady stuff, especially for a lowly computer programmer on loan to the company. Pickens never knew it, but this was actually my first encounter with him, or at least his organization.

Over the years, I learned more about him. Pickens rewrote his autobiography three times, but the early part of the story remained unchanged. He started his career at Phillips Petroleum in Amarillo, but he only lasted a few years. He bristled at the staid corporate bureaucracy and executives' unwillingness to consider new ideas. The frustration got to be too much, and he quit and set out on his own. He was twenty-six years old and would later claim he was the youngest independent geologist in the Texas Panhandle.[1]

His life as an independent oilman didn't start out glamorously. He rattled around the dusty plains of West Texas in a 1955 Ford station wagon, consulting at well sites for seventy-five dollars a day. He often slept in his car and shaved at gas stations. Heading into the 1960s, the independent petroleum industry was facing tough times. Since the days of Spindletop, the site in East Texas where the modern energy industry was born, oil companies had shared the same interests regardless of their size. But by the 1960s, the majors began looking for oil abroad, and imports were rising. The biggest players used their lobbying power in Washington to adopt tax rules and other provisions that favored their new business model at the expense of independent producers. As a result, as oil imports rose, domestic production declined. Another oil industry legend, Michel Halbouty, once estimated that by 1964, the number of independent producers in the United States had fallen by 60 percent in just seven years, from thirty thousand to just twelve thousand.[2]

Despite the industry challenges, Pickens managed to get a few investors behind him and form a company called Petroleum Exploration Inc., or PEI. He cobbled together drilling prospects in the Panhandle and by 1964 he had twenty-three employees. He took the company public, changing its name to Mesa Petroleum, after the vistas of the Panhandle. Four years later, Mesa was a $6 million company, but the growth wasn't fast enough for Pickens. He knew that for Mesa to hold its own it had to get bigger quickly. This meant it either needed a big discovery or a big acquisition. Drilling was expensive and risky, so he decided to look for a deal.

Hugoton Production Company was based in my home state of Kansas, in Garden City. It had substantial acreage in the Hugoton Field, then the largest gas reserves in the United States. The company was fifteen times bigger than Mesa, but it wasn't growing. It had exactly what Pickens was looking for—a large block of reserves that was poorly managed. When Hugoton refused Pickens' offer to buy the company, he did something that was a rarity in the energy business in those days: he launched a takeover against the wishes of the company's management. The strategy would become his calling card two decades later.

He amassed stock in Hugoton, eventually controlling 28 percent of the outstanding shares, then made an offer to the other shareholders to buy the rest. They accepted on April 7, 1969. Pickens would later say buying Hugoton was one of the most important deals he ever did—and also one of the most profitable. It gave Mesa the financial heft to compete for acreage against larger rivals. I never asked him how it stacked up against the Red Bull, and now I wish I had.

The good times didn't last—they never do in the Oil Patch. To keep growing, Mesa bought offshore leases in the British North Sea and the Gulf of Mexico and wound up losing as much on them as it had made on the Hugoton purchase.[3]

Sitting at Pickens' Mesa Vista Ranch that spring day in 2018, I couldn't help reflecting on what I'd learned about the oil and gas business after observing it for almost thirty years: it's a treadmill. Companies make money from production, of course, but for every barrel they produce, they must find another one to replace it. Otherwise, the company shrinks. The problem facing many independents in the 1970s and 1980s was that replacing those barrels was getting more expensive. The cheapest oil had already been produced and drilling costs were rising. Pickens did an analysis and predicted that by 1985, Mesa would have to spend a billion dollars on new drilling just to replace the reserves it already had.[4] If it wanted to grow, it would need even more capital. Growth takes money: this also became a critical concept in the Red Bull case.

Pickens was always shrewd with numbers, and he could calculate reserves and production rates in his head with lightning precision. Being good at math was one of the things we had in common. During our preparation for the Red Bull case, we were discussing those calculations when he got off on a tangent and started preaching about unnecessary college courses.

"Chrysta, who ever needed calculus?" he said. "I never needed calculus in geology."

We hadn't been working together that long, but I couldn't help myself. "Mr. Pickens, do you know that every time you calculate the barrels of oil under a decline curve you are using calculus?" He looked at me incredulously. I couldn't make up my mind whether he was astounded that I had dared to challenge him or if he couldn't decide whether I, a blond woman several decades his junior, was right. In dealing with clients over the years, I've found both to be true. Powerful men often don't like being challenged—especially by a woman—on a subject with which they think they're familiar.

Pickens' fast head for figures and the success of the Hugoton deal taught him it was "vastly cheaper to look for oil and gas reserves on the floor of the New York Stock Exchange than to explore for them in the Gulf of Mexico or some other untapped frontier."[5] So, taking a page from the Hugoton experience, he developed a plan to "seek out the most vulnerable, undervalued, poorly managed companies, then target one and make a major investment in that company." He would acquire an equity position and try to force the managers to increase returns. If they refused, Mesa would launch a takeover. It wouldn't be hard to find candidates: the stocks of most major oil companies were selling at a fraction of the companies' asset values by the early 1980s.

By 1982, Pickens had identified his next target, Cities Service Co. of Tulsa, Oklahoma, a company six times Mesa's size. "Cities Service was a case study in what was wrong with Big Oil's management," Pickens wrote in his 1987 autobiography. The company's refineries and chemical plants were losing money, and Cities had been depleting its oil and gas reserves for a decade. Pickens wanted to get control of those reserves, but Cities was too big for Mesa to buy.

He lined up partners to make an offer. At the time, the idea that a smaller independent producer would buy one of the major oil companies seemed outlandish. Mesa may have pulled that off with Hugoton, but this was the big leagues of American business. Pickens' bid upended the natural order of things. Size would no longer protect management from its own complacency.

Rather than submit to Mesa, Cities found a buyer it liked better: Gulf Oil Co. Gulf agreed to acquire Cities later that year. Cities bought back its shares from Mesa, whose original offer had caused Cities' stock to rise. Mesa made a $30 million profit on the deal. Gulf later withdrew its offer, and Occidental Petroleum Corp. bought Cities for $4 billion in 1982.

The Cities deal whetted Pickens' appetite for the takeover game. In August 1983, he made his most famous bid, for Gulf itself. At the time it was the sixth-largest U.S. oil company. Pickens again put together a group of investors, which acquired 11 percent of Gulf's stock. Just as Cities had run from Pickens into the arms of Gulf, Gulf ran to another buyer, Chevron, which then was known as Standard Oil of California. Pickens lost the bid but claimed victory anyway. Gulf shareholders made $6.5 billion on the deal—money that would have gone unrealized if Pickens hadn't come on the scene. Mesa's portion of that profit was $760 million. Gulf shares almost doubled in value, to $80 after the deal from $41 before Pickens began his run. Pickens profited personally, too. That year, he was the highest paid corporate executive in America, with more than $20 million in salary and deferred compensation.[6]

Pickens was now among an elite group of business celebrities—the corporate raiders—a term he despised at the time but later made peace with. The raiders prowled the canyons of Wall Street looking for undervalued assets and cheap financing. Back in the 1970s, Michael Milken, a young trader at the investment firm Drexel Burnham Lambert, began underwriting bond offerings of companies with poor credit ratings. These companies typically couldn't get financing, or if they could, the interest rate was so high they couldn't afford it. While most underwriters wouldn't touch this kind of credit risk, Milken argued that a diversified portfolio of these so-called junk bonds would offer rewards that far outweighed the risk.[7]

Milken found investors who were willing to buy this high-risk—and high-yield—debt and used their investment to fund takeovers. One of his first deals was Pickens' raid on Gulf, for which Milken raised almost $5 billion.[8] By the time the takeover era was in full swing, Milken hosted an annual soiree for his corporate raider clients in Beverley Hills that he dubbed "The Predators' Ball." Pickens attended the event in 1986.[9]

Pickens may not have liked the "raider" label, but he loved the takeover game. The rough-and-tumble nature had all the thrill of wildcatting without the disappointment of a dry hole. Even if his takeover attempt didn't succeed—and few did—he usually walked away with *something.* He embraced the media's portrayal of him as a hero for the shareholder, the little guy too often shunned by Corporate America. It was a story ripe for Hollywood—a self-made millionaire from Amarillo, Texas, who'd once started his day shaving in gas station restrooms, scaring the pants off the captains of industry.

Pickens unsuccessfully targeted Phillips in 1984, Unocal Corp. in 1985, and Diamond Shamrock in 1987. He urged companies to "maximize shareholder value" a decade before the cliché became corporate boilerplate. He formed a group, United Shareholders of America, to champion investors.

Wall Street bankers and the media began to question his motivations during the Phillips bid. To thwart Mesa's advance, Phillips adopted a recapitalization plan that included buying

Mesa's shares. Mesa took the buyback, which many considered "greenmail"—a payment that came at other shareholders' expense to make him go away. Pickens claims that although Phillips offered him greenmail, he never took it. He ultimately accepted the same deal offered to other shareholders.[10] Still, many business-watchers didn't see it that way. "I was seen as the financial barbarian with little regard for shareholders, employees, or consumers," Pickens wrote later.

A *Time* magazine cover story in 1985 likened him to J.R. Ewing, the wheeling-dealing villain of the TV show *Dallas*. "To his victims, mostly entrenched corporate executives, he is a dangerous upstart, a sneaky poker player, a veritable rattlesnake in the woodpile. To his fans, he is a modern David, a champion of the little guy who can take on the Goliaths of Big Oil and more often than not gives them a costly whupping."

Many independents cheered Pickens for getting even with Big Oil, which had promoted cheap imports over domestic crude. "On one level, his campaign, for that's what it was, represented the revenge of the independent oil man on the hated majors," oil historian Daniel Yergin wrote in *The Prize: The Epic Quest for Oil, Money and Power*. Indeed, for the rest of his life, Pickens would push politicians—especially the Republicans he supported—for energy policies to reduce dependence on foreign oil.

Above all, Pickens pioneered the concept that management should answer to shareholders for a company's performance. Today, the idea is commonplace, largely because of his efforts. The corporate raiders of yesteryear haven't gone away. Today, they're known as "activist investors."

Pickens unfailingly saw himself as a champion of the shareholder—or more broadly, of the little guy. He may have been a billionaire, but he could be remarkably down-to-earth at times.

While eating dinner in the capacious dining room at Pickens' ranch during our visit in 2018, the cooks served ham loaf, a Midwestern dish reminiscent of meatloaf, but made with minced ham. They'd prepared it from a cookbook of Pickens' favorite recipes. As we finished the main course and waited on the cobbler for dessert, Pickens reflected on his shareholder activism days. "I remember dealing with the oil company management back in those days. They never realized they weren't the real owners of the companies they served. They'd go play golf and work short days and never understood that it wasn't their company—it was the shareholders'." He spoke more slowly than he once did, but the concepts he'd trumpeted over the decades were still fresh in his mind.

As we prepared the Red Bull lawsuit, Pickens repeatedly reminded me that we were fighting for the little guy by helping to enforce the law. Pickens felt that if he could get cut out of an oil deal, anybody could, and they might not have the resources to fight back.

I thought about how far he'd come between the 1980s and 2018. I knew he'd fallen on hard times and risen again. "I should have quit the takeover game after Gulf," he once said. "I was a folk hero at the time, and that should've been good enough."[11]

Ha, I thought. Everything I knew about Pickens said he could never have settled for "good enough." As Wall Street chronicler Michael Lewis noted in a Bloomberg News column in 1999, before Pickens and the corporate takeover battles, huge financial ambition was uncommon.[12] By the end of the decade, it had become normal. Without the zeal of Pickens and others in the 1980s, there would likely have been no tech boom in the 1990s. "Would it have occurred to Jeff Bezos to create Amazon if it had not first occurred to him, while he worked on Wall Street, that there was nothing absurd in trying to make $100 million for himself?" Lewis wrote.

Earlier in the 1980s, the federal government had adopted laws to deregulate how natural gas was sold, traded, and transported. Demand for gas was rising, and many in the industry, including Pickens, believed that it would become the fuel of the future, perhaps even unseating oil. "It's the best end of the hydrocarbons," Pickens said. "It's the cleanest and the cheapest, and it's easier to find than oil."

But as the markets opened up, and more gas became available, prices fell in the late 1980s and early 1990s. Pickens had restructured his company as a partnership, and his investors were expecting substantial dividends. By 1991, his big bet on natural gas had become a crippling albatross. The company borrowed heavily to meet its financial obligations, and by the mid-1990s, it was stumbling under more than a billion dollars in debt as its market value plunged.

Pickens became the target of the very same takeover threats he had launched in the 1980s. Many of his Big Oil adversaries reveled in his comeuppance.

In its weakened state, Mesa caught the eye of David Batchelder, a former Pickens lieutenant. Batchelder, by then running his own money management firm in San Diego, lined up backers and made a hostile bid for Mesa. Mesa responded with some of the same anti-takeover measures that Pickens had criticized less than a decade earlier. He turned to a white knight: his friend Richard Rainwater, the superstar investor who'd made billions running money for the Bass family of Fort Worth.

Rainwater agreed to recapitalize Mesa. But as he and Pickens worked out the details, Rainwater became convinced that Mesa needed new leadership. Pickens claimed he had tried to do right by his investors. But there was no escaping the fact that by 1996 he not only had fallen short of that goal, he had become more like many of the entrenched managers he once attacked than he would admit.

After Pickens was forced out, the company rebranded itself as Pioneer Natural Resources. Ironically, Pickens' predictions about natural gas eventually proved true. Surging gas prices in the early 2000s catapulted Pioneer into a major player in the Permian Basin, the region of West Texas that would become the centerpiece of the lawsuit bringing us to Pecos twenty years later.

Pickens found himself setting out on his own again at age sixty-eight. In media interviews, he tried to sound upbeat. He had no intention of retiring, he looked forward to the next chapter, and so forth. But in reality, he felt his world crashing in on him. His twenty-six-year marriage to his second wife, Beatrice, ended at about the same time. Pickens would later reveal that he was diagnosed with depression.

He was done with takeovers and public companies. A few months after being ousted from Mesa, he lined up investments from wealthy friends and set up an energy hedge fund, BP Capital, in Dallas. Unlike Mesa, the company was private and out of the limelight. The partnership struggled in its first few years. Distracted by the divorce, Pickens wasn't at the top of his game.

The fund racked up big losses in the first few years, and by January 1999, it had less than $2.5 million left of the $37 million Pickens started with. Faced with the prospect of losing it all, he slowly came out of his funk. He intensified his physical workouts, started seeing a therapist, and began to find excitement in work again. In 2000, he spotted early signs that natural gas prices would rise, and he positioned the fund to profit. The strategy worked. Gas quadrupled that year, and BP Capital ended 2000 with a balance of $237 million.

Things just kept going up. Natural gas topped thirteen dollars per thousand cubic feet in 2003 and by 2006, Pickens became a billionaire at age seventy-six.

His fortune made, in 2008 Pickens returned to an earlier theme with a strategy to wean the United States off imported oil. His "Pickens Plan" proposed relying primarily on wind power and natural gas. The plan turned him into an internet sensation, aided by the creative genius of his PR man, Jay Rosser. A younger generation who knew little of the 1980s takeover battles loved the story of an old-school oil guy embracing renewable energy. As an octogenarian, Pickens suddenly found himself with millions of followers on social media.

The Pickens Plan made for some strange bedfellows. A longtime Republican donor and friend of party stalwarts such as Bob Dole and John McCain, Pickens now found himself allied with environmental groups. He had given millions to defeat Democratic presidential candidate John Kerry but after the Pickens Plan, Kerry reached out in hopes they could find common ground on climate change issues. Pickens may have been a diehard Republican, but he could set aside partisan differences to achieve common goals. After all, he hired me, a vocal Democrat and one-time Congressional candidate, as his attorney.

I was glad that Pickens had long ago left behind his corporate raider days and had become more of an environmental advocate by the time I became his attorney. It made it easier to portray him favorably to the jury, and it also made it easier for me to be around him.

That weekend at the ranch, after our tour, I decided to go for a run and experience the ranch from the perspective of the dirt roads that wound their way to its lonelier parts, away from the grandeur of the buildings. It was March, so the air was still relatively cool and dry, unlike the stifling heat the summer months would bring. The peacefulness of my surroundings enveloped me, interrupted only by the sounds of my own footfalls. To get out into the wild of the countryside, I ran past the beautiful yet simple stone chapel that Pickens had built near the grave of his grandson, who died at age nineteen of a heroin overdose. It had a picture window that overlooked one of the many lakes. Pickens, too, had planned to be buried on the ranch, but that changed after he decided to sell it. His relationship with his family had been fraught for a long time. Like many hard-charging executives, it seemed his family suffered because of his ambition. Yet in his later years he reconciled with some of his five children—four from his first marriage and the fifth, Liz, the daughter of his second wife whom Pickens adopted.

As I ran, I thought about how while I knew of Pickens' reputation as a Wall Street raider, it didn't gel with the reality of the elderly gentleman I had represented at the trial. The man I'd read about decades before seemed at odds with the man who was my client. Perhaps things were different now: he had the perspective of another forty years, and the corporate raider days didn't come up much anymore. He certainly didn't dwell on them. Our discussions always turned to our Red Bull case, which he loved to relive every chance he got.

My shoes crunched on the caliche of the ranch roads. The rocks of the roadway and the grasses and groundcover that surrounded me would be here, like the rest of this vast expanse, long after Pickens was gone. I'd like to think he came to understand that before he passed away on September 11, 2019. I think he realized that when you become a billionaire in your seventies, the money doesn't matter that much. For men like Pickens, the thrill was being in the center of it all. Money was just a way to keep score.

Having made so much of it, the only thing he could do with his fortune was to give it away. Living in Dallas since 1985, I'd seen his philanthropy firsthand. Pickens had donated money to the downtown YMCA that now bears his name. I worked out frequently there as I prepared for the Red Bull trial, and each time, I passed the portrait of Pickens next to the main staircase. The picture memorialized him as a lanky college basketball player some seventy years earlier.

I would come to learn many surprising things about T. Boone Pickens, but perhaps the most surprising, at least for a lawyer, is that he'd had relatively little experience with the legal system. You might think that a billionaire who'd made his fortune in the Oil Patch, where lawsuits are as common as the dust on the streets of Pecos, knew his way around a major court case. But neither Pickens himself nor his top lieutenants could recall him being involved in a significant trial.

Sure, he'd employed lawyers to help with his takeover battles, review contracts, handle his five divorces, and oversee other personal matters. I'd even represented him in an earlier lease dispute, but he'd never been caught up in the courtroom drama in which many business leaders inevitably find themselves. And while he may not have fully understood what he was in for with the Red Bull case, it didn't seem to diminish his expectations that I would win big for him.

Another surprise about Pickens: he's often referred to as a "legendary oilman." But I learned during my time with him that much of the legend had little to do with oil. "I never found much oil," he said in 2016.[13] "I probably had no more than five really great years. It's a competitive, risky business every day."

Since 1980, the price of oil has been cut in half five times, he liked to point out. It's a market driven by unforeseen events— bad weather in the Northeast, the whims of a Middle Eastern autocrat, the value of the dollar on world markets. Of course, for every one of those steep declines, you're likely to find an equally dramatic rise. But he'd never seen an upswing as dramatic as what he would see with the Red Bull.

As fickle as oil is, natural gas can be worse. It was so unpredictable that traders on the floor of the New York Mercantile Exchange used to call the gas futures contract "the widow maker" because it had wiped out so many of them who'd bet wrong and lost it all. Pickens counted himself among the natural gas victims. He may not have had many good years in oil, but his downfall as a producer came from natural gas. "Natural gas—hell, it cost me my job at Mesa," he said.

Even so, once oil seeps into your blood, it's hard to get it out. While Pickens made more money than ever with trading, he couldn't resist doing oil deals. He won back the rights to the original Mesa name and used it to invest in private deals, including the Red Bull.

Pickens got wind of the Red Bull in late 2006 through a call from another wealthy Dallas oilman, Jimmy Thompson. Dallas wasn't the oil town it had been in the 1980s. Most of the business had consolidated and shifted offices to Houston. Those who stayed behind formed a close-knit group. Thompson had known Pickens for years and offered him a 15 percent stake in a Permian Basin oil deal that looked promising.

Pickens didn't know it at the time, but the Red Bull would return him to the spotlight for an encore performance. As our trial unfolded in 2016, he found himself in the headlines once again. By then, in his late eighties and with failing eyesight and hearing, he girded himself for one last fight.

Chapter 3

"THE CHAINSAW"

I didn't set out to be a lawyer. Growing up in the suburbs of Wichita, Kansas, I liked math and science. I came by my interests honestly. My dad was an aeronautical engineer who worked for decades at Beech Aircraft, which was later bought by Raytheon and is now known as Hawker Beechcraft. My sisters, Cathy and Cheryl, and my little brother, David, also studied engineering, and most of us married engineers. Law wasn't in my DNA.

My parents were the first in their families to graduate from college. My mother became an elementary school teacher, dissuaded from the sciences like most women of her generation. Later, she became a banker. She told me that she hoped each of us would, at the least, graduate from a two-year college. Education was important to her. Yet, I don't recall her ever telling me to do my homework, or monitoring my grades, or being overly involved in my schooling. She was not a helicopter parent by nature. And besides, she had four children to raise in addition to her job. She simply didn't have time to hover that closely.

Left largely to my own imagination and resources, I learned an early lesson that guided my adult thinking, including my preparation for the Pickens case. In fifth grade, our teacher told us to create a commercial about something—I don't recall what. I threw myself into the assignment. Perhaps the future engineer was excited by the chance to build something, or perhaps the future lawyer didn't want to leave anything to chance. I worked for five hours that night crafting a miniature stage and figurines and wrote a script. I was surprised that none of the other kids had done as much work. Most were content just to get by. I knew that wasn't me. I had too much energy and a penchant for polishing my work until I liked it enough to show to others.

By high school, I was making straight As, I had good scores on my college entrance exams, and I participated in almost every extracurricular activity the school offered—track, softball, cheerleading, drum major for the marching band, mathlete, orchestra, and some clubs. Most schools don't have varsity cheerleaders who are mathletes, but my senior squad had three. For a town of less than fifteen thousand people and a high school graduating class of four hundred, that wasn't bad.

When it came time for college, I applied to Kansas State and Texas A&M and got accepted at both. Then, a Harvard recruiter came to our campus. I applied, and I was accepted there too. Harvard seemed like a bigger challenge and that appealed to me, so I set off for Cambridge in the fall of 1981.

I decided to study engineering because I knew I could get a good-paying job. I didn't really understand what my dad did. His work was classified, and he's a man of few words, unless the subject is sports. But I had participated in an engineering summer camp for high school girls at Notre Dame in 1978 and had some idea of what I was getting into. I liked that engineering, unlike social sciences, involved correct answers—you solved the problem, or you didn't. There was no subjective view. Plus, I discovered that I could learn math and physics just as well from textbooks as I could the odd assortment of lecturers who taught us as freshmen. That was a bonus: I could attend about every third class and still get good grades. Professors didn't take attendance in those days. You passed or failed based on your own efforts. I think it was easier to be a kid back then.

In the early 1980s, Harvard didn't offer a true engineering degree. To get one, I'd have to commute to the Massachusetts Institute of Technology in my junior and senior years. It would be complicated, but I could do it. Then, everything changed. One February morning during my sophomore year, my parents called and told me that they couldn't keep paying for Harvard. I'd won grants and scholarships and worked a series of part-time jobs delivering newspapers, washing dishes in the cafeteria, and tending pigeons in a psychology lab, but my education was still costing twice as much as their monthly mortgage payment. Plus, my sister, Cathy, was about to graduate from high school and would also need college tuition. They simply didn't have the money. I loved my time at Harvard, but I didn't relish the idea of taking on a load of debt. After all, I'd been accepted into other good schools. I felt confident I could get a degree somewhere else and still earn a living. My pragmatism beat out Harvard prestige.

I transferred to Kansas State with a full scholarship. Having finished most of my fundamental courses in Cambridge, I decided to specialize in industrial engineering, which is basically a math degree. It also had the least amount of lab time. I hated labs. Lab courses required me to stand around for hours waiting for chemical reactions or other physical processes to happen. It felt like too much wasted time. I had a lot of things I wanted to get done.

There was another factor in my choice of Kansas State. My high school boyfriend was an engineering student there. We got married the summer before I graduated, which wasn't all that young if you lived in Kansas in the 1980s.

I had a number of job offers when I graduated, but my husband had landed his dream position working in robotics for the General Dynamics aircraft plant in Fort Worth, which made F-16 fighter jets. We moved to North Texas in December 1985, and I began looking for engineering work.

On the morning of January 28, 1986, I was sitting in a Sonic drive-in on Forest Lane in Dallas. I'd just finished an interview and had been offered a job at Electronic Data Systems, the computer services company down the street. I liked the idea of cutting-edge technology and solving other companies' software problems. I'd just ordered a cheeseburger when I heard on the car radio that the Space Shuttle Challenger had exploded after liftoff. I recall thinking that the miracle of technology can sometimes also result in the shared heartache of national tragedy.

EDS hired me to investigate and document the client's business processes that we were automating with software. The first step in designing software is determining what it should be doing. Companies' business procedures often evolve over time and they aren't always logical or efficient. Many firms justify certain procedures by saying "that's the way we've always done it." EDS hired industrial engineers like me to figure out how to do it better before automating those processes.

I worked on some interesting projects at EDS, including one at the Minneapolis headquarters of Northwest Airlines (which was later acquired by Delta Air Lines). It had no automation at the time. None of the carrier's business processes, such as crew and aircraft scheduling, were automated. Instead, clerks wrote schedules for each pilot, flight attendant, and aircraft on thousands of cards that they filed in long drawers. The drawers filled up several rooms and required dozens of clerks to keep track of them. Mind you, this was 1986, not the 1930s, but the company's owner had resisted installing computers, fearing that workers would watch television on their monitors even though this was decades before broadband internet service or video streaming and none of the monitors could receive a broadcast signal. I thought it seemed crazy at the time, but decades later it's something employers worry about.

Arthur Andersen, an EDS rival, lured me away about a year later. In 1986 they put me to work on the project for Pickens' Mesa, helping prepare its computer systems to handle the records of the company's new partnership structure. The job market for software engineers was far hotter at the time than anything having to do with energy. A couple of years earlier, the oil industry had entered one of the worst busts in its history. In fact, because of that bust, I'd turned down one of the first jobs I was offered out of college, with a pipeline company that's now part of ConocoPhillips.

Despite the career potential, I realized the day-to-day job of computer programming wasn't enough excitement for me. I loved the problems I was trying to solve but I really hated sitting for hours writing lines of computer code. I wanted to work on bigger projects at a higher level, and I didn't see software development helping me achieve those ambitions. I was only twenty-four, but I felt like I needed to reboot my career.

I thought an advanced degree would help, but business school seemed boring. I opted instead for law school, figuring that as a lawyer, I could solve business problems without ever having to write another line of code.

I'd already missed the law school application deadline for 1988. Not wanting to wait an entire year, I applied anyway—to

Harvard, the University of Texas, and Southern Methodist University in Dallas. Harvard put me on a wait list, but UT and SMU accepted me. UT had the better law school at the time, but SMU offered me a full scholarship. Free, after all, was free—and I didn't have to move.

I liked law school and did well at it. It was less difficult than engineering, although the anxiety level was a lot higher and it was far more competitive. In law school, the only thing that matters—in terms of future prospects for employment—is graduating at the top of the class. Because I had good grades, I was offered a summer clerkship with a premiere law firm. I was pregnant when I started it, and my son Scott was born on what was supposed to be my last day at the position. Since I was at the hospital, in labor, the law firm only paid me for four days that week. I got an early lesson about being a working mom.

A month after Scott was born, I was diagnosed with invasive melanoma. I was twenty-eight years old, with a newborn, and suddenly I didn't know if I would survive to see him walk. I was told I had an 80 percent chance of living five years, but that 20 percent seemed like an enormous risk. I slowly came to terms with the idea that I might, in fact, die young. Such a realization radically changes your outlook. Obviously, I survived. But I learned to put risks in perspective. The turmoil of emotions also probably contributed to my divorce from my first husband. No business risk can compare with these sorts of personal trials. Once you stare death and divorce in the face, everything else seems pretty harmless.

I graduated and went to work for the same law firm that docked me a day's pay for going into labor with my son. It had a unique group of smart lawyers and let me work part-time in exchange for reduced pay. Three days after I got my law license, I argued my first appeal. My supervising partner, David Godbey, who's now a federal judge, had me write the brief. At the last minute, the argument in the court of appeals was reinstated after a stay from bankruptcy and the client wasn't paying the bills. A nonpaying client meant opportunity for me. The firm would write off the bill regardless of the outcome. My time was cheaper than a senior partner's, which meant the loss was less for the firm. I would benefit by gaining valuable experience. So, I stayed up all night and gave my first oral argument the next day. I was terrible, but I learned to jump in and do my best on whatever preparation I had. And, like my fifth-grade experience, I learned that the more you prepare, the better you will do.

I moved around and practiced law for several large firms over the years, focusing on cases that required engineering expertise, such as products liability, medical device litigation, and oil and gas contracts. I particularly liked those. They usually involved larger-than-life people and the stakes were always high. And, I must admit, I enjoyed the surprised looks from the men who didn't think a "blond girl" could ask intelligent questions.

I took every litigation case I was offered, remembering advice from a woman law partner about getting "out on the skinny branches." She'd meant that you have to take risks and embrace every challenge if you wanted to get ahead—especially if you were a woman. The secret to success was saying yes to the opportunity first, then figuring out how to accomplish the task after committing.

It goes without saying if you're going to be a woman in the male-dominated world of trial lawyers, you have to be tough. I got used to walking into a conference room, prepared to cross-examine the witness in a deposition, and being asked if I was the court reporter. I also got used to older male lawyers protesting my objections in depositions in ways they wouldn't if I were a man. Once, the opposing counsel stood up and yelled, "Don't you tell me how to practice law, little missy!" Another time, after making what I considered a persuasive argument to a judge in Fort Worth, he said, "I like your earrings," accompanied by a creepy stare. But after ten years, I learned to view condescension and chauvinism as background noise. You never get comfortable with it, but you learn to get past it.

I had a good client who sent me a variety of cases over the years. He called me "The Chainsaw." I pondered what to make of the title at the time, and I still do. I didn't really think I was that fierce, but apparently, he did. I readily admit that I can be hardheaded, although I'd like to think I have a pleasant demeanor to offset my tenacity. After considering it for a while, I decided that he called me that because a chainsaw is effective at what it does. Not much stops a chainsaw.

I'd taken on a particularly difficult, emotionally charged case in 2011. It culminated in a nine-week trial late in the year. I wound up losing. Even worse, during the proceedings, we were under intense media scrutiny every day. We not only lost the case in court, we also lost the battle for public support, which can often be won by communicating the right message at the right time. I knew that there was more to practicing law than what happened in the courtroom, and I also knew that as the lead lawyer, I could not wage the public relations fight all on my own. I vowed to find a PR firm that would support my clients the next time I had a case like that.

But I was also exhausted after that trial. I realized I'd grown disenchanted with Big Law. I had been a partner in a large law firm for more than a decade and I felt as if my career was stagnating. While I was doing well, the firm wasn't giving me the financial recognition I felt I deserved. I'd just settled a case that resulted in a $5 million fee for my firm, but little of it was shared with me—less, I still believe, than a male partner would have received. And, I had to completely rebuild my practice and client base after the trial. Under the best of circumstances, even if you win, a big trial is like a tsunami that runs backwards: First, the ocean rushes in and you are absolutely swamped. Then, it all runs back out again. Sometimes you wonder whether the surf—the next client engagement—will return. It always does, but it takes a while. Trial lawyers call it "refilling the pipeline." Maybe they just say that in Texas because we are so dominated by oil.

I was frustrated by not receiving equal pay for the work I was doing. Big Law's only real currency is, well, currency. The worth of each lawyer is measured in cash. Women lawyers would joke that a Y-chromosome added 30 percent to your salary and bonus. No matter how much business I brought in, the male partners always seemed to come out ahead in the compensation battle, which is the only measure of success in Big Law.

As I ended my trial in 2011, a new congressional district was formed in the Dallas-Fort Worth area. I had no previous plans to run for Congress, but I'd been working as an organizer for a couple of decades to encourage more women to run for public office. I'd donated to their campaigns and supported Democratic politics at all levels. I firmly believed we needed more women in Congress, and it didn't appear any women were planning to run.

The Texas Legislature, which sets the boundaries of congressional districts, drew new districts based on the results of the 2010 Census. Lawsuits immediately followed. Republicans have controlled the state government since the early 1990s, and they have engaged in numerous geographical contortions to ensure that Democrats dominate as few districts as possible.

They designed the 33rd Congressional District as a Democratic concession, but its boundaries demonstrated the absurdity that redistricting had become. The new lines scooped out the center of Dallas and the poor, predominately African-American neighborhoods south of downtown. The district wound up with an arm that stretched west, through central Irving, across northern Grand Prairie and Arlington—where many residents worked at the General Motors assembly plant, aircraft factories, and other blue-collar jobs—into the heart of Fort Worth's poorest neighborhoods. The area not only stretched across two counties, it looked like two separate districts strung together by a thread of Democratic voters that spanned the Dallas-Fort Worth Metroplex. The whole idea was to pack as many Democrats as possible into just one district, keeping as much of the surrounding area as possible safe for Republicans.

The litigation over the district boundaries threatened to drag on past the candidate filing deadline, so party leaders agreed to an interim compromise establishing the borders of the 33rd in early 2012. The last-minute deal left candidates only a few weeks to declare their intention to run. Eventually, ten men and one other woman signed up. My campaign theme was that if you want something done, elect a woman to do it.

When the primary results came in, I was in the middle of the field of eleven candidates. Marc Veasey won the seat that year and still holds it. One of the male candidates spent $4 million of his personal fortune and came in fourth. The other woman in the race, whom the *Fort Worth Star-Telegram* reported had just forty-two dollars in her campaign fund but had served on city council, came in third and got six times as many votes as I did. I was largely unknown to most of the voters, and because of the timing, the election cycle was short. I learned that in politics, name recognition matters a lot and that you can't build it quickly.

However, Veasey's campaign consultant complimented me for a well-run campaign, and I felt good that I made the attempt.

Part of me was relieved that I didn't win. It would have required an even bigger personal sacrifice than campaigning had been, and I would have had to give up my law practice entirely. Here's the truth about public service: done right, it's a *huge* personal sacrifice. It requires relinquishing your career, your free time, and your anonymity.

Plus, my husband, John, hadn't wanted to move to Washington. John is a fellow lawyer. We met through our respective law practices, and we shared a Harvard education (he finished law school there) and the love of ideas. The real glue in our relationship is that he's wicked smart and invariably makes me laugh out loud. We married in 1995, making our two identically aged sons, Scott and Joseph, stepbrothers. John also has a bachelor's in political science and a master's in public policy, and he's acutely interested in politics. But when it came to running for office, he left that up to me.

The end of my congressional campaign didn't make me any more eager to return to Big Law. But what else was I going to do?

One thing had stuck with me from the case I'd lost in 2011: I needed to learn how to protect future clients in a public relations war. As it happened, I ran into one of my former paralegals, Tim Fortenberry, who was working as the office manager for the Dallas branch of the Brunswick Group, an international PR firm. Tim connected me with one of the partners, who told me the firm had several high-stakes litigation clients. The executives appreciated my legal background, and the more I talked with them, the more I became intrigued by the possibilities of learning the PR business myself. Instead of using them as my service provider, I signed on to be a partner.

I didn't exactly know where the public relations stint would take me, and I wasn't completely settled on the idea of never practicing law again. But I came to think of the new job as a trial separation from my legal work.

The PR firm put out a high-quality publication called *The Review*. It covered topics related to corporate reputation management, such as how to handle crises, how to talk about social change, and how to reach different stakeholders. When the call went out to the partners to pitch ideas for the next quarter's issue, I suggested an interview with T. Boone Pickens. I knew that the senior partner in the PR firm, a former *Wall Street Journal* financial reporter, would love the idea of interviewing Pickens. I also felt that Pickens' general counsel, Sandy Campbell, would help me get the interview.

Back when I was still a partner at the law firm, I'd crossed paths with Pickens once again, this time more directly than I had decades earlier working as a software programmer. In about 2007, Campbell had hired my firm to represent Pickens in an oil and gas lease dispute. The senior partner on the account wasn't able to take on the case right then, so it fell to me to handle. It was another example of how taking every opportunity pays off, because the case established my client relationship with Pickens and ultimately led to the Red Bull case years later. Pickens had invested with a company drilling in the Barnett Shale, northwest of Fort Worth, where the fracking boom began. The driller had its hands on a big lease in what was supposed to be the best remaining acreage in the whole play. The company was negotiating with the landowner to extend the lease but at the last minute, Chesapeake Energy, an aggressive independent producer out of Oklahoma City, swooped in and "top leased" the acreage. This cut off the rights for anyone else, including Pickens, to drill.

I filed a lawsuit asking for the court to decree that the Pickens lease was the controlling one and that landowners had breached it when they signed with Chesapeake. The court agreed with me, which is unusual for a state court in Texas, where a plaintiff doesn't often win on summary judgment. As it turned out, the defendants moved for reconsideration after hiring a local lawyer, who managed to undo the judgment.

Still, as a result of that case, Sandy Campbell and I had developed a good relationship. I asked him to set up the interview with Pickens for the piece in *The Review*. Pickens has always been great about knowing the value of publicity. His communications chief, Jay Rosser, saw to it that Pickens was regularly featured in the press on such favorite topics as natural gas powered vehicles, the "Pickens Plan" for energy independence, "Booneisms" (a collection of aphorisms that Pickens perfected over the years), wide-ranging financial issues, and philanthropy. Philanthropy was a big PR theme for Pickens, who had given away billions of dollars by then. His money basically built Oklahoma State's football team. He attended almost every home game in the stadium that bears his name.

On the day of the interview, my firm's senior PR partner and I were ushered into Pickens' enormous Dallas office. We gathered around a smaller table in the corner of the room.

I expected Pickens would give us twenty or thirty minutes, but we spent more than two hours there. We intended to focus on Pickens' shareholder activism days, viewed from the lens of the ensuing thirty years. But we covered so much more, including many of those Booneisms. Time and again, Pickens would call in his long-time assistant, Sally Geymuller, to remind him of people and places. He had an amazing memory, but Sally would fill in the smaller details if they slipped his mind. She had worked for Pickens for so long she usually knew what he was going to say before he said it.

I was surprised by the attention Pickens gave us during the interview. Most CEOs don't allow anyone to occupy that much of their time. When Pickens walked me out of the office, he said, "Let's look for our next big case together. We will have another big case together." Mentally, I pulled up short, thinking that he had become confused about who I was and what I was doing there.

"Mr. Pickens, I'm no longer practicing law," I said. "I'm a partner in this PR firm and I'm focusing on international crises."

I wasn't sure he heard me, because he looked at me and said again, "Chrysta, we will have another big case together."

I didn't know what to say. I wondered if perhaps he was mixed up, but the moment stuck with me. Looking back, it still gives me chills. Maybe that sort of prescience is how he made so much money in the markets. When I reminded him of it several years later, he dismissed the incident as nonsense.

After a year or so in the PR business, I began to miss the courtroom. Public relations was fun and I got to travel all over the world, but I wasn't getting any traction of my own. Plus, I wanted two things again: to lead the high-stakes commercial cases I had handled before I left Big Law and to offer opportunities to other women. I knew that my first objective would be easier to accomplish if I went back to a big firm, but I also knew that the second wouldn't happen if I did. I decided to go it alone, starting The Castañeda Firm in July 2014. I crossed my fingers and hoped for the best.

One of the first things I did after opening my doors was schedule a lunch meeting with Sandy Campbell at a restaurant near Pickens' office. I told him about my plans and how I was trying to build my own law firm from the ground up. He was encouraging, and he mentioned that Pickens might have "a small contract matter" that they could have me evaluate. He planned to meet the potential adversary a few weeks later, and they would know for sure whether or not it would head to litigation. It involved a drilling prospect in West Texas known as the Red Bull.

Chapter 4

THE RED BULL PROSPECT

My lunch with Sandy proved to be auspicious. A few weeks later I met him again at Pickens' BP Capital offices. He introduced me to Alex Szewczyk, whose last name is pronounced "says check," but everyone just calls him Alex. Alex had been in charge of monitoring Pickens' investment in an oil deal called the Red Bull Prospect. We sat down to discuss the deal and what might have happened to Pickens' interest in it. Pickens had bought a 15 percent interest in the Red Bull in 2007, but they'd heard nothing more about its development since 2009. That had been five years ago. I found this extremely curious.

Pickens' main business at the time may have been trading on the stock and commodity exchanges, but he couldn't resist doing side deals in the Oil Patch that he found intriguing. He controlled a partnership bearing the beloved Mesa name, Mesa Petroleum Partners. He used this vehicle to invest in those opportunities. One of the deals was the Red Bull.

The Red Bull covered oil properties in an area that spanned Reeves and Pecos counties in West Texas. The town of Pecos, where we would eventually gather for the trial, is in Reeves County, not Pecos County. Texas has a habit of naming counties and towns after the same people or things, but not necessarily in the same place. The town of Burleson isn't in Burleson County, for instance. It's a little confusing, but you get used to it.

The Red Bull deal started small with a single well and lease. By 2014 it had grown to include hundreds of leases, tens of thousands of acres, and more than seventy-five wells. A Midland-based company, Baytech, had first organized the deal after identifying an area where it thought a rich layer of oil had yet to be discovered. The company needed to raise money from investors to lease enough land and drill enough wells to show that the oil was there. These initial efforts are known as "exploration," because a company is literally testing the ground to see if oil is present. The Red Bull would be built out over time, with incremental investments from others so that Baytech could drill more wells and reap the profits from the deal for itself and its investors. Ventures like these cost hundreds of millions of dollars, but if they succeed, they can generate billions of dollars in oil production and asset value. Having investors spreads the risk, which means no single investor or company has to fear losing all those millions. It also means that if they hit it big, those same investors are supposed to get their share of the profits.

Baytech first turned to Dallas oilman Jimmy Thompson's company, J. Cleo Thompson. It would invest in the prospect and also serve as the "operator," drilling the wells and producing the oil. Baytech would continue to oversee the leasing of land.

J. Cleo—as we came to refer to the company during the trial, to distinguish it from Jimmy Thompson, the man who had once owned it—had decades of expertise operating in the Permian and other areas. Jimmy Thompson would work his connections in the oil and gas community to find additional investors for the Red Bull. One of his connections was Pickens. Because they knew each other and had done other deals together, Pickens decided to take a 15 percent stake in the Red Bull in early 2007. The agreement Pickens signed with Thompson and Baytech called for Mesa to pay 15 percent of the costs for acquiring future leases and drilling future wells. Before each acquisition or drilling project, the companies were required to notify Mesa, which could choose to participate or decline to make an additional investment. In exchange, if it elected to participate, it was entitled to 15 percent ownership of the lands as well as the profits from any oil produced.

When J. Cleo became the operator, it also took over the bookkeeping for the Red Bull leasing and drilling programs. It distributed the bills for the costs of those activities, and it was supposed to distribute the oil revenues once they came in. It also performed the critical and customary function of notifying the investors, including Mesa, of opportunities to participate in the new leases and wells. This responsibility meant that J. Cleo should have notified Pickens and let him decide whether Mesa wanted to invest 15 percent of the cost for each new lease and well that became available. But the firm stopped sending the notices after a few years, and Sandy and Alex didn't know why.

In 2014, seven years after he'd first signed the Red Bull deal, Pickens realized that he hadn't heard from anyone about the project's further development. That's not necessarily unusual. Some deals die off because the oil isn't there or there isn't enough of it to justify additional leasing and drilling costs. Pickens didn't know what had happened, only that the notifications had ended. The Mesa team knew that there had been several profitable wells drilled in the area, though, so Pickens asked Alex and Sandy to investigate.

First, Alex took a look at recent drilling activity in the area. He learned that drilling had accelerated dramatically near the Red Bull. If Baytech and J. Cleo had been drilling wells, they hadn't notified Mesa. Alex set up a meeting with Rick Montgomery, Baytech's lawyer, in Midland. Rick listened to Alex's questions and promised to investigate the status of Mesa's Red Bull interest.

Montgomery came to Dallas in October 2014 for a second meeting with Alex and Sandy. He told them that he'd examined the records and that Mesa had "opted out" of the Red Bull deal in 2009. Alex and Sandy were confused. Neither of them had heard of an "opt out" in a deal like this, and they didn't know what that meant in regard to the Red Bull. The contracts they reviewed didn't reference the term, and Pickens hadn't signed any paperwork saying he'd opted out. The more that Sandy questioned Montgomery, the more annoyed Montgomery seemed to get. Eventually, Sandy told me, Montgomery left the meeting in a huff. By then, Sandy had decided that Mesa needed to file a lawsuit.

This was big, exciting news for me, but it also made me anxious. It had been almost three years since I'd tried a case. I missed legal work, and if ever there were a case to reignite my passion, this mystery "opt out" was it. I relished having my own firm, because I could focus on the case and do what I needed to do without worrying whether my partners thought I was billing enough for the work. At a big law firm, the requirements to bill a lot of hours and collect a lot of fees are always hanging over your head, even when the size of the case doesn't justify it. Here, I could spend as much time as I wanted investigating because I controlled the costs.

I dug into the Red Bull contracts. The first was called the Participation Agreement. It covered Baytech's efforts to buy leases and the mechanics of notifying Mesa and the other investors of their participation rights in those leases. The other contract was called a Joint Operating Agreement. It governed the procedures for drilling the wells and the requirement that J. Cleo send notices to the investors of their participation rights in those wells.

The first Red Bull well was known as the Lyda. It had been drilled long before Baytech put the prospect together. Oil wells are named by the operators who drill them, and often those names refer to the original landowner. The well at Spindletop that ushered in the modern oil age in 1901 was named the Daisy Bradford #3, after the woman who owned the land that would eventually become the largest oil field in the world. Texas rancher William Thomas Waggoner named an entire field of wells for his daughter, Electra, after oil was discovered on his half-million-acre ranch west of Fort Worth in 1911.[1]

I never did learn who the Lyda well was named for, but I assumed it was for someone's wife, daughter, mother, or lover.

When Pickens signed the Red Bull deal in 2007, he paid more than $125,000 for his interest and rights. That covered the cost of buying the Lyda well and refurbishing it, known in the industry as a workover. It also covered the purchase of land around the Lyda well and the section next to it. The payment further included a kicker for Baytech, known as a "promote." This is basically a fee you pay to the company that assembles the project.

I could see from the paperwork and canceled checks that Mesa had paid Baytech the initial amount of $125,000. I also found that after Pickens signed the first contracts, he had received additional notices that the parties were leasing more acreage. Mesa had elected to participate in those purchases and had made some additional payments after being billed for them.

Pickens' elegant cursive signature was attached to each notice Mesa had been sent, signifying Mesa's agreement to participate in each new acquisition for its full 15 percent. The record also showed that someone had placed credits on Mesa's bills, but I couldn't tell what they represented.

I knew just from reading the newspaper that by 2014, the Delaware Basin formation of the Permian, which the Red Bull was targeting, had become the hottest oil play in the country. But, of course, that didn't mean that the Red Bull itself had necessarily benefited from the extensive Delaware Basin drilling that had gone on. I couldn't tell from the documents I had before me whether the group had simply failed to find the oil that was now known to exist in the Delaware Basin or whether something else had happened. Either way, it appeared that all the communications about acquisitions and new wells had stopped even though the bills had not. I had to find out why.

The visit from Montgomery, Baytech's lawyer, only confused things further. When he met with Sandy and Alex in Dallas, he gave them a copy of a letter addressed to Pickens dated March 2, 2009. It said that Mesa had "opted out" of additional Red Bull acquisitions in late 2008. However, Pickens hadn't signed it, and it wasn't clear from the meeting that he had even received it. In the letter, Baytech also offered to buy Mesa's remaining interest in the project, which Baytech said was limited to the Lyda well alone, for about $160,000. The letter was signed by Baytech's CEO, Ben Strickling.

Alex told me he recalled discussing the possibility of Baytech buying Mesa's interest, but he was certain the deal never took place. Neither he nor Sandy recalled seeing Montgomery's proffered letter before the meeting. Far from settling anything, the letter only raised more questions. Had Strickling actually sent the letter to Mesa at the time? Did they have anything that Pickens had signed saying that Mesa was getting out of the project? If so, why hadn't they presented that document? More importantly for Pickens, what had happened to Mesa's 15 percent interest in everything but the Lyda well after 2009?

I drafted a letter to Montgomery that outlined these questions. I pointed out that I found nothing to indicate the deal had been amended or that Mesa had sold its interests. I was pretty sure somebody at Mesa would have kept copies if those types of documents existed, but I asked Montgomery to preserve all the relevant material they had so we could examine it if a lawsuit ensued. I sent a copy of the letter to J. Cleo as well, since its name was also on the contracts. Maybe it, as the entity responsible for the billing, had information on what had happened.

I've reviewed a lot of oil and gas deals over the years, and sometimes, you can just tell on a first look that something isn't right. You may not know why, but your gut tells you there's a problem. This was one of those cases. Of course, it could have all been a simple misunderstanding, but it didn't feel that way. Montgomery's presentation of the March 2009 letter, unsigned by Pickens, was the first whiff that things could get ugly. That's not the way business is usually done, even in the good ol' boys' network of the Oil Patch.

Another red flag: several weeks went by without Montgomery responding. When I called his office, he told me that that Baytech had retained a lawyer, Stuart Hollimon, for the lawsuit the company knew was coming. Hollimon was a well-respected oil and gas attorney and a partner with the large firm of Andrews Kurth. He'd chaired the state bar association's oil and gas section a few years earlier. You don't get to do that without knowing your stuff.

If Baytech had hired a high-powered law firm and was already girding for a lawsuit—yet another red flag—this dispute wasn't going to get resolved easily out of court. If we wanted to find out what happened to Mesa's investment, we were going to have to take legal action—the outcome that Sandy had predicted after his meeting with Montgomery in Dallas. Something had definitely happened to Pickens' interest in the Red Bull Prospect, and I intended to dig in and find out what the trouble was.

Chapter 5

THE LAWSUIT

After discussing the options with Sandy, we decided to sue Baytech and J. Cleo in state court for breaching their contracts with Mesa. At that point, I thought the lawsuit boiled down to these simple facts: Mesa signed two contracts that gave it the option to own 15 percent of everything that was purchased or drilled by Baytech and J. Cleo in the Red Bull area. The companies were supposed to notify Mesa when acreage was purchased or when wells were drilled, but they stopped doing that in 2009. About the same time, Baytech had tried to buy Mesa's interest. Beyond that, we knew that Mesa had stopped getting notices about new developments with the project but didn't know why. Mesa had continued to receive Red Bull bills from J. Cleo, but they contained errors and credits. In the meantime, Alex and Sandy learned that in 2014 the drilling around the Red Bull had increased significantly, which meant that Mesa's interests may have been worth a lot more than they were in 2009. But I needed more information.

Once I filed the initial papers, I began a formal search for material to better understand what happened to Mesa's Red

Bull interests. This meant I would have to ask for and scrutinize every document that Baytech and J. Cleo had relating to the Red Bull. There could be dozens; there could be hundreds of thousands. That's not unusual in a business dispute like this.

Documents were only part of the case. I needed to talk to people. Many—perhaps most—wouldn't want to talk to me. I was looking at taking dozens of depositions to secure witness testimony before a trial. If the case actually went to court, I would likely need to hire several different types of expert witnesses: geologists, accountants, and others familiar with oil and gas operations and contracts. Getting a case like this through the trial stage could take years, and that's before the inevitable appeals.

The problem was that The Castañeda Firm consisted of one person—me. I'd ventured out on my own only four months earlier. I'd wanted to do things my own way with my own firm and now, with my first major case, I was already confronting the potentially overwhelming limits of that strategy. Undeterred, I forged ahead.

No one hands you the answers as a lawyer. The number one job of a good trial attorney is to figure things out. You may have to stare at a document time and again until you fully understand it. You may have to read tens of thousands of pages yourself to determine which ones are important. It may take years before you really understand what those documents are telling you. It's like putting together a giant jigsaw puzzle or untangling a huge knot. You have to start somewhere but you have no idea until you get into it whether you've started in the right place. Sometimes, you have to retrace your steps.

Being a good trial lawyer is not about giving the best speeches in court, it's about having command of a thousand details when you need them. It's being able to think on your feet and to pivot on a dime when a witness doesn't say what you expect. It's thinking through all of the possibilities and mapping out a strategy for dealing with every one of them. And it's having a plan for all of the ones you can't possibly think of.

Late in 2014, after filing the lawsuit, I requested dozens of categories of documents from the defendants. I obtained them a few months later. In particular, I asked for copies of all the leases that had been purchased and files for all the wells that had been drilled in the Red Bull. I got what I asked for, but now I faced the massive task of sifting through it all.

Help arrived early in 2015 when I enlisted Debbie Eberts to assist me with the case. Debbie and I had been friends since law school and we were associates together at Jones Day Reavis & Pogue, a large firm I'd worked for in the 1990s. Debbie had retired from the law and moved to Minnesota to raise her two boys with her husband. Now divorced, she had returned to Texas as a single mother and needed a job. This presented an opportunity for us both. After all, part of the reason I started my own firm was to create more positions for women. She agreed to help.

Debbie and I flew to Midland to review the Baytech documents. Midland is the hub of the Permian Basin. Most of the oil companies that operate in the region have field offices there, but it isn't a big city. In 2015, it had about 133,000 people. Almost all of them either worked in the energy business or were related to someone who did. Midland has more restaurants, movie theaters, and other amenities than towns further west like Pecos, but it's far from a metropolis. We landed at the Midland International Air and Space Port, an overly futuristic name for an airport still served mostly by regional jets and, to my knowledge, no actual spacecraft.

We headed straight for lawyer Rick Montgomery's offices to view the material he'd collected for us. Montgomery showed us to a conference room with a long table where he'd laid out about twenty boxes packed with papers, then he left us alone to look at them. I immediately was struck by the significant number of files relating to the Red Bull. If the communications with Pickens had stopped in 2009 because the project went bust, there wouldn't be so many documents.

It only took a few minutes to find pay dirt. It turned out that Baytech and J. Cleo had indeed continued to expand the Red Bull. Then, in 2013, as oil prices climbed, they'd sold a portion of it for hundreds of millions of dollars. The Red Bull, it turned out, was in the sweetest drilling spot in the Permian Basin. And the Permian, in turn, was one of the best places in the world to be drilling for oil.

This told me two things: first, Pickens was entitled to 15 percent of the proceeds from the sale of that piece of the Red Bull, and second, his remaining interest in the Red Bull was worth far more than any of us thought. I made a rough calculation and figured that his portion of the sale alone could be worth about $40 million. Not a bad return for an initial investment of about $125,000.

I thought back to my conversation with Pickens' attorney, Sandy, when he first handed me the Red Bull file. "Take a look at this, Chrysta," he'd said. "We don't know if it's worth pursuing." It was definitely worth pursuing.

Before we left Montgomery's office, we arranged to make electronic copies of all of the files. Once we got them, we loaded them into a huge computer database where we could search for key terms. It took a few months to sort through this treasure trove.

Then, as is typical in a court case, we started taking depositions. The first person I wanted to question was Mike Hedrick, the Baytech employee who oversaw the Red Bull leasing efforts.

I could tell from the documents that he was an important witness. His role was to identify new acreage to lease and then report the purchases to Cliff Milford, J. Cleo's chief financial officer. Milford, in turn, would bill the Red Bull investors for their share of the costs.

Hedrick worked closely with Baytech CEO Ben Strickling, keeping him apprised of the Red Bull activities. As we dug through the documents, we found a key email from July 2008. In it, Strickling told Hedrick he wanted as much of the Red Bull interest as possible. But all the interests in the deal had already been apportioned to the original investors, with Pickens among them. For Baytech to increase its stake, one or more of those investors would have to sell. Hedrick approached a few of them, and one sold to Baytech. Then, he turned to Mesa and tried to make a deal to buy its 15 percent.

Unsurprisingly, Baytech's desire to buy all of the Red Bull interest it could get its hands on corresponded with oil hitting a high of more than a hundred dollars a barrel. But I found it curious that Mesa's alleged desire to "opt out" wasn't mentioned in any paperwork until much later, and then, only in documents written by Baytech or J. Cleo.

When I questioned Hedrick about this in his deposition, he testified that Baytech had tried to buy Mesa's interest because Milford, J. Cleo's CFO, had told him that Mesa wanted out. He added that Milford had also said that Mesa hadn't paid its share of the additional leasing costs after the initial buy-in. Hedrick stated that he believed Mesa's rights were limited to 15 percent of just the Lyda well.

The documents showed that Hedrick had, in fact, approached Alex about buying Mesa's interest in December 2008. The men had a few conversations over the next few months, but the talks ended in March 2009 without a deal. Hedrick had taken detailed notes of the last conversation. According to those notes, Alex had told him that Mesa had bought more than just the Lyda well. They revealed that Alex told him that Mesa had paid $515,738 up to that point for its Red Bull interests—far more than just its initial $125,000 investment for its interest in the Lyda well and two original sections of land. But Hedrick was only authorized to offer Mesa a little more than $160,000 for its interest, a sum that Alex rebuffed.

Hedrick's notes about his discussion with Alex contained another detail that struck me as odd. He seemed surprised that Mesa said it had paid for its interest in more than just the Lyda well and original two sections. At the time, I couldn't figure out why he cared what Mesa had paid for. A cryptic line at the end of his notes held the potential clue. Hedrick was questioning Mesa's level of ownership in the other Red Bull leases Alex claimed Mesa had paid for because Baytech itself had already paid J. Cleo for Mesa's stake in those same leases in February 2009—*a month before Hedrick's negotiations with Alex fell through.*

I couldn't believe what I was reading. It appeared that Baytech had paid J. Cleo to transfer Mesa's interests *before* Baytech's negotiations to buy out Mesa's rights had concluded. If Hedrick's notes were correct, it looked to me as if Baytech and J. Cleo had removed Mesa from the deal first, then later tried to build a paper trail to back up the transfers. This appeared to be a key piece of evidence, or as we call it in the litigation business, a "smoking gun."

I discovered an even more disturbing development. A few days after his final conversation with Alex, and nearly a month after Mesa's Red Bull interests had been transferred to Baytech on J. Cleo's books, Hedrick emailed Milford complaining that Mesa didn't want to sell its Red Bull rights because Pickens' company thought oil prices would rise again. But the need to buy out Mesa's remaining rights had taken on new urgency because J. Cleo was attempting to revive another Red Bull well the next day.

The Colt well had been drilled before the Red Bull deal was put together, but it didn't produce much oil. The Red Bull partners—Mesa included—elected to purchase it so that it could be "recompleted." Recompletion is like a do-over. If a well isn't producing at a particular depth or formation, it can be either drilled deeper or plugged back to try to get oil from a shallower depth. The process is usually cheaper than drilling a new well. In this case, J. Cleo planned to recomplete the well to a shallower depth in the Delaware Basin formation. The group had already seen that the Delaware Basin's oil-laden shale layer existed in the Lyda well (even though it didn't produce much oil there). If the same oil-producing rock layers, or benches, also existed in the Colt well, the results of the recompletion would show that the whole area was rich with oil. It might turn out to be the ticket to a huge discovery.

There was no dispute that Mesa had been offered its 15 percent share of the Colt well. And more important to Mesa's case, there was no question that Mesa had elected to participate in buying and recompleting the Colt well, in accordance with the agreements. I had the documents with Pickens' signature attached to prove it.

But Hedrick's email to Milford added an unexpected twist. It showed that Hedrick was worried that if Mesa got word that the Colt workover turned out to be a success, Pickens would become more determined than ever to stay in the deal—eliminating any further possibility that he might want to sell to Baytech. Hedrick wanted Milford to give Mesa its money back pronto. "This has to be done fairly quickly because you are fracking the Colt well tomorrow and don't want any information about it to affect their decision," Hedrick wrote. Later, in his deposition, Hedrick was steadfast in his contention that Mesa wasn't entitled to any information about the Colt well because it had "opted out" of receiving it.

The first time I encountered them, I read the notes and email several times over in disbelief. It appeared to me that Hedrick knew in March 2009 that Baytech hadn't actually bought Mesa out of its rights in the Red Bull deal, even though it had just paid J. Cleo for Mesa's stake. That was bad enough. But the email that advocated hiding information about the potential for big results from the Colt well workover—material information to which I believed Mesa was entitled by law—was truly incriminating in my mind. Juries don't like to see companies or people hiding information.

Things were getting interesting. I concluded we had some evidence that Baytech took Mesa's interest without paying Mesa for it. I thought Hedrick's emails with Milford showed that Baytech knew that it didn't have clear title to that interest. And it appeared that we had discovered a plot between the two of them to cover it up.

I was staring at what I believed were the elements of a conspiracy. I had already calculated Mesa's damages in the case to be at least $40 million, based on the value of the piece of the Red Bull that had been sold. Considering that most of the Red Bull was still held by the original investors, I felt as if Pickens' share of the sale and his stake in the remaining property could easily be worth triple that amount. Now, given the new details we'd uncovered, it appeared we had a case for punitive damages, too, which could add two to three times that amount. To top it all off, the land rush in the Permian was making Pickens' interest in the remaining Red Bull properties and wells more valuable by the day.

These revelations put a whole new perspective on Pickens' case. Eventually, after we'd gathered all the documents and had our experts analyze the value of the Red Bull lands and wells, I decided to amend our lawsuit to claim damages in excess of $1 billion.

It was that big of a deal.

Chapter 6

"THE WRONG GUY TO ELIMINATE"

I needed more answers about what had happened to Mesa's Red Bull interest and decided to depose Cliff Milford next. Though he held the title of chief financial officer for J. Cleo, he really served as a jack of all trades. Jimmy Thompson, the company's namesake and founder, had died three years before we filed the lawsuit, so I couldn't depose him. But there were details about Thompson and his company, J. Cleo, that were important to the case. Milford might be able to fill in some blanks.

Thompson had graduated from SMU's law school several decades before I had. But he'd gone into the oil business instead of practicing law. Despite his legal training, rumor had it that Thompson had operated the company out of his back pocket, keeping track of its deals and finances on a small pad he carried with him. The J. Cleo company appeared to have been run as an extension of Thompson himself. Even after his death, it didn't have a large staff. Milford kept the books and oversaw the land and lease files until 2013, when the company hired more full-time staff.

Oil deals run on accurate records. Companies must know what land and wells they and their investors own. Those investors, also called "working interest owners" or just "partners," may buy and sell their interests. To keep track of all those transactions, companies maintain "interest decks" that list all the fractional ownership interests in each property and well. It's a complex business, and I couldn't imagine someone keeping it all straight in a notebook in his back pocket.

Based on Hedrick's testimony, I knew Milford had never seen a document signed by Pickens in which Mesa gave up its Red Bull rights. I also knew that the deal documents required that all changes to the agreement be made in writing and signed by Pickens. I further discovered that nothing in the Red Bull contracts mentioned an "opt out" provision, which apparently was Baytech's defense for taking Mesa's share. The documents also showed that Baytech had taken over Mesa's 15 percent interest in early 2009, and that Baytech had paid J. Cleo to make that transfer.

What I didn't know was why. Why had J. Cleo agreed to stop sending Mesa its Red Bull notices? Why had it transferred Mesa's 15 percent interest to Baytech? What was the source of this "opt out" contention that arose at the same time Baytech was looking to buy more Red Bull interests?

Milford was a difficult witness to depose. I concluded from his demeanor that he resented me questioning him. I could also sense that he thought he knew more than I did about the two contracts in the case. It wasn't the first time a male witness thought he could show me up, and it probably won't be the last. After he told me not to "smart off to him" about how the contracts worked, I set about, with gusto, to prove that I had studied their every detail. Despite the seemingly incessant objections from the defense lawyers—a foreshadowing of what

I would face at trial—Milford eventually conceded that Mesa should have received a legal document transferring ownership of its share of the original Red Bull land sections and that Baytech and J. Cleo hadn't provided it. He became more pliable after losing that battle. Most witnesses do after losing a few skirmishes.

Milford acknowledged that no one notified Mesa that its interest had been transferred to Baytech. Milford said there was no need, because Pickens already knew he was giving up on the deal. Milford testified that he had personally heard Pickens say that he was getting out after walking into Thompson's office during a phone call between Thompson and Pickens. But Milford couldn't say when the call happened. And by now, Thompson wasn't around to corroborate any details.

"How do you explain the fact that Pickens didn't sign anything?" I asked him. He said that he didn't think he needed to. After the call, Milford simply put a credit on Mesa's bill for everything but the Lyda well charges. I had seen multiple credits with varying descriptions on Mesa's bills, and one that simply said "current adjustment" that would turn out to be a key to the case. But I also knew no one at Mesa but Pickens could agree to take a credit instead of the ownership interests. Milford said that Baytech had agreed to buy out Mesa's interest in the Lyda well, and Milford and Hedrick believed the credit would take care of everything else.

The problem was, as I pointed out to Milford, Mesa didn't know any of this was happening.

"Shouldn't J.Cleo and Baytech have notified Mesa that they transferred Mesa's interest?" I asked.

"How did they transfer it?" Milford asked in response.

"Well," I said, "apparently they did because they stopped sending Mesa its election notices."

"At Mesa's instructions." Round and round we went, with Milford repeatedly insisting that Mesa "opted out" of the deal based on the phone call he overheard between Pickens and Thompson. I started to ask another question, and as I did, Milford added: "we can do this all day."

And we pretty much did. The deposition went on for hours, with Milford claiming he had little knowledge of what had happened, little recall of key conversations, and little familiarity with the documents I put in front of him. He also insisted he had no reason to question Baytech's alleged purchase of Mesa's stake.

Eventually, I got him to acknowledge that J. Cleo had received a payment from Baytech for Mesa's interest. Then, I asked if he ever talked to Mesa about receiving it. It took two tries.

"Did you tell Mesa, either Alex or Mr. Pickens, that you had accepted a check from Baytech for the 15 percent of the leases?" I asked.

"I had no conversation with them after we received a check," Milford said.

I finally had a what I needed: he agreed that neither J. Cleo nor Baytech had told Mesa what they were doing.

While we seemed to have cleared up that point, the bills J. Cleo sent to Mesa that listed the mysterious credits continued to confuse things. The bills were a mess. Milford agreed that some of the documents mixed up the Red Bull records with other, unrelated, deals between J. Cleo and other Pickens-related entities. In one billing error, Mesa was charged for payments it had already made, creating an error of several hundred thousand dollars. It didn't take long for me to realize I would need an accounting expert to unravel the books.

I couldn't just depose defense witnesses, of course. To build a strong case, I'd interviewed the employees who'd been involved in the deal for Mesa. And I needed to hear from Pickens himself. I started with Alex, since he had overseen the Red Bull investment in his role at BP Capital, Pickens' other company. Unfortunately, he wasn't much help because he couldn't remember most of what had transpired. He'd played a number of roles while working for Pickens, and he'd since moved on to start his own investment fund with some other former BP Capital employees. He did clearly remember that Baytech had offered to buy the Mesa interest and that the two companies didn't reach an agreement. Beyond that, he didn't know why Mesa stopped getting notices, and he didn't remember anything about the mysterious credits.

The defense counsel asked to depose Alex and Pickens, too. We agreed to do that at my office, which at the time was located in Dallas' West End, a district of old warehouses just west of downtown that had begun to decline early in the twentieth century. During the oil boom of the 1980s, developers converted a bunch of these structures into office and retail space. The building where I'd set up my law firm had been formed out of three factories that shared ancient brick walls. Some of the walls and floors had been knocked out to create a huge five-story central atrium with glass-fronted offices facing it. I loved having my own space and one so different from the high-rise law firms I had inhabited for the past twenty years.

But the acoustics weren't good—or more to the point, it was impossible to speak without being overheard. When Pickens attended the depositions, I frequently had to keep him from speaking too loudly during a break, which he liked to do because he was hard of hearing. The conference room we used for the depositions was huge and seated at least thirty people. Given the number of lawyers involved in our case, it was nearly packed for every deposition.

Rick Montgomery always attended for Baytech. Stuart Hollimon was Baytech's lead lawyer, but Tim McConn, a younger litigator from Hollimon's firm, often attended in Hollimon's place. Geoff Bracken, who represented J. Cleo, was the head of litigation for a major Texas firm and had a lot of experience as a trial lawyer. He was accompanied by Paul Rudnicki, J. Cleo's current chief financial officer—he'd replaced Cliff Milford—and Rick Hodges, the vice president of land, who'd been hired in 2013 to take control of the land records.

I had Debbie, my associate, order pastries and brownies each time for the assembled crowd. It can be a long and dull experience to sit through a deposition. I wanted to keep the process friendly, hoping the defendants would agree at some point to pay Pickens his fair share of the Red Bull profits without going to trial. You can usually catch more flies with honey than vinegar.

Besides Alex, the other side wanted to depose the man himself, of course. Not only did the defense lawyers relish the idea of cross-examining Pickens, they knew this case would bolster their own careers. Lawyers live for big cases, and even more so for cases involving celebrities. McConn was already listing the case in his biography on his firm's website, making sure to cite "T. Boone Pickens" rather than the actual plaintiff, Mesa Petroleum Partners.

Pickens was a challenging witness. He couldn't hear or see well. He'd told me he'd been diagnosed with macular degeneration, and he wore hearing aids in both ears, which made it difficult to prepare him to testify for a document-intensive case. I had to blow up the material I wanted him to review so that he could read it, and I had to sit next to him so he could hear me.

These weren't the only hurdles. I approach every case like I did my fifth-grade advertising project—I prepare. I don't want to leave any detail to chance. For witness testimony, that means I want to help them anticipate all the ways their words can be used against them. I want to cover key points and have the witnesses practice talking about them. Pickens would have rather eaten broccoli with a straw.

From the moment I filed the case, Pickens had been fully invested and attentive to whatever I needed. He was good at communicating, and he felt comfortable in front of an audience, whether it was a packed auditorium or twelve people in a jury box. But he detested preparing for his testimony. For all of his focus on the case, he had no patience for sitting and running through hours of what-if scenarios.

It didn't help that we both were sure we were right about how to proceed. Fortunately, we saw the case the same way most of the time, but when we didn't—and luckily those instances were rare—things got heated.

In a case in which a witness can't prepare or doesn't want to cooperate, you take your chances. With Pickens, it was a bit of both. He was eighty-eight, after all, and he found it exhausting to read documents with his deteriorating eyesight. Even worse, he thought he knew how to handle everything already.

We arrived at my offices for his deposition well before the 9:00 a.m. start. I wanted to show him around, thinking that he would like the old building and the giant murals on the first floor with scenes of commerce conducted at the turn of the last century. I also knew that others in the building would enjoy meeting a genuine business celebrity. So, after showing him the conference room, I walked him over to the offices next door. I thought shaking a few hands and telling a few war stories might make him more comfortable and take his mind off the deposition. It seemed to work.

Just before nine, I took him back to the large glass conference room where his interrogators, and their entourages, were
waiting. All of them looked as eager to meet Pickens as the
people in the next office had been. It was their first time confronting the legend.

After the handshakes and introductions, Pickens sat down
at the end of the table with a microphone attached to his lapel.
He faced a video camera that would record all of the proceedings and sat next to a stenographer who would transcribe his
testimony. I sat on his right side, as always, so he could hear
me. My main job during the deposition was to object to inap-
propriate questions, but I was concerned. I hoped that he was
prepared enough for the questions he would face.

Bracken, the J. Cleo lawyer, started with routine questioning—name, age, what he did for a living and so forth. He asked
if Pickens was a sophisticated businessman, and Pickens said
he was. I knew that would be a theme at trial—that Pickens
couldn't have been in the dark about what had happened with
the Red Bull because he was too sophisticated.

After nearly thirty years of being a lawyer working with
CEOs, CFOs, COOs, directors, and anybody else who occupies a
"C-suite" position, here is what I know about the sophistication
of businessmen: none really knows what they're doing. No one
gets it right all of the time, and no one is immune from making
mistakes. It doesn't really matter how long you've been doing
your job. You're still going to inevitably and regularly face new
challenges. You'll have to figure it out without knowing everything you need to know, and there's always the risk that things
will go badly. Business legends like Pickens are no different.
They don't make decisions knowing the outcome, but they have
track records that give them the confidence to think things will
work out. And, of course, for someone like Pickens, they also

have the financial means to protect themselves if they're wrong. In later years, Pickens often said that while he was right in a lot of his predictions, especially the rise of natural gas, he was wrong on the timing. Few people could have made such a big bet or afforded the billions of dollars that being wrong that time cost him. But Pickens jumped back in and tried again, making more money than ever.

Pickens' mistakes, like his successes, played out on a large stage. Sure, he understood business, and you could say he was sophisticated, but if sophistication was sufficient protection against misunderstandings, mistakes, and misdeeds, I wouldn't have a job.

J. Cleo's Bracken and Baytech's McConn picked away at the specifics of the Red Bull investment, asking hour after hour of detailed questions. Pickens said he signed the deal, he intended to participate in all of the purchases, and he paid for them. "If you send us a bill, we pay it," he said. "That is the direction I always give Dick Grant," referring to Mesa's chief financial officer. I knew he was right. I wasn't working for a contingency fee on this case; I was paid by the hour, and Mesa paid every bill with a check sent by return mail.

Pickens admitted he didn't know a lot of the details. He had left most of those to Alex, his Red Bull overseer, and Sandy, his lawyer. He did recall someone trying to buy his Red Bull interest, and he'd said he'd sell for all they had put into the deal, which was about $515,000. He also knew he never sold it because he didn't sign anything.

They wanted to know why he hadn't asked about the Red Bull between 2009 and 2014, when he finally realized he hadn't heard any news about the deal for some time. He'd "had a lot of things going on, and it just didn't come around," he replied. The deal was a "peanut investment that we had at the time that turned into a lot of money." Then, in typical Pickens fashion, he added that the defendants "were sorry people to do business with, and I should have watched closer."

Pickens had a talent for knowing when to concede a point and at the same time turn it into a strength. With that answer, he both acknowledged that he should have watched the investment more diligently and pinned it to the fact he didn't trust the defendants. I knew it would be tough for the defense lawyers to clip that piece of videotape into a sound bite that they'd actually want to show to a jury.

Time and again, the defense lawyers pressed him on whether he'd told Jimmy Thompson he was opting out of the deal. Pickens was emphatic that it hadn't happened. He glared at Bracken, the J. Cleo attorney, his steely blue eyes boring into him. "You know we didn't get out of the deal," he said. "I mean, you guys have a silly story. I never got out of a property in my life that had value that somebody didn't pay me and I signed something passing ownership. Show me what I ever signed. Show me the check. You just eliminated me from the thing, and I'm the wrong guy to eliminate."

I'm the wrong guy to eliminate. The words echoed in the room long after they left his lips. I knew that he was dead serious, but I wondered if these younger men, who had never encountered Pickens in his full corporate battle mode, could see past his current visage of a near deaf and blind elderly gentleman. For a moment, there was a flash of classic Pickens, the same guy who'd gone toe-to-toe with corporate titans and made them blink. The defense attorneys blinked too. Whether because of Pickens' celebrity status or his age, I felt as if they didn't push him as hard as they probably wanted to.

Pickens held up well during the rest of the deposition. We finished with McConn asking Pickens to name every "malicious" act committed by the defendants against Mesa. I hadn't prepared him for that specific phrasing, but Pickens perked right up and shot back, saying they "went together and figured out a way they could cut us out of the deal. I truly believe they stole the properties."

It was the late afternoon when the defense attorneys finally concluded their questioning. Pickens looked to me for validation that he had done a good job, which frankly kind of surprised me. He hadn't been terribly cooperative about the preparation, but now he seemed to want my reassurance that he'd done well. He might not have been in many courtrooms for trials, but he'd sat for dozens of depositions during his takeover days, when lawsuits swirled like flurries in a blizzard. And he'd mentioned some of the New York law firms that represented him in the past: Sherman & Sterling, Wachtel Lipton, and other Wall Street heavyweights—a Who's Who of the legal world. He'd had many lawyers more important than me on his cases, but there he was, seeking my approval. "You did a great job, Mr. Pickens," I said. And I meant it. He had made his points and done so despite his age, memory, or physical challenges. He looked pleased with the answer.

After taking a few more depositions of defense witnesses, I'd learned a lot about the Red Bull deal. I knew that it had grown to more than a hundred square miles and that Baytech and J. Cleo had leased more than 60,000 acres. That should have entitled Pickens to the value of 9,000 of those acres. Given that leases were going for as much as $40,000 an acre, Pickens' stake in the raw land could have been worth as much as $360 million back in 2014. In addition, J. Cleo had drilled seventy-six wells, and the defendants had determined that each of the wells accessed rich reserves. As a result, we argued that Pickens was entitled to his 15 percent share of all that oil, adding up to a tidy billion dollars, by my calculation.

The term "reserves" refers to the quantity of oil that a company expects to recover through drilling. Calculating reserves is based on a bunch of variables, such as how many zones (or "benches") of oil shale you plan to drill; how likely you are to hit oil, and how many barrels you will find; when you plan to drill the wells; how much the wells cost; how fast you think you'll deplete the oil through each well, known as a "decline curve"; what you think you'll get for the price of oil when you sell it; and something called the "discount rate," which is used to compare the value of future dollars with today's dollars.

All of those variables go together to produce a "reserves report," which is the basis on which oil companies borrow money and attract investors to a deal. For publicly held companies, it affects their net worth and other financial metrics. It can also be wildly subjective. A company can make a property worth more simply by stepping up the drilling schedule, for example, or by increasing the estimate of oil that will be recovered.

Because of concerns that public companies inflated reserves, the Securities Exchange Commission cracked down.[1] It now requires that companies count reserves only on wells they are likely to drill in the next five years based on past performance. In addition, companies must review their assumptions periodically and revise their reserves value downward if they haven't drilled the number of wells that they said they would. Because the industry is governed by boom-bust cycles, and the price of oil and natural gas fluctuates so wildly, an unexpected price drop can curtail a drilling program and deflate a company's value. The SEC wants that volatility factored into the stock price.

No similar rules, however, apply to private companies like Baytech. Because private companies are allowed more latitude, inflated reserves numbers can drive a lot of investments, asset deals and company mergers. In this case, Delaware Basin

Resources, or "DBR" as we called it, had compiled the reserves report on the Red Bull. I'd never heard of DBR before I filed the lawsuit. Early on, I had served an interrogatory, which is basically a question that the defendants had to answer in writing, asking what had happened to Mesa's Red Bull interest after 2009. I got back the sworn answer that Baytech had taken it and transferred it to DBR, which had been formed for the purpose of holding Baytech's Red Bull interests. That, too, was shocking to me. Taking Mesa's 15 percent and putting it in a company we'd never heard of would help to obscure the title records. As soon as I learned of the transfer, I promptly added DBR to our lawsuit. Even more suspicious: Baytech and DBR had the same chief executive officer, Ben Strickling. It was starting to look to me as if he was personally involved in whatever had happened, so I decided to sue him, too.

Strickling, who's in his mid-fifties, is soft-spoken and shows little emotion, even in stressful situations like his deposition. I decided to question him about the email that he'd written to Hedrick July 2008, when oil prices were at a record high, telling Hedrick that Baytech "wanted all of the Red Bull interest, if possible." Before that email, I'd found no mention of an "opt out" by Mesa in any of the documents, but after that, the phrase began showing up frequently and eventually evolved to the point that in March 2009, Strickling was telling Pickens in a letter that because of the "opt out," Mesa's interest was limited to the Lyda well alone. But all the documents that supported these claims were coming from Baytech, DBR, and J. Cleo, not Mesa. To me, that was highly suspicious.

The Lyda well was expensive to operate and generated little revenue. As long as Pickens owned 15 percent of it, he'd have to continue to pay that part of the costs while getting little in return. After studying the bills that had been sent to Mesa—with the help of expert accountants—it looked to me as if Pickens had paid J. Cleo almost $1 million for Mesa's share of the Red Bull bills by the time we were actively preparing for the trial. J. Cleo had continued to send invoices for project expenses, even as it had stopped notifying Mesa of new acquisitions. This helped explain why Mesa thought all along the project was still active but small. Yet Pickens had little to show for it other than an interest in the single subpar well the defense would credit to him, the Lyda.

When I deposed Strickling, I pressed him on the opt-out defense. He claimed to remember little about it, saying it started with Milford and Thompson. Of course, he couldn't distance himself from the documents and emails. Emails always catch people out in litigation, popping back up long after they've forgotten they wrote them. In this case, I confronted him with his message about wanting all the Red Bull interests possible. I juxtaposed it to the fact that oil prices were at an all-time high.

"Why did you want all of the interest if possible?" I asked. He said that Baytech and DBR were bringing in other investors and they needed a bigger piece of the pie to make it more attractive. Baytech had taken Mesa's 15 percent for itself in February 2009, and then later that year Strickling and Montgomery set up DBR to hold the Red Bull properties and rights, transferring them from Baytech and giving the investors they'd courted a stake in the new company.

You don't often get one smoking gun—let alone several—in a business case, and you certainly don't usually get a direct statement of intent. With the admission that Baytech and Strickling had needed Mesa's share for their plans, I believed I now had the motive for the taking of Mesa's interest.

Chapter 7

LINGERING DOUBTS

So far, everything was going smoothly, but I knew that wouldn't last. In fact, the more smoothly things go, the more I worry. I wonder if I'm missing something. The law is complicated, and my biggest fear is always the argument or the tactic I don't see coming. But I knew I had the law and the facts on my side, which was a plus. In some cases, you have neither. I also had a pretty good paper trail showing that my client had been cut out of his ownership rights in a high-dollar, high-stakes oil project. And I had some good testimony admitting that the defendants hadn't paid him for it.

But I also felt anxious on a couple of fronts. I was surprised that the defendants weren't more willing to settle, given the evidence I'd assembled against them. I'd underestimated the power of billions of dollars to drive decision-making. Given how the defense lawyers had been acting, it seemed clear we were headed to trial, and the fledgling Castañeda Firm was understaffed for the effort that would require.

The team was now Debbie, two paralegals and me. We needed more help. I wanted to show Pickens that I could handle the case. He might not have been involved in other trials like the one we were headed for, but he had certainly paid legions of lawyers over the years. He expected results. The bigger this case grew, the more worried I became that he would turn it over to another lawyer—probably an elder statesman of the Texas bar. Most oil and gas trial lawyers are men. I knew that Pickens could be old-fashioned about certain things—he still believed in dressing for dinner, for example—and I worried he might be equally old-fashioned in his views of traditional roles for women. If so, would he really let me see this through to a verdict?

Pickens had never hinted he was thinking of replacing me, but my years in the business fueled my worry. Frankly, there just aren't that many female lead trial lawyers for business cases, and I had never seen another one in all of the oil and gas cases I had handled. Sure, others were out there, but we were few and far between. Besides, Pickens had no women professionals working as managers at his companies. From what I'd seen, all of the women there were assistants to the men.

Perhaps I was being paranoid, but I even asked Sandy whether I was at risk of having the case taken away because of my gender. He insisted that Pickens frequently hired women professionals—accountants, lawyers, and others—and that he treated them respectfully. That may have been true, but I never saw any other woman entrusted with the kind of role I'd been given.

Pickens frequently told me how much he admired strong women, particularly his mother and grandmother. Based on his telling, they had ruled the household and set his life on its future path. I could see he meant it. This gave me some solace, although I couldn't tell if his admiration protected my role in the case. But he seemed sincere, both in his respect for me as a professional and in his regard for women, especially those with grit.

He'd sometimes refer to me as a bulldog when we were talking about the case. I think he meant it as a sign of respect. One of the women in politics he held in high esteem was Condoleezza Rice, the former Secretary of State under President George W. Bush. Pickens used to say, "she pisses ice water." If his measure of female worth was whether a woman could be as tough as a man, he seemed to have formed an opinion that I was tough enough to handle his case. But I could never fully dismiss the possibility that he would want to call in a male lawyer, as the stakes multiplied, and we drew closer to trial.

Several incidents heightened my uneasiness. During Pickens' deposition, his cell phone started ringing. He'd just gotten the phone and he couldn't figure out how to turn it off. It was disrupting the questioning, and I needed it silenced. "Hand it to me," I said, reaching across the table. He obliged. I turned it off and gave it back. "Another pushy woman," he quipped. He was chuckling as he said it, and I knew he was kidding, but the other men in the room broke out in grins. Tim McConn, the Baytech lawyer, looked at me and asked if I wanted to object. I forced a smile, but before I could answer, Pickens said, "Just for the record, I have had five wives. I know what I am talking about." His comments wound up on the official transcript of the deposition.

A few weeks after his "pushy woman" comment, I ran into Pickens and his fifth wife, Toni, at the Ritz Carlton. I'd been having a cocktail with Ann Marie Painter, a good friend and labor lawyer who spotted Pickens as he walked by. Even at eighty-eight, Pickens was still a recognizable celebrity about town. I figured I should be polite and say hello, so I followed them to the hostess desk. While they were waiting to be seated, I introduced myself to Mrs. Pickens.

She was cordial enough, but I could imagine in her eyes the calculation that women frequently make about each other. *If you are working with my husband, can I trust you not to threaten my marriage? Or should I do something to get rid of you now?* It seems like women should have moved beyond thinking that way, but some of them still do. Sometimes instinct is stronger than reason, I guess. I've seen women's career opportunities challenged by the wife of a male partner who didn't want the female associate traveling with her husband. And then there are the men who think like Vice President Mike Pence: they won't have a meal alone with a woman who's not their wife. I returned to finish my drink, and I confided my thoughts to Ann Marie. She told me I was nuts, but I think she said it out of friendship. I certainly didn't fully believe the issue was imaginary.

Much later, after the case was over, I learned my worries had some merit, although not for the reasons I'd suspected. Ron Bassett, Pickens' right-hand man for forty years and the vice president of all of Pickens' companies, told me that if they had known what the Red Bull case was worth at the time, they wouldn't have hired me. Unlike Pickens, Bassett is a soft-spoken behind-the-scenes kind of guy, but like his boss, he has a keen intellect and solid business acumen. He meant that they would have felt compelled to hire a big law firm, rather than taking the risky move of trusting it to a solo practitioner. I'm glad he didn't tell me that until the case was over. I'm also glad that he, Pickens, and the other folks at Mesa had no idea what the case was worth until I had already demonstrated I could handle it.

My first chance to prove my value came in the fall of 2015. Baytech, J. Cleo, and DBR filed more than a dozen motions asking for summary judgment—asking the judge to end the case before it went to a jury. Typically, a summary judgment means the case is so lacking in evidence, or support in the law, that the judge can just make a decision without the trouble and expense of a trial. Essentially, the defendants were asking the judge to throw out our case before it even got started.

I no longer had time to worry about whether Pickens had concerns about my gender or my abilities. The first shots had been fired, and I wanted more firepower on my side. We would have to file hundreds of pages of briefs to respond to the summary judgment motions. And although the defendants had beat me to the punch, I intended to file our own summary judgment motion because I thought our case was that solid.

Debbie could do some of the briefing and research, but I would need the help of a more experienced lawyer as well. I hired David Coale, a Dallas appeals attorney whom I had known since my clerkship at the same law firm that didn't pay me while I was in labor. He had interned there too. For this case, I wanted an experienced appellate lawyer involved from the beginning, because if we succeeded as well as I hoped, the defendants would probably appeal, and the appeals process could go on for five years. (In fact, Geoff Bracken, the J. Cleo attorney, told me that he had been in a case that had bounced between the trial and appellate courts for more than a decade, which I took as a signal that he would try to extend this one out, too.) David knew the ropes and could help me mind the issues that would come up later on appeal. David's partner was Mike Lynn, who would eventually serve as my co-counsel at trial.

David was extremely creative and persuasive in legal argument. He's one of the brightest lawyers I know, but also one of the quirkiest. He always carried a deck of tarot cards, and outside of court, he might offer you a reading. At the time of the trial, he also was obsessed with the online game Pokémon Go. Somehow, he could play the game and follow the proceedings simultaneously. Every year, for his Facebook friends, he wrote an intricate Christmas yarn that was basically a shaggy dog story featuring the Grinch, a host of characters from mythology, and, occasionally, Vladimir Putin. David would not only play a key role in the case, he'd also ensure things never got boring.

I also hired my sister, Cathy Mallonee. Like almost everyone else in my family, Cathy had an engineering degree—electrical, in this case—as well as a master's in geology. The ink was still fresh on the master's diploma. She had gone back to school after staying home to raise two daughters. She had aced every class in grad school, but she was still waiting for a solid job offer. No industry makes it easy for a woman to return to the work force after child rearing.

Cathy had no experience as a legal assistant, but she knew geology, and she's extremely smart. I knew she could figure out any task I gave her, so I set her to work to find the best evidence in the hundreds of thousands of documents that the defense had turned over.

I still recall the day she dug up the emails on the Colt well. I knew the defendants didn't want Mesa to know about the results of the well's workover. But Cathy's attention to the geology made me go back and look at the situation a second and third time. She spotted that a previous operator had drilled the well to the Devonian formation—far deeper than the main pay zones of the Delaware Basin. She realized that Baytech and J. Cleo planned to re-enter the well in 2009, plug off the lower portion of the well bore, and perforate—or punch holes in the side of the well casing—at the shallower shale formations of the Delaware where they believed oil resided. Other than the Colt, the Lyda was the only other well in the Red Bull that had been worked over. I called Ricardo Garza, a petroleum engineer and the expert witness who would explain the geology to the jury, to discuss the find. At trial, Cathy's scrutiny of the Colt well geology refocused our attention on that workover and would prove critical to the outcome of the case.

I hired Kara Guillot as a paralegal and professional assistant. Kara had worked in the land department of a midsized Oklahoma oil company and understood the documents oil companies use to track land transactions and ownership. She was Debbie's cousin, and she'd just moved to Texas.

With both a geologist and a land records expert in my lineup, I felt better prepared. I also felt better that I had my younger sister working with me. Only nineteen months separate us, and we've been a team since before I can remember. Mostly, I don't notice that I'm trying to do hard things that other people might believe or hope I will fail at doing. But when I do notice, it's always helped to have Cathy there for moral and emotional support.

Debbie, Cathy, Kara, David and I worked around the clock to file hundreds of pages of briefs on the summary judgment motions. David spent a lot of time at my office, going over the legal points. Cathy supplied the snacks that kept him engaged through the long hours. Debbie was an excellent writer, which helped as well. As a team, we prepared for an all-day hearing on the dozen motions for summary judgment that was scheduled just before Christmas 2015.

One legal point troubled me. I couldn't find case law that directly dealt with the kind of contract we had. The Red Bull Participation Agreement was known as an "area of mutual interest" agreement, or AMI. The essential feature of an AMI is that it's built out over time. The parties start with an initial lease, then try to acquire more land in a target area over a specific number of years. During that time period, all the investors are supposed to be notified of their right to participate in each acquisition. The Red Bull AMI had run from 2007 to 2012, but the defendants had expanded it after Mesa was cut out of the deal in 2009 to encompass more target areas and extend it through 2018.

The defendants were arguing that we had only until 2013—or four years after Baytech had taken Mesa's 15 percent, in February 2009—to file the lawsuit. We hadn't filed until December 2014, more than a year later. They were trying to get the case thrown out of court entirely based on the argument that we filed too late. I knew their argument wasn't correct, but I couldn't find the case law that said so.

We had spent hours and hours sifting through electronic legal databases looking for the right case to address the point. I was pretty sure the Texas Supreme Court should have dealt with the subject before 2015. We needed to know when, exactly, do you start counting the four years for the limitations period when you haven't even acquired all of the AMI property? Shouldn't it be at least four years from the end of the AMI period? That would have meant we were good if we had filed the lawsuit by early 2016, but I was perplexed that the answer wasn't easy to find.

When I can't find what I need online, I head to the books at SMU's Underwood Law Library. Sometimes, the people who turn legal opinions into searchable text miss the point. I would have to spend a day or two looking at legal digests, pulling the cases they cited, and seeing if I could find it myself. Sometimes, old school works better.

As I finished that first day in the library, feeling like I was back in law school, I got the results I sought. I found the 1957 Texas Supreme Court case that dealt with the exact point. It said that the four years didn't begin to run until the defendants notified us of *each acquisition*. If they never gave Mesa the notice in the first place, then the limitations period would never begin to run. The case said that what we were dealing with was a series of option contracts, and the defendants had to allow us to exercise each option. The four years would begin to run anew with each notice of acquisition, and they hadn't even sent most of them yet.

Bingo. I could prove we'd filed Pickens' claim to his share of all of the Red Bull in a timely manner.

I was excited to tell the legal team as well as Pickens. Every couple of weeks or so, I would drive to his office and discuss the myriad details of the case. Every one of those meetings made me feel more comfortable about my role as Pickens' lead lawyer. He devoted his time and attention in the case to such a degree that it surprised me. I had expected he would sit for his deposition, then follow the proceedings from Dallas, leaving it to others to fight. After all, he had extensive business interests to tend to, and even though the case had grown in size, I remembered his comment about it being a "peanut investment." I figured he might show up for part of the trial, but I never expected him to attend preliminary pretrial hearings. Instead, he told me he was going.

Pickens wasn't one of those business guys who tried to show how humble he was by flying coach. He'd gotten in the habit of using private planes back when he worked out of Amarillo, a city that had limited air travel in those days. More recently, he needed a way to get between his home in Dallas and his beloved Mesa Vista Ranch in the Panhandle some three hundred fifty miles away. He offered me a seat to the preliminary hearing in late 2015 on his Gulfstream, and I wasn't going to say no. The jet was personalized with his initials and fully stocked with snacks and beverages, including his favorite drink, Dr Pepper. I had never experienced anything like it.

The Reeves County Courthouse is, by Texas standards, unremarkable. In many counties, the courthouse sits prominently in a square in the center of town. In Pecos, the courthouse is just off one of the major thoroughfares, tucked away from the main row of shops almost as if it were an afterthought. Built in 1937, its beige brick exterior signals the last century yet somehow seems timeless. On the inside, it's a tribute to World War I. Apparently, a lot of locals were involved in that war. As far as Texas courthouses go, it's in pretty good repair. The courtroom is upstairs, its entrance wedged between the rising staircase and a narrow hallway that leads to the district clerk's office. One bench, for public seating, is outside, at the top of the stairs.

As we walked into the courtroom, I was greeted by the court reporter, whose last name, ironically, is Record. I'd later learn that he'd been married to another court reporter whose maiden name was Court. She became Mrs. Court-Record. (I know what you're probably thinking, but no, I'm not making this up.)

Breck Record was a friendly guy who wore western attire, including long duster coats and bolero ties. He liked to show visitors pictures of his pet parrot and his motocross bikes during breaks in the proceedings. He was also extremely competent and timely with transcripts, which you don't always get from court reporters in understaffed and underfunded Texas courts.

State District Judge Mike Swanson, who presided over our case, had a job that required him to move around among courthouses in Pecos, Monahans, and Mentone. Mentone is the seat of Loving County, which has a population of just 134—or one person for about every five square miles. It's the second least-populated county in the country behind Kalawao County, Hawaii, on the northern tip of Moloka'i. Swanson was the only judge in a district that spanned more than four thousand square miles, an area almost the size of Connecticut. The trial would be conducted in Pecos, the seat of Reeves County, but for pre-trial hearings, we went to Swanson's base of operations in Monahans, forty miles away.

Judge Swanson took his seat behind the bench. He was not a small man, and I wondered if he had played football when he was younger. Most boys in West Texas did. Some towns didn't have enough high schoolers to field a team, so they played a variation known as Six Man. As the name implies, the teams were half the normal size and the game moved much faster than traditional football.

Swanson had close-cropped graying hair and wire-trimmed glasses. He was new to the bench, and I knew that the Red Bull case was going to be his first trial. His predecessor, Bob Parks, who had presided over the district for decades, had died of cancer a year earlier. Texas' Republican governor, Greg Abbott, appointed Swanson to fill the bench.

We settled into our seats and the attorneys for the defendants began arguing their first motion. Except for Pickens, no other executives came for the hearing, only the lawyers. As anticipated, their primary attack was that Pickens had waited too long to sue them and that the claims were all barred by the statute of limitations. When it came my turn to respond, I pointed to that 1957 Texas Supreme Court ruling. Because the defendants hadn't sent the required notices to Pickens, the clock hadn't even started to run yet on the statute of limitations, I argued.

When I presented Mesa's own motion for summary judgment, I asked the judge to rule for us based on the undisputed facts. We knew that the contracts required the defendants to give Mesa notices of lease purchases and wells drilled, and they hadn't. We knew Pickens had never signed a contract amendment relieving them of that responsibility, and executives for the defendants had already admitted that in their depositions. In my mind, that was all the court needed to find that Baytech, J. Cleo, and DBR breached the contracts. We didn't need a jury to sort out the facts relating to whether they had done so.

The judge took all the motions "under advisement," which meant he would study the arguments and rule on them later. I figured we'd hear after the Christmas holidays, and certainly well before we got close to the trial setting. Winter came and went, the spring of 2016 gave way to the blistering heat of the Texas summer, and still no rulings came. Only when the winds carried the first wisp of fall across the baked plains of West Texas did the judge give us his decision. Although he would limit some of our claims, we were going to trial.

Part Two

THE TRIAL BEGINS

Chapter 8

MORNING IN MONAHANS

The start of a trial is rarely the true start of a trial. Before the jury hears the case, judges first establish the ground rules, such as what evidence can be admitted. They also consider last-minute attempts by the defense to get the case thrown out. Our case was no different. About ten months after our big summary judgment hearing, the court faxed a ruling upholding some of the defense's statute of limitation claims. This decision essentially cut our potential damages—the billion dollars I believed Pickens' interest was worth—by at least half. We would have to recalculate to determine exactly how big the cut was. And the defense wasn't done trying to avoid the trial entirely.

A few weeks before our court date, the lawyers all gathered at the courthouse in Monahans, another dusty Permian Basin oil town west of Midland. It was an important meeting, a hearing on the two fundamental issues that would set the parameters for the entire trial.

Once again, I made the tedious journey from Dallas Love Field to Midland, this time without the comfort of Pickens' Gulfstream. I rented a car—Hertz gave me a midsize, although you never knew when flying into Midland if you might end up with a pickup—and drove the fifty miles to Monahans. Interstate 20 was clogged, as usual, with trucks and semis hauling pipe, tools, and other equipment used in the Oil Patch. The boom was in full swing, and an endless flotilla of vehicles pounded mile upon mile of roadway. Maintenance crews couldn't keep up with the potholes, and the steady stream of heavy traffic turned the posted speed limit of eighty miles an hour into an unattainable goal. That wasn't all bad. Even at seventy miles an hour, the trucks were so big, and spaced so close together, that many drivers of passenger vehicles felt as if they could be run off the road at any moment. The locals bear a heavy price for the oil that is produced around them.

I pulled into the parking lot of the Ward County Courthouse. The blocky white facade was just three years younger than its counterpart in Pecos, but the strips of vertical windows that bisect the exterior give it the feel of modernity from a bygone era. I made my way into the courtroom and settled into my seat at the table next to the jury box. There would be no jury today, and probably few spectators.

As we prepared for trial, Judge Swanson was gearing up for his first election. Fortunately, he had no opponent, so I didn't have to worry that a campaign would distract him from our trial.[1] I wanted him focused on our case, because even with his full attention, it would be a complicated proceeding.

On that day's docket, Swanson would determine if the defense could argue that Pickens orally "opted out" of the written contracts. The defendants claimed Pickens not only told a dead man, Jimmy Thompson, that he wanted out of the deal sometime in 2008, but they were asking the judge to allow Cliff Milford, who said he overheard the conversation, to testify about it. Essentially, they were asking the judge to let their witness share hearsay.

Our response to their opt out argument was the second issue Judge Swanson would consider. We had asserted the Statute of Frauds defense. It dates to sixteenth century England, and it's designed to prevent people from claiming property that isn't theirs. It's why when you buy a house, you need a written contract signed by the prior owner giving you title. Otherwise, your next-door neighbor might decide that you've "opted out" of your house the next time you go on vacation, arguing that if you wanted to keep the property, you shouldn't have left it. Having a signed, written agreement transferring title prevents that.

I felt good about our chances on both issues. The law was usually ironclad about two things: you don't get to put into evidence what a dead person said or heard because they can't be cross-examined, and you can't get out of a written agreement without another written agreement. As for the first concept, it's known as the Dead Man Statute. I expected the judge would rule that the defendants couldn't make claims about the oral "opt out" and that they wouldn't be able to bring in Pickens' alleged conversation with the dead man.

They say judges simply call balls and strikes. If that were true, these defense pitches were certainly nowhere near the plate.

I opened my briefcase and began pulling out notes and files. Because these issues all seemed straightforward, I expected a short hearing. In fact, I'd made plans to meet my husband, John, for a long weekend in Marathon. The town is even smaller than Monahans or Pecos. It's situated near the entrance to Big Bend National Park, about three hours south of the courthouse. I'd have to work most of the time, but I was planning to squeeze in a few hours to run one of my favorite races out there, the

Marathon to Marathon. With any luck, I'd get a short break before the onslaught of the trial.

I knew that the proceedings would keep me away from home for a month or more. John had been a trial lawyer before becoming a nonprofit executive, and he understood what the job entailed. Over the years, he'd been supportive of my work and the demands it put on our family. What's more, I could run ideas by him and get his input, and he had valuable insights about trial themes and evidence. Still, neither of us was thrilled at the long separation the trial would require, and we were looking forward to spending some time together in Big Bend. I just needed to wrap up this hearing.

The judge allowed both sides as much time as they needed to make their points. He listened politely and asked a few questions. Then, he took all the arguments "under advisement" again. Sometimes, judges do this because they don't want to issue their rulings in front of the parties, which can lead to more arguments. But I knew that Swanson rarely ruled from the bench, regardless of the circumstances, so I wasn't worried. I was confident in our arguments because we had the law on our side. I packed up, headed down to the car, and began the drive to Marathon feeling good about the prospect of the upcoming trial.

Marathon is in the high desert in one of the most remote parts of the state. Only the vast expanse of Big Bend separates it from the Mexican border. Of course, in that part of the world, "only" is relative. The Big Bend National Park comprises more than twelve hundred square miles—more than the size of Rhode Island. It's hot and dry most of the year, and although it might not sound like it, it's a great place to run a race, especially in the fall. Participation was usually meager, given the remoteness of the race, and runners could meander down a state highway on a cool morning, past cacti and scrub, and watch the sun rise over the Chisos Mountains. It was exactly what I needed to get my head set for the trial. I decided to run the 10K because I knew I wasn't in shape for the longer half marathon I'd usually have run. I'd spent months holed up in depositions and scouring documents, which didn't leave a lot of time for training.

I run for the relief it offers. It shifts my entire mental focus to something other than the thousand trial exhibits and upcoming judicial rulings. My brain goes still while my body focuses solely on moving forward. I'm not a fast runner, and I do not win. Perhaps that's why I love it so much. My job requires me to win; running doesn't. It's a relief to engage in a pursuit in which winning isn't essential. With running, I can be content with simple competence.

Every time Pickens heard that I had run a race, which was pretty frequently, he'd ask whether I won. Each time, he seemed surprised when I said I hadn't. I think he actually expected a fifty-three-year-old woman to be able to beat the field. Or maybe he simply didn't understand why I would enter if I didn't intend to win. I appreciated his faith in me and hoped that I'd live up to his expectations that I would win his trial.

John and I rented a house in Marathon through Airbnb. Like most of the available lodging in the town of four hundred people, it was quirky. It had two small buildings separated by a paved courtyard. We took the main house. The furnishings were spare but functional. John brought his bicycle, and while I was running the race, he planned to ride into Big Bend, heading down the two-lane highway toward the park entrance sixty miles away. He hoped to get in a hundred miles by early afternoon. I reminded him, as I always did, to take his driver's license in case he got stopped at the border patrol station a few miles south of town. He'd never been asked for it on the many times we had made this trip, but he's Hispanic, and things had definitely changed on the border, even for U.S. citizens. I tried not to worry about him.

On Saturday morning, I got up before sunrise and gathered with the other runners at the Gage Hotel to catch a school bus that served as a shuttle. The hotel was the only one in Marathon. It had been built by a ranching baron in 1927, and it was said to be a favored hangout of western writer Zane Gray. It fell into disrepair over the years but was restored in the late Seventies and has become a popular retreat for Big Bend visitors and others who enjoy spending time in the desert.

Like most other things in that part of the world, the race was loosely structured. You picked your distance—from the 5K to the full marathon—and the school bus would drop you at the appropriate point. It was up to the runner to get back to town for the post-race barbecue, hosted by the local volunteer fire department.

In my first few strides, I began to feel the effects of too little training, too little sleep, and more than four thousand feet of elevation. It was also warmer than usual; not cool like I'd hoped. I passed a large Hispanic family walking the 5K together wearing matching t-shirts that said "Abuela's Crew." Abuela means "grandma," and she was proudly walking with more than a dozen members of her family. They and the other participants took my mind off what was turning out to be a painful run into town. I made it through the distance, and as I crossed the finish line, I found a place to sit down and wait for John, who would join me at the barbecue.

In my post-race fatigue, my mind inevitably drifted back to the upcoming trial. I tried to put it out of my head, but it kept bubbling back to the surface of my consciousness. It wasn't just the trial itself or the legal strategies we'd employ that I was fretting about. It was the logistics. My life, my daily routine, everything was about to be put on hold. I would be moving to Pecos for an indeterminate amount of time and living out of the Best Western Swiss Chalet. I would be spearheading a huge trial effort with a team I'd never led. And I still didn't know exactly what we'd be doing, because Judge Swanson hadn't made many rulings on important motions. Most of the motions from both sides were still "under advisement."

I didn't talk to Pickens that weekend. I wanted a few days of calm before we entered the storm of the trial. We'd spoken frequently all summer. He typically called from his office speakerphone several days a week, usually between 8:00 and 8:30 a.m. while I was driving to the office. Pickens arrived early to his office, even in his late eighties. His work ethic was legendary, and he was showing few signs of slowing down. He usually spent an hour working out in the office gym at 6:30 a.m. with his personal trainer before sitting down at his desk. By the time he arrived, his market analysts had prepared an update for him to scan. They typically held a brief strategy session to discuss how they wanted to trade around whatever was happening that day and its anticipated impact on the commodities markets. By the time he called me, he might have already made a dozen million-dollar decisions. Talking to me was like taking a break, a chance to deal with something else.

I'd catch him up on the latest events in the case, and I'd try to reiterate the key themes we needed him to present at the trial. Given his reluctance to prepare before his deposition, I wanted to use every chance to reinforce the main points until they were engrained in his subconscious. I wanted them to become second nature to him. Almost every call, he would repeat how the defendants took him out of the deal and how he never signed the paperwork. Then he'd go over the value of the barrels of oil that were attributable to his 15 percent interest in the Red Bull, recalculating out loud based on the current price of oil and where he expected it to go. I had math skills, but he could do that arithmetic faster than I could. He'd been doing it his whole life.

The weekend in Marathon wound down, and I felt my little oasis of calm melting away. I said goodbye to John, not knowing when I would see him again. He headed back to Dallas, and I set out for Pecos. After more than twenty years of marriage, I knew he wouldn't watch the trial. He'd get too anxious for me, which would stress us both out. It reminded me of when I was a kid and my dad tried to coach me in softball or basketball. He was too personally invested to be a good coach and it usually frustrated both of us.

A few days later, the lawyers in the case gathered in Pecos for another pretrial hearing. The defense wanted the judge to keep our experts from testifying for one reason or another. Without experts, we couldn't present our claims for damages, and our entire case would fail for a lack of evidence. We were literally a few days from the start of a huge, expensive trial, and I was working from an unfinished script. In Texas, judges aren't required to rule on the pretrial motions before a trial starts, and we'd received almost no pretrial rulings.

I was the general in this war, but without knowing where the battle would be fought, it was difficult to organize the troops. We had only one option: be ready for anything.

Chapter 9

PREPPING PICKENS

The trial was scheduled to begin on Halloween of 2016, which was on a Monday. I'd arrived in Pecos the week before for the hearing on the experts and spent the rest of the week preparing for the first day in court. Putting on a trial of this size is a huge undertaking. I'd assembled a team of ten lawyers and paralegals, and we needed a place to work when we weren't in court. We could meet in the Swiss Chalet's solitary conference room, but we couldn't leave our files and other materials there. I knew we'd never find a place to rent for a month. Because of the fracking boom, every available space in Pecos, from empty lots to office buildings, was leased. It seemed as if anyone with a patch of dirt had offered it for drilling equipment storage or "man camps" of trailers and RVs where the roughnecks and other rig workers lived.

Fortunately, I knew a friend at a Dallas-based oil company that let us use its field office about a mile outside town. The building was brand new, with six or seven large offices, a nice kitchen, some conference rooms, and a huge garage for oilfield trucks.

Most of my team arrived by the Thursday before the trial. The locals must have thought we were a small invading army. We had a fleet of rented vehicles—a minivan, a few SUVs and a white panel van carrying more than a hundred boxes of files and supplies. Cathy had rented the van in Dallas and we filled it with almost everything in my law office except the furniture. Dozens of the boxes held thousands of evidence files. Dozens more held supplies for the trial: pens, Post-It notes, tape flags, highlighters, binders, white out, extra batteries. We also had a few dozen props and demonstratives: unwieldy "trial boards" that contained enlarged documents affixed to foam backing, each measuring three by four feet. We brought extra technology too: computers, printers, and spare ink cartridges. We couldn't leave anything to chance. If a computer crashed, we didn't have time to repair it; we needed an immediate replacement. The nearest Best Buy was almost a hundred miles away.

Cathy and I had packed the panel van ourselves with the help of our dad, who happened to be in town. We experienced a wave of panic when our stuff wouldn't all fit the first time. We'd unpacked and rearranged everything like some giant Tetris exercise, eventually managing to shove it all in and close the doors. Then Cathy got behind the wheel and set out on the six hundred-mile trek to Pecos along Interstate 20. I drove my Audi A3 hatchback separately, packed with enough suits to last through weeks of trial and my own personal trial materials. I used the long drive to relax before battle.

Our fleet pulled up in front of the borrowed building on the outskirts of town and the team unloaded everything. In traditional lawyer fashion, we began referring to the facility as the "war room." Lawyers, paralegals, and support staff grabbed every available corner as personal workspace. In addition to the team members who would be there throughout the trial, we would also use this space to prep more than a dozen fact and expert witnesses.

I looked at the legal firepower I'd assembled with pride. Pecos was famous for another legal legend. Since moving to Texas in the mid-1980s, I'd heard about Judge Roy Bean, "the Law West of the Pecos." The saying refers to the Pecos River a few miles east of town, which had marked the edge of Bean's dominion and authority. I was disappointed to see it's barely a creek. Its place in history is bigger than its place in the world. The same could probably be said of Bean.

After some rough early years in California—Bean's neck bore scars from an unsuccessful attempt to hang him, instigated by the friends of a Mexican military officer Bean had killed—he moved to San Antonio and became a prosperous businessman. As the railroad expanded west from San Antonio toward El Paso, Bean decided to follow it. He set up the Jersey Lilly saloon in Pecos County, which is west of the town of Pecos. Because the sparsely populated region needed someone to keep order, the county commissioners appointed Bean to serve as judge even though he had no legal experience. His rulings became famous. He once threatened to hang a lawyer for using "profanity" after the man spoke the Latin legal phrase "habeas corpus." Most of the cases he oversaw were misdemeanors—few involved serious crimes like murder. Nevertheless, Bean developed a reputation for harshness, meting out sentences from the porch of the Jersey Lilly, often while drunk. Thankfully, he never presided over a case as big as ours.

I recalled how in the 1990s, a group that wanted to reduce big jury verdicts created an annual list of "Judicial Hell Holes." These were counties, nationwide, where the group believed defendant corporations faced the potential for out-sized verdicts and judgments against them based on "runaway juries." Reeves

County, where Pecos is located, made the list one year. It had the characteristics that made defendants nervous, primarily a struggling local economy that could use the boost that typically came with major verdicts.

Big Oil took over Pecos again in the mid-2000s, capitalizing on the fact that the town had little in the way of industry other than oil. Its best-known product was the Pecos cantaloupe, a local melon that became a staple of stores and farmers markets across the state each June. Without high-paying jobs or a solid industrial base, potential jurors were more likely to view out-of-town corporate defendants as potential cash cows.

In reality, the reason verdicts tend to be large in places like Reeves County has nothing to do with cantaloupes or the lack of good jobs. It was because of oil. Oil money, especially in boom times, tends to add two or three zeroes to the cost of everything it touches. If a breach of contract case involving any other business resulted in a ten-million-dollar verdict, it might generate a hundred-million-dollar verdict if the same contract dispute involved oil.

Regardless of Pecos' reputation in the legal community as being plaintiff friendly, I couldn't leave anything to chance. After all, my client was a famous billionaire, and I needed him to appear sympathetic to cantaloupe farmers and other local residents. I couldn't assume the jury would side with us just because they rarely sided with the defense in civil cases. They might also decide that someone as wealthy as Pickens didn't need the money for damages. I needed to understand who the jurors were and how they might think. For that, I'd hired a couple of local lawyers as jury experts, Bill Weinacht and his wife, Alva Alvarez.

Bill, who was about my age, had his own personal-injury firm in Pecos. He'd grown up in the area, and he knew almost everyone in town. He talked fast but lacked the stereotypical west Texan drawl. His mind moved as quickly as his speech, jumping from subject to subject, which made it difficult to know if he was catching all the important parts of a conversation.

Alva, a beautiful Latina in her mid-thirties, had also grown up in Reeves County and graduated from Harvard and the University of Texas Law School. She'd returned home in 2006, hoping to use her law degree to help the hardworking people of Pecos—people like her father, who drove a truck for an oilfield services company, and her mother, who was a teacher's aide. Soon after she came back, the former county attorney was indicated for theft and Alva took over the job. In Pecos, the county attorney is an elected official but the job is part time, so Alva kept her law practice going on the side.

Pecos' sparse legal community meant there were few other choices for local counsel, but I would have picked Bill and Alva regardless. They were both accomplished lawyers, respected and well-known in the area. Bill wasn't eager to join our team, however. I got the impression that he'd made a lot of money acting as local counsel in contingency fee cases, in which the winning side received a percentage of the plaintiff's damages. He told me that he and Alva wouldn't take my case unless they received such a fee. When I explained that I wasn't getting paid that way—I was working by the hour—he said he wasn't interested.

I persisted. First, I tried the telephone. "Bill, this is T. Boone Pickens we're talking about," I said. He seemed unimpressed by Pickens' name or fame, and again said he'd pass. "Bill, the case may be worth a billion dollars," I said. "When I win, this could be the biggest verdict ever handed down in Reeves County." That piqued his interest, but he still wouldn't commit. I told him I had a hearing in the case coming up and offered to visit him in person. He agreed to meet me in Midland and talk during a break in a mediation he was involved in. Mike Lynn had come with me on the trip, and I brought him to the meeting. We ended up cooling our heels outside the mediator's office while Bill and Alva finished their case. We talked for ten or fifteen minutes, then Bill agreed to join us only if we paid him an astronomical flat fee—solely for helping with jury selection. Bill said he might be willing to help with closing arguments, too, but only if he and Alva were back from a trip to Peru by then.

I reasoned that they would probably spend less than a full day's worth of billable time and the hourly rate would be extraordinary, but we really had no other option. I recommended to Pickens that he pay their fee, and he agreed. I secretly fretted about whether I'd made the right recommendation, adding it to the long list of things I was worrying about.

As it turned out, Bill and Alva provided guidance far beyond the trial itself, as we would see when Pickens arrived. Pickens' Gulfstream landed on Friday, October 28. He planned to sit through the entire trial, which I still found extraordinary. It wasn't just his age. It was exceedingly rare for a CEO to devote so much attention to a single case. But something about this deal stuck in his craw. He wasn't about to leave it to others. Accompanying Pickens were his two closest advisers. Ron Bassett, his right-hand man and Mesa's vice president, had worked with Pickens since the 1970s, and Pickens trusted him for guidance on almost any subject. Jay Rosser, Pickens' head of communications, carefully monitored and guarded Pickens' public image and presence. Jay stayed on top of who was writing what about Pickens and who should be writing about him.

Before the plane landed, Bill had a suggestion. "Give the locals a show," he said. "We don't get many billionaires out here in Pecos. Or people who fly in on their own planes. Take a picture, call the paper. Let people know something important is happening here in town." It wouldn't be long before the town was abuzz with the news that T. Boone Pickens had arrived.

I met Pickens, Ron, and Jay at the Pecos airport, which was really just a runway with a part-time facility manager. Dee Janice, one of our paralegals, snapped a quick picture of Pickens and me together. I wore an orange top in honor of Oklahoma State, Pickens' alma mater. I knew he usually dressed in the same color—orange ties or orange fleece pullovers—and it would make a good photograph.

We swung by the Swiss Chalet so they could check in, then headed straight to our war room about a mile out of town. From the time Pickens arrived, I had a singular focus: preparing him to testify. I'd remembered how difficult it had been to get him ready for his deposition. He'd made it through that largely on his wits and the force of his personality, but I couldn't risk such a cavalier approach to trial testimony. Pickens might be fine, but my nerves wouldn't. For my own sanity I needed him to focus and prepare. Fortunately, this time I had Bill and Alva to help me.

I knew that with their involvement, we'd at least get Pickens familiar with the sensibilities of the local jury pool. More importantly, I'd get feedback from Bill and Alva about how Pickens would appeal to jurors and how much they would trust him. We'd also hired jury consultants for that purpose. It would take an entire team to gear Pickens up for the stand.

I wasn't worried about how he would answer the questions that I posed to him. A direct examination of a friendly witness will usually go well, as long as your witness remembers to cover key topics and can pick up on your cues. That wouldn't be a problem for Pickens. I was more worried about the cross-examination, when the other lawyers could grill him about the details that he hadn't studied as thoroughly as I'd wanted him to. He would be shown papers that, because of his deteriorating vision, he wouldn't be able to see. That's why I had wanted him to review every key document in the case.

I also had to worry about the judge. What if Swanson didn't allow Pickens to testify the way he wanted to? What if he carved out certain topics and kept Pickens from saying what was on his mind?

As a lawyer, I can't change the facts or the law. All I can do is present a case that makes sense based on the evidence we are allowed to use and hope the jury will see my client's side. Part of that is making sure witnesses understand their role in the trial. Only they can tell the jury the truth about what they know, and only they can explain any inconsistencies between their testimony and the other evidence. If witnesses can't communicate clearly, then the chances of winning decline significantly. When they take the stand, you want them to champion your cause.

Pickens was known as a master communicator. He'd been interviewed hundreds of times, both on TV and in print. He'd written books. He'd been in magazines. He'd appeared in CNN's "The 80s" just a few weeks earlier. He clearly had the experience presenting himself as an authoritative businessman. But being a good interview on television isn't the same thing as being a good live witness in a trial. A typical TV interview only lasts a few minutes—maybe a half hour at most. Trials can be long and tedious, and rather than telling a story, witnesses may have to pick through boring documents. If you're suing over a contract, as we were, you have to walk the jury through each term, one at a time, without losing their attention. A dull witness, droning on about terminology, isn't exactly riveting.

Pickens signed the contracts that formed the backbone of our case, so he had to be the person to explain them. My problem in putting him on the stand was that he hadn't studied them since he signed them almost a decade earlier—and he didn't want to study them before the trial. He was sure he knew what the case was about. He did, but I needed him to understand that the jury wouldn't just take his word. He needed to *show* them. I needed him to master the concepts and refresh his memory through repetition.

I did everything I could to get him to focus. I carefully scripted the questions I wanted to cover so he'd understand the flow of the testimony. I rehearsed him on the stand a dozen times, including in a mock courtroom back in Dallas several weeks before trial. Mike Lynn played the cross-examiner so Pickens would see how a slipup could lead to unwanted questions on cross examination.

Success was fleeting. I could get him to focus for a while, but after about fifteen minutes of going over my questions, he would veer into the things *he* wanted to say: he'd signed a deal, he'd paid his money, and they took his 15 percent without him signing a document to say that they could. How is it that they could walk away with his interest when there were billions of dollars at stake? Every time he talked about how the other participants got to stay in the deal, but the defendants had taken him out, he'd punctuate it with the same looping motion of his right hand. He'd point his index finger straight at me, then twirl it around counterclockwise so it ended up sideways, as if he were pointing toward the door. He did it so often, I began to imagine it with a sound effect: "…they took me out." *Swoosh*.

In Pecos, that weekend before the trial, Bill and Alva watched as I tried to keep Pickens on track. We were all in a big room with whiteboards on the walls. I'd take a marker and draw concepts on them, hoping the visuals would engage Pickens' attention so that we could drill through a few questions. Bill and Alva would offer some practice questions, reinforcing with Pickens the concepts that they thought the jury would want to hear. But the outcome was the same. He'd turn back to the things he knew best, and away from another point we needed from him to make our case.

We'd run through it again, and the same thing would happen. After about fifteen minutes, he'd bring up his list of grievances, ending with the swirl of his finger: "…they took me out." *Swoosh*. He was getting frustrated and so were the rest of us. I knew what we needed to do, he knew what he wanted to say, and once again, we were both sure we were right.

"Mr. Pickens, you're absolutely right about that point," I said, trying not to let my frustration come through in my voice. "They did cut you out of the deal and they did leave others like you in the deal. *But* we have to cover a lot more territory than that. I need for us to focus on what the defense is going to grill you about. For example, let's talk about the issue of the credit they put on the Mesa bills."

"Chrysta, the jury isn't going to care about the credit," he shot back. "They're going to know that I got cut out of the deal and that I never signed anything."

Round and round we went. I wasn't making any progress in choreographing the dance he and I were going to have to do once he took the stand. I was going to have to do something differently. There's an old story that Ginger Rogers did everything Fred Astaire did, only backwards and wearing high heels. As the lead trial lawyer, I was supposed to be Fred Astaire and lead the dance at trial. Clearly, that wasn't going to happen with my star witness. I'd have to become Ginger Rogers and follow Pickens' lead. My best hope was to anticipate his testimony and come up with the next question on the fly, based not on where I wanted to go, but where he did. I realized Ginger had it easy, because she knew the choreography before she went on camera. Our dance at trial would be improvised.

Chapter 10

DAY ONE

I woke up at 5:00 a.m. the first day of the trial and flipped on the TV to the morning news shows. Absentmindedly listening to them, I showered and dressed. I wouldn't face the jury on the first day, so I wasn't as careful in staging my outfit as I would be the first time the jury saw me. If you think getting dressed for a formal event is an ordeal, you've never been a woman trial lawyer getting ready to try a big case. Every item is thought out: the suit should be professional but not too imposing; shoes, comfortable but stylish; makeup—subtle but completely necessary in a place like Texas; wedding ring needed to be just that—a band, no flashy diamond—and the same for the rest of the jewelry—minimal, no bling; haircut, professional, styled and not too girly. I wore my hair in a short bob, but my bangs were already getting too long. I'd skipped my last cut because I hadn't had time during the trial preparation. How did I know my bangs were too long? Pickens told me. He mentioned it in the days before the trial when he was annoyed with me. He told me to get them cut so I'd stop pushing them out of my eyes and messing with them. I'd wondered if he'd ever told Sandy Campbell or his other male lawyers to get a haircut and decided he probably had.

When I got to the breakfast area in the lobby, I saw Pickens holding court with the landmen and other oilfield roustabouts who were loading up on the hotel's free breakfast. From the moment we arrived, Pickens was treated like a celebrity by the hotel's staff and guests. When we'd checked in to the Swiss Chalet, the desk clerk knew who we were, because we'd been working with the manager for months to get the large block of rooms we needed. "Can I meet him?" the clerk asked, referring to Pickens. He'd studied business and had read Pickens' books. As my sister Cathy observed, Pecos was an oil town, and Pickens was one of the biggest oil guys on earth. His arrival was like Elvis showing up at Graceland. It was no wonder that in the mornings, over breakfast, the oilfield workers would gather around him to hear his stories.

Pickens was happy to oblige. He'd query his audience, asking which companies they worked for, what operations they were about to perform that day, and telling them about his expertise on whatever they were planning to do. He loved it.

I wasn't hungry that morning, and I didn't eat anything. Instead, I took a roll call of the troops, making sure everyone was ready and my paralegals had everything packed up. I also made sure Pickens was in a good mood and ready to roll.

We loaded up our six-vehicle convoy and headed to the courthouse, winding through the residential neighborhoods to get to the center of town. I left my Audi at the hotel, because it would appear conspicuously out of place. Better to be seen in the assortment of American-made SUVs and minivans.

We pulled up in front of the courthouse at 7:30 a.m. and began unloading our file boxes, computers, and presentation materials that we would use to illustrate our case. The lobby of the Reeves County Courthouse isn't much bigger than a typical living room. Its black flooring had lost its sheen decades ago. As if the entrance weren't small enough, several rows of folding tables took up most of the space in the lobby just outside the county clerk's office. In another half hour or so, those tables would begin filling with landmen (some of whom were women), who would carefully sift through oversized books of title records checked out from the clerk. Like many rural counties, Reeves hadn't yet computerized its filing system. Title information was still logged by hand in massive, cloth-bound books. The landmen would request the book from the clerk, then bring it to the table, flip through it, examine the information about a particular piece of property, and record it on their laptop computers. Landowners, lease holders, drilling companies, and other opportunists involved in extracting oil and natural gas from the ground hired those landmen to track down ownership details. No one gets the right to drill for oil without engaging in this detective work.

In Texas, mineral rights to the oil and gas can be held separately from surface rights. In other words, you may buy a house that sits atop, say, a half-acre of land. But unless you also bought the mineral rights, someone else could sell the right to drill on that land to an oil company, and you'd have to simply put up with it.

The landmen in the lobby paid little attention to us, but their job was critical to our case. Oil companies hire them to examine title records verifying that the operator has obtained the legal right to drill, known in the industry as "clear title." Drillers were spending anywhere from $4 million to $10 million or more to drill a well. If they didn't have the right to drill on a particular property—usually because of a problem with the "chain of title," or the history of buying and selling a piece of land—they could end up drilling a successful, highly profitable well only to hand over all the profits to the real owners. So, they hired the landmen to make sure the title was clear and that the people who claimed to own the mineral rights actually did.

The trial courtroom—the only one—was on the second floor. We weaved our way past the tables of landmen and lugged our boxes and supplies up the stairs. The courtroom itself was spacious but trapped in the 1970s. On my first trip to Pecos, the gallery chairs, which had been installed at least forty years earlier, were upholstered with alternating avocado and harvest gold fabric. A few months before the trial, the county commissioners had apparently paid to redo them to a nice shade of purple that reminded me of the signature color of my alma mater, Kansas State. Perhaps, I thought, it was a good omen.

Normally, the gallery chairs would be filled with dozens of people waiting for hearings on criminal drug possession charges, tax foreclosure cases, or child custody matters. Because Judge Swanson presided over a court of "general jurisdiction," he heard and decided almost every type of dispute that went on in Reeves County. When we came to Pecos for pretrial hearings, we would often sit in the gallery waiting for the civil docket to begin. We watched county jail inmates in orange jumpsuits paraded before the judge for sentencing and saw the local tax authority foreclose on someone's home because of unpaid property taxes. Once those cases were adjudicated, the judge would move on to more complicated civil cases such as ours.

Because the judge still hadn't ruled on the pretrial motions from the hearings of the past two weeks, we still didn't know exactly what case we would be allowed to try. We didn't know whether the defense could argue that Pickens had orally opted out of the Red Bull agreement, or whether we could assert the Statute of Frauds and require the defense to produce a written document to support its "opt out" claims. We didn't know whether our experts could take the stand to present the damages we were seeking, which at this point amounted to more than $600 million. And, we were waiting on rulings for a number of claims that the defense had moved to dismiss. After filing the initial lawsuit, I'd added dozens of different legal theories as the case developed. We asserted claims for breach of contract, theft, breach of fiduciary duty, fraud, conspiracy and collusion, among others. In a case like this, you show up prepared to try everything that the judge hasn't thrown out on summary judgment.

Despite the uncertainty of how the judge would rule on these issues, I entered the courtroom amped up but not anxious. I knew we'd done everything possible to prepare. I'd hired some of the best expert witnesses around. They'd gone over the evidence in exacting detail, rendering reports on what had gone wrong and what damages Pickens deserved to recover. I'd hired the best local counsel, Bill and Alva. Mike Lynn and his firm added to our legal fire power, and we had the possibility of appeals covered thanks to his partner, David Coale. Mike had brought a whole team of attorneys and paralegals to assist me and had given them explicit instructions to follow my lead as if I were one of his own partners at his firm. We were as ready as we could be.

Judge Swanson came in, and we all rose. He motioned us to take our seats. Remember when I said the start of the trial is rarely the start of the trial? Well, the same thing was true even on the day the trial is supposed to begin. In reviewing the defense challenges to our experts, the judge decided each one should take the stand before we picked a jury so that they could prove that they were qualified and that their opinions were sound.

Testimony from experts proves things that aren't within the routine knowledge of the jury or the judge: engineering or accounting issues, disputes about land titles, industry practices, and other oil and gas topics. For a case like ours, we needed experts to testify on dozens of issues.

Again, our case was a little unusual, because I intended to call Pickens as both a fact witness and an expert. I wanted him to discuss his expert opinion on the fair market value of Mesa's 15 percent interest in the Red Bull, based on his decades of buying and selling such interests. Among our other experts was the vice president of land for another operator who would testify that J. Cleo's refusal to recognize Mesa's interest in the Red Bull was a gross deviation from industry norms. We also had a title attorney who had reviewed the title records to the disputed Red Bull acquisitions and who would conclude that Mesa still held a 15 percent share. Ricardo Garza, the petroleum engineer, would talk about how many barrels of oil were attributable to Mesa's 15 percent. Rodney Sowards, an accounting expert, would put a value on all the oil that had been produced and would be produced in the future, subtract the costs of getting it and calculate Mesa's 15 percent as damages. The defense had asked the judge to strike all of them to prevent them from even taking the stand.

The hearing took hours. For each of our five witnesses, the defendants first argued the points that they had presented in their written papers. Then we had to call each witness to the stand and question them. The other side got to cross-examine, and then we got to "redirect," or question them again. It was as if the witnesses themselves were on trial, which in a way they were. It was a mini-trial to decide who got to testify in front of the jury once the real trial started.

The defense's challenge to Pickens as an expert was particularly infuriating. They were claiming that his lack of day-to-day experience as a geologist in recent decades meant he couldn't testify about the details of the Red Bull case. Obviously, they hadn't spent hours watching my attempts to prep my client, who *only* wanted to talk about the very matters they hoped to keep him from discussing. Pickens knew the geology inside and out, and he'd spent sixty years in the business evaluating deals and prospects. It's hard to image a better expert. Still, if the defense succeeded in their challenge, it would make managing Pickens that much harder for me because he couldn't talk about the technical aspects of the case the way he wanted to.

The whole process was tedious and smothered the adrenaline that typically comes with the start of the trial. We hadn't even picked a jury yet. We'd spent the entire day arguing over expert witnesses, and even then, we didn't know the outcome because the judge didn't make any rulings. Instead, he decided to consider all our arguments and issue his decisions later.

That meant we were starting the trial without any idea of which experts we could use to support our case.

After we finished that day, I raced down to the first floor to do a stand-up interview with a TV reporter from Midland. A trial in the heart of the Oil Patch involving a legendary figure was certain to draw media attention, and while Pecos was too remote for the national press, the locals were all over it. I'd learned a few tricks during my stint in public relations. As I saw it, the media attention could only help our cause. Our trial was going to be on the news, in the paper, and the talk of the town. We had no "gag order" that prevented us from speaking about the case to the press, and Jay Rosser put me in front of every camera he could find.

I made a few forgettable comments to the Midland reporter— something along the lines of what we had already said in our court papers, which is about all a trial lawyer can say. I have no clear recollection of my comments, but that wasn't the point anyway. It's like Kevin Costner said in *Bull Durham,* you gotta learn your clichés. Publicity during a big case is fine as long as the other side can't claim you're trying to influence the jury. The point of my interview was to keep our trial in the news, especially if it was going well, without doing anything that would jeopardize our case.

My standup on the courthouse steps had a second purpose. I wanted to get the attention of the defense, and it worked. In the middle of my interview, Rick Montgomery, the Baytech lawyer, burst through the front doors of the courthouse and into the glare of the late afternoon sun. He'd seen me scamper out of the courtroom and down the steps, and he wanted to know what I was doing. He wasn't happy to see me talking to the press, which wasn't surprising. What I said on TV mattered less than the mere fact that I was saying it. I'd learned the hard way that trial strategy isn't limited to what happens inside the courtroom. Montgomery's face told me the defendants were worried about what was coming.

They should have been.

Chapter 11

THE "GUIDANCES"

The judge announced that he had other court business and gave us the next day off. He might have wanted the time to decide some of the pending motions in our case, because we received a fax with a flurry of orders attached late that afternoon.

He struck our Statute of Frauds argument, meaning that the defense could argue that Pickens orally "opted out." He ruled that the defense could introduce the purported conversation between Pickens and Thompson and Cliff Milford's overhearing of it. It was an unprecedented ruling, in my experience. I rationalized that if the judge hadn't ruled that way, the defense would have no case left to try. He wasn't going to do that; we were already all here and ready to go.

Worse yet, he struck three of our expert witnesses. The title attorney, selected to testify that Mesa still owned title to its share of the Red Bull, and the operations expert, chosen to offer opinions regarding J. Cleo's conduct as an operator overseeing the Red Bull, would not take the stand at all. Even more distressing, the judge ruled that Pickens himself could not testify about his expertise in geology, only as a fact witness to what he had observed. Fortunately, our petroleum engineer, Ricardo Garza, and our accounting expert, Rodney Sowards, would still be allowed to testify. As is the practice in Texas state courts, the judge didn't give his reasons; he only granted or denied the defense requests.

Even so, the judge included a cryptic note at the end of the order: Garza and Sowards would have to establish that their opinions about damages due Mesa were based on "fair market value immediately before and immediately after any breach." It was not clear what the judge thought that meant.

Often, a court will announce a ruling and leave it to the parties to figure out whether they are complying with it. The judge will then entertain arguments for and against whether the parties complied with the ruling after the jury has returned its verdict. Judges do this to save time and effort: once the jury rules, a lot of the legal posturing falls away. Texas juries vote against the plaintiff more than half of the time, which ends a lot of the bickering immediately. As a result, many experienced judges will let a case go to the jury and sort out any remaining legal arguments afterwards. Based on my decades of experience, I assumed the same would be true here, and that the judge was done ruling on whether our expert testimony was admissible. He had certainly taken some unusual steps in kicking out three of our experts already.

But, so far, Swanson's rulings weren't like anything I'd ever seen before. They weren't clear parameters, as shown by the cryptic line about "market value." We wound up calling his rulings "guidances," a term the judge himself used. They proved difficult to interpret. It was like being given a horoscope instead of a map.

It took me a while to figure out why Swanson was seemingly so vague yet so active in giving guidance. I could tell he was meticulous in weighing the evidence and arguments before he ruled. A few mused about whether someone with influence was getting to the judge (such speculation happens in nearly every case, regardless of the judge), but I dismissed that notion. It was true that the other side had hired the top county official in Ward County as their local attorney, and that official had some sway over Swanson's pay. But I decided that wasn't the issue. This was our judge's first trial, and it was a big one. I concluded he was trying to balance the positions of both sides, managing the case in a way that he thought would minimize an appeal. If he allowed us to pursue a billion dollars in damages and the jury gave it to us, the appeals court might have felt that he had presided over a runaway jury. And that might increase the possibility that his decision would be reversed. Some judges take reversals by an appeals court personally, like they're a rebuke.

Whatever the "guidances" meant, I felt that the rulings were bad for us. I knew I had to stay focused. We still had two damages experts who could testify, Garza and Sowards. And while Swanson had disqualified Pickens as an expert witness, he could still take the stand and hopefully convince the jury of his position.

For Pickens himself, the judge's limitation on his testimony would be frustrating, if not impossible. As an owner in the Red Bull, he couldn't even say what he thought his property was worth. About a hundred years of Texas case law said he should have been able to do that. Pickens was still our star witness, of course, but Swanson's rulings added to the challenges I'd face when Pickens took the stand. Given Pickens' stubborn insistence on returning to his favorite points about the case, right down to the swoosh of his hand when he said "they took me out of the deal," it meant that somehow, I was going to have to keep him from straying into expert witness territory or risk running afoul of the judge.

My team was discouraged after the rulings, but I was ready to get started in earnest. I told them we still had a lot of daylight left and we could manage without the two experts. Pickens' opinion about the worth of the Red Bull was not as critical as Sowards' and Garza's. I told them to keep their spirits up, because the next day we would select the jury. These twelve people would decide the outcome of what would prove to be T. Boone Pickens' final court battle.

Chapter 12

PICKING THE JURY

More than eighty local residents filed into the boxy courtroom gallery on November 2, 2016. Fall tends to come late to Texas, and the day was warm, with the sunlight interrupted by occasional clouds. The group was answering the county's summons to serve as potential jurors in the trial of Mesa Petroleum Partners versus Baytech, J. Cleo Thompson, and Delaware Basin Resources. The candidates were predominantly Hispanic. Some had high school diplomas while others had post-graduate degrees. They worked at jobs that included prison guards and schoolteachers. We all rose as they entered the courtroom and made their way to the gallery seats. There were so many that some people had to stand along the back wall. I eyed them closely, looking for anyone who seemed friendly and interested, and for anyone who didn't.

Jury selection is as much art as science, and most trial lawyers have their own theories for how to approach it. The process is named for the old French term *voir dire*, which literally means "speak the truth." In Texas, it's pronounced "vore dire"—phonetically—not in the French way, "vwär dir," like the dictionary and rules of French pronunciation show it should be.

The prosecution and defense teams each get to address members of the jury pool, ask the candidates questions, and urge them to give truthful answers. As a lawyer, eliminating jurors who are against your case is job one. It isn't like being elected to the student council; you aren't looking to win votes. You want to pick off and remove the potential jurors who will side with your opponents. It sounds simple enough, but it isn't.

The only way to expose the jurors who will favor your opponent is to discuss the flaws in your own case. That way, you can determine which jurors won't look past those flaws when voting on a verdict. But every communication with jurors—even if they haven't officially been seated yet—can be critical. *Voir dire* is the first time the potential jurors will hear you speak, and you're pointing out the weaknesses of your own case. As an advocate, the purpose of *voir dire* runs counter to every instinct you have about winning in the trial.

That's only half of the juggling act. You also want to signal to the other jurors—those who are potentially sympathetic— your case's merits, even as you're trying to weed out those who are against you. In legal parlance, this is known as "jury commitment." It's nearly impossible, and it's risky. If you spend too much time selling your theory of the case, you won't identify who you need to remove. And there's an added complication: you aren't supposed to discuss the law or the facts of your particular case directly. If you're wondering how you conduct *voir dire* when you can't even talk about the case, you've asked the right question.

Bill Weinacht and I decided to split *voir dire*. I'd hired Bill because he knew almost everyone in town, and he knew what messages would resonate with the jurors. He would go first and hammer home a key theme of our case: the need for paperwork. He'd couch it in easily relatable terms. Want to get married? You need paperwork. Want to get a divorce? You need paperwork. Want to buy a car? Sell one? Buy a house? Sell one? It all requires paperwork. This is a universally understood experience, and Bill thought this theme would resonate with jurors.

After Bill stressed the paperwork aspect, I would follow with the more standard approach of asking probing questions about the weaknesses in our case. In the process, I would hopefully figure out who would vote against us.

I love talking to potential jurors. I genuinely enjoy the interaction, but I also can't remember what they say. We would rely on two jury consultants who would record the responses, analyze them, and determine who should be off the jury. This case was too important to take any chances. The bailiffs lined up the members of the jury pool by the numbers they'd been assigned earlier in the morning. We used the numbers to cross-reference each person to the background information we'd received— name, gender, age, employment, education level, and so forth.

Judge Swanson gave a patriotic speech intended to make people feel better about spending the entire day at the courthouse. (Actually, only those who got dismissed would be there for the day. Anyone who actually was selected was going to spend every day for the next several weeks in the jury box.) He reminded them that the right to serve on a jury is guaranteed by the Constitution. Second only to serving in the Armed Forces, being a juror is the highest civic duty any citizen can render on behalf of the country. I've heard similar speeches at every trial I've ever had, but it was clear Swanson believed what he was saying, and I found his words more moving than I expected. This was a big, important case, and his speech amplified its seriousness.

After his speech, Swanson introduced all the lawyers and gave the potential jurors the standard instructions—don't talk to anyone about the case, don't read about it in the news, don't look for the lawyers or the witnesses on social media. He reminded them that they must decide the case solely on the evidence they heard in court.

Before the selection process could get started, however, one of the defense lawyers, Stuart Hollimon, asked the judge if he could survey the room and see if anyone had seen me on television the night before. I had no objection. After all, it would only remind the jurors that this was an important case—important enough to be on TV. Of course, we ran the risk that someone we wanted on the jury would say they *had* seen me, and that it did influence their views of the case, but that risk was low. By raising the issue, it was like showing the broadcast to everyone in the room. A miscalculation, I thought.

I was surprised, though, that when the judge asked the question, about a dozen hands went up. Small town, big trial. Swanson wrote down the numbers of those who raised their hand for later questioning. Even better, I thought.

Bill Weinacht stood up and turned toward the gallery. As he started to speak, he began moving slowly across the front of the room. Because he knew most of the jury pool, he also knew that many of them were nervous. Most had never been in court, and none had served on a trial like this. But he knew how to put them at ease. "One thing before we start," he said. "I'm going to pace around up here like a cat in a cage...and there's a big plug on the floor. If I trip and fall down, don't leave—I'll get up and be right back with you." He paused, and there were some chuckles from around the room.

"I'm here to talk to you about your thoughts and beliefs about some things. And the other side is going to do that too.

I'll be straight with you: both sides are looking to find the jurors who will be strong for us and get rid of the rest. So, I'll love you if you tell me everything you hate about me. If you hate my tie. If you don't like my wife. But if you get on this jury and you didn't tell me those things, I'm going to hate you. So, tell me everything. Sing it out like you're in church, man."

Now, Bill moved into the process of actually questioning jurors, hitting the paperwork theme. Normally, attorneys questioning potential jurors refer to their sheet with their names, but Bill could address everyone in the room without looking. It sent a powerful, subliminal message: We're one of you. We know you.

"Let me talk to you about your lives, about the paperwork in your lives," Bill continued. "Mr. Gonzalez, you're a corrections officer at the prison, right? You go in and out of that jail all the time? You sign a paper to get in, and you sign a paper to get out? If you don't sign out, you're still in, right?" Gonzalez agreed.

He turned to another juror whose background information showed he'd once signed an oil and gas lease. "Mr. Thomas, do you go and look in the county records to see what is going on with your lease? How do you know if anything good has happened on that land?"

"Only if they tell me about it," Thomas replied. We were laying the foundation of our case without talking about it.

A third man had received a deed for his mother's house. A fourth had gotten a divorce. Bill wasted no time finding the humor in that one: "You wanted out of that marriage, right? You probably wanted out before you got the divorce decree? No matter how bad you wanted out, you weren't out until you got that paperwork signed, right?"

"You are so right!" the juror replied.

By the end of his hour, Bill had woven a magic spell over the panel. Every time he called out, "What do you need to get in?" he'd also silently raise the paper in his right hand, and the jurors would call out "Paperwork!"

"What do you need to get out of that deal?"

"Paperwork!"

"Order supplies?"

"Paperwork!"

"Sell a car?"

"Paperwork!"

Real-life trials may fall short of television drama, but this was as close to a Hollywood moment as I've seen in court. We were off to a great start. Based on my recommendation, Pickens had paid Bill and Alva a small fortune to help with *voir dire*. I hoped it had been worth every penny, but we wouldn't know until the end.

Bill had gotten the jurors committed to our position, but we still didn't know which ones would vote against us. I had the more nuanced job of figuring that out. Unlike Bill, they knew I wasn't a local, and I wanted to dispel the "big city lawyer" stigma. I told them that I had grown up in a town smaller than Pecos, and then I seized on an element of local pride. The marching band had just made the state competition.

"How many here are proud of that marching band?" I asked. Almost every hand went up. "I was in marching band long ago," I said. "I was actually the drum major. Who here has been in marching band?" Several hands shot up, and I moved on to my point, picking a name from the list of potential jurors. "Ms. Ramirez, what happens in marching band if someone isn't following the chart?" The chart is the term used for the script that shows the music and designates where each band member is supposed to be for every beat. It's the choreography that defines a marching band show.

"Everything goes wrong," she said. "The whole show falls apart."

"You're depending on other people to follow the rules, right?"

"Absolutely."

"Who here remembers the book *Everything I Needed to Know I Learned in Kindergarten*?" I asked.

No hands. Either these folks weren't readers, or the book had been published too long ago for them to remember it. It didn't matter. The title was really the message. I was planting the idea that if the defendants had just followed simple rules of fairness, they wouldn't be here. I kept going. "The point is, most of what people need to know about how to act in the world they learn really early on: Share. Don't steal. Tell the truth. And my favorite: cookies are best served warm with milk." That got a few smiles.

Having made my point about fundamental fairness, I moved on. Pickens was sitting in the jury box, watching the whole process. I glanced over at him to see how he was faring because it was a long haul and he wasn't used to sitting still without taking charge. Now was the time to focus on the man himself.

I told the potential jurors about how Pickens worked his way up from nothing to riches. I asked whether they could treat him fairly and award him money if the evidence showed he was owed it, even though he was wealthy already. I asked whether they had any properties that they rarely checked on and whether they thought it would be fair for someone to take their property while they were gone. I asked about the 2008 recession and how it affected them. The defense was going to claim that Pickens wanted out of the Red Bull in 2008 because of the economic downturn, and I wanted to gauge how jurors might react to the argument.

The questions would give us a lot of insight into the jurors' minds. I just hoped it would be enough. The jury consultants who were recording the answers would decide who to pick, and therefore, who to remove, or strike. Ultimately, a jury consists of those who are left after both sides excuse the people they don't want. The trick is, you only get six strikes, and so does the other side. The jury ends up being the first twelve people after both sides have used their strikes.

The defense took its turn as well, though I wasn't paying that much attention. I was already running through my opening statements in my mind. Besides, my consultants would be following the defense questioning. The other side didn't have an attorney like Bill, and without him, I doubted they could establish the rapport that he had. Several hours later, we'd narrowed the panel down to twelve jurors and a few alternates. Nearly all of them were Hispanic and they were slightly better educated than we'd anticipated.

No matter how carefully you conduct *voir dire*, there's always a risk. Juries are made up of people, and people can be unpredictable. As we packed up our things for the day and loaded our vehicle convoy, I hoped we'd gotten a group that would give us the verdict we needed—or at least were open to hearing the whole story.

Chapter 13

A TOUGH ACT
TO FOLLOW

We didn't get to our opening arguments until the first Friday after the trial started. Wednesday had been taken up by jury selection and Thursday was consumed by more arguments over evidence and whether we could present any of our remaining claims. At the end of the day, Judge Swanson threw out all our claims except breach of contract, accepting the various defense arguments about why our claims were legally deficient. We couldn't argue fraud, conspiracy, collusion, or theft.

I was tremendously frustrated that we were now four days into the trial yet hadn't yet actually started it. I was reeling from the judge's ruling and how much of our case he'd wiped out with the stroke of a pen. I was also worried. Things weren't going our way. Rulings that I thought should have easily been made in our favor were undercutting our case at every turn. I kept telling myself that once we got in front of a jury, the momentum would shift. Now, we were about to find out.

With a case of this size, you really don't want to leave anything to chance. A few months earlier, we'd assembled the entire legal team to stage a mock trial to test how sample jurors might rule. We'd presented our case just like we would in the real courtroom—opening and closing arguments, witnesses' video-taped depositions, and so forth. We'd listened to the "jurors" deliberate and reach their conclusion. The exercise had taught us that while some of the jurors would give us every dollar we wanted, a substantial number would only award Pickens what he had in the deal as of March 2009—a little over $515,000. That would be disastrous. He had spent far more than that in attorneys' fees already.

I had taken the plaintiff's side of the case in our mock jury trial. The attorney I'd hired to assist me, Mike Lynn, and his partner, Andres Correa, had taken the defense. A few weeks later, Mike confronted me. He was concerned about how the mock trial had gone. "Chrysta, I'm going to be blunt," he said. "You can't win. You need to let me give opening and closing arguments." I wasn't persuasive enough, he said. He thought he could do better. And if I didn't let him essentially take over the case, he didn't think we'd win. Our deal had been that he and his firm would support me, not vice versa.

It's not the first time I've had a man try to upstage me. It's happened more than I care to admit. But when the stakes are as high as they were in this case, I couldn't allow my own ego to get in the way of the right decision. I had to step back and look at this objectively. What if Mike was right?

As the lead lawyer, I had to decide what strategy gave us the best chance to win, even if it meant diminishing my role. Mike had tried hundreds of cases, and he'd won that half-bil-lion-dollar judgment a couple of years earlier. Factoring that in, I decided to compromise. We'd split opening statements—he would address the claims, and I would present the damages.

When we actually got to Pecos, however, plans changed again. Bill and Alva had another idea. Bill had seen Andres make an argument at a pretrial hearing, and he was impressed. Andres was from Chile, a former actor who had appeared in telenovelas. He was bright, personable, and Latino, all of which would appeal to Pecos jurors. The drawback was he had never tried a case. Bill didn't care. He thought the jury would love Andres and that he should have a prominent role in the trial. "Give him *all* the witnesses," Bill said. "It doesn't matter if he doesn't know the evidence and has never done it. The jury will be with him. It might even be better if he screws it up. The jury will want to mother him."

Bill might have been right about the jury, but that's not the only consideration in trying a case. In any trial, there are actually three audiences: the jury, the judge, and the court of appeals. The jury decides the facts and gives its verdict, but the judge decides whether the law supports it and enters the judgment. The appeals court reviews everything that was done during the trial. Trying a big business case is like playing three-dimensional chess—you have to keep track of what's happening on all of the levels. Even if Andres won over the jury with his charisma, that wouldn't likely work with the judge, and he certainly couldn't produce the record necessary to survive the appeals court. After all, he'd only been involved in this incredibly complex case for a few months.

I liked Bill's idea, but if we were going to give Andres a more prominent role in the opening statements, it would have to come at Mike's expense. I was the only one who understood the ever-evolving damages model, so I felt like I had to take that part. Besides, as lead counsel, I had no intention of surrendering the entire opening argument to others. The jury would expect me to speak, and I intended to. I decided Andres would take over Mike's role.

I met privately with Mike later that day at our war room and explained what I wanted to do. I knew it would sting Mike's ego, but I also knew he'd do what was best for the case. He wasn't happy, but after mulling it over, he accepted the plan. Andres and I would open the case.

It was a risky approach. We were leading off with a young lawyer, untested in the courtroom. What would Pickens say if he blew it? Pickens wouldn't blame Andres, of course, he'd blame me. Then again, throughout his business career, Pickens had surrounded himself with bright young talent, up-and-coming financial whiz kids, many of whom had gone on to build their own fortunes. Pickens once said he had a bias toward youth. During his heyday in the 1980s, when he was approaching sixty, the average age at his company was thirty-six. "Forget about age, which means giving young people a chance," he said.[1] I hoped he'd see this decision the same way. Actually, I hoped Andres would be so good that Pickens would never think about the decision at all.

We all rose as the jurors we'd selected filed into the jury box and took their seats. Once they sat down, I stood to speak. I introduced Pickens to the jury, and then the defense attorneys introduced their clients, including Ben Strickling, the chief executive officer for Baytech and DBR; Jimmy Thompson's widow, Dorothy, and one of his daughters, Christy. They were now the owners of J. Cleo. None of them looked happy to be there.

With the introductions out of the way, I turned the floor over to Andres. I hoped I'd made the right decision putting him in the prominent role of presenting our opening argument. We were risking everything on the bet that he would connect with the jury. If he didn't, we'd have wasted a critical opportunity.

Andres stood up, as confident as if he had tried dozens of cases. He rose deliberately from his seat, looked directly at the jury, and prepared to speak. He was poised, exuding an air of authority that masked his inexperience. I knew he must have been nervous—every lawyer is the first few times they address a jury—but his actor training kicked in. He seemed at ease with his audience.

"Ladies and gentlemen, there are three things we want you to understand about this case," he began. "Number one: We had a written deal. We had a piece of paper that Mr. Pickens signed, that Baytech signed, that J. Cleo signed. And that written deal, that contract, said that Mesa got a share of an area of land, an area that had oil. We got 15 percent.

"Number two: Baytech and J. Cleo wanted us out of the deal. That deal said if you want to change it, you had to get it in writing. Mr. Pickens had to sign. But they wanted us out. Mesa said no. Mesa, the evidence will show, said if you want us to sell, pay us. Sign a document.

"Number three: The evidence is going to show that when we said no, Baytech just took it. And they worked together with J. Cleo to just take our 15 percent. And not just take it but hide it from us. And that's why we're here."

He went on to explain that in 2008, Baytech needed more money to fund its own piece of the deal but didn't have a big enough piece to attract the kind of capital the project required. That's why they needed Pickens' 15 percent—to lure enough private equity to pull the whole thing off. I was pretty proud of that little piece of information. I still remember the day I discovered it. My associate, Debbie, and I had been reading thousands of emails, and suddenly, I found myself staring at the one piece of correspondence that made the entire case clear. It explained everything that had happened. Breach of contract cases don't often reveal a motive, but seeing that email between Strickling and Hedrick saying "we want all of the interest if possible" was gold. It was sent just days before the "opt out" position suddenly cropped up in the documents, which in my opinion undermined the "opt out" defense.

While I was reliving that moment, Andres explained that Pickens would take the stand later in the trial. He would testify that the defendants wanted him out of the Red Bull, and that he agreed that if they were willing to pay him back what he had put in the deal, he would sell. He negotiated with Baytech from late November 2008 through March 2009. As Andres recounted the facts leading up the lawsuit, he also repeated a key theme of our case: pressure. Baytech needed cash, and the company wanted to force Pickens out of the deal so it could sell a piece of the Red Bull to another buyer.

"So, it's February," Andres went on. "And they're scared. They know they need the interest." On February 26, Baytech sent a letter to Mesa outlining what it wanted to buy back and sending a proposed agreement to purchase it. "The agreement listed a series of tracts that were at the core of the case—Lyda, Hardin-Simmons, Colt, La Escalera Ranch, the Lloyd Estate," Andres said. "They're going to tell you, 'oh, the only thing Mesa owned was the Lyda.'" Andres said. "Well, if that's the case, ladies and gentlemen, you're going to have to ask yourself, then why are you putting all of this other stuff in the agreement? Why are you putting Mesa's 15 percent in this agreement if you didn't think we owned it? Makes no sense."

The jurors were listening intently to what Andres was saying. That wasn't surprising. Jurors are usually engaged at the start of a case. But Andres was poised and careful in his delivery, and he did seem to have a connection with the jury. I had to hand it to Bill and Alva; letting Andres take part of the opening statement had been a good call.

Andres was explaining that Pickens refused to sign the letter unless he got his asking price for the properties "On March 2, at 9:20 a.m., Mike Hedrick, the Baytech employee who handled the Red Bull, sends Bill Strickling, the CEO, an email that says Pickens and Mesa 'are starting to back up on me.' They're starting to back away from the deal they thought they might get."

Andres paused for a moment, for dramatic effect, emphasizing the next point: "Baytech *knows* Mr. Pickens hasn't signed. They know it. And they panic. They panic because now it's been months and no deal with Mesa. And they need Mesa's 15 percent."

He paused again, then began speaking more conversationally.

"Let me tell you why they were panicking. They were panicking because for months before that, they had already been working—Baytech had been working with J. Cleo—to take Mesa's 15 percent. Maybe they didn't care if Mesa signed or not. Maybe they thought Mesa was going to sign at some point. But the evidence is going to show you that one month before March 2nd, Baytech had paid J. Cleo more than a million dollars for our 15 percent. Not Mesa—J. Cleo. The evidence is going to show you that they had already transferred the 15 percent, even though we had not signed a piece of paper."

"When Pickens refused to sell at the price they were offering, Baytech and J. Cleo decided to just take Mesa's interest and paper over what they had done. They had decided," Andres went on, "Don't pay him anything. Create this fairy tale about him just giving the property away."

Then he gave them the kicker: "A few months after that, Baytech went to their investors with Mesa's 15 percent—with our share—and got forty million dollars." He said the number again—"forty million dollars"—and let it linger. The courtroom was as quiet as a library on Sunday morning. You could almost see dollar signs floating in the room. Andres' acting experience was paying off. He knew how to build the drama of our points and keep the jury focused on them.

Andres went through other details of our case. He noted that Strickling and his partner got two million dollars personally from the investors. Further, the defendants kept negotiating with Mesa even after they sent Pickens the letter saying he was out of the deal and J. Cleo applied the mysterious "current adjustment" in the billing paperwork. "We'll show you the bills," Andres said, and then added, "I don't know if you're going to be able to tell what they say, because Mesa couldn't."

I was still troubled by that detail. I still hadn't figured how to conclusively disprove that the "current adjustment" credit that J. Cleo had put on the Mesa bills took Mesa out of the Red Bull completely. J. Cleo hadn't given us enough documents to explain the "current adjustment"—the backup apparently didn't exist—and no one recalled the details. Based on the scant information we had, even our accounting experts hadn't figured it out. I hoped the fact that even the pros couldn't understand the accounting entries would bolster our claim of having been kept in the dark, but it was a gamble. I also was worried that the defendants might suddenly come up with a plausible explanation.

Andres was laying out the narrative of our case well, and most of the jurors were still with him. One, though, I couldn't be sure about—a man between thirty and forty years old, sitting in the front row of the jury box. He had his sunglasses on in the courtroom, and over the next four weeks we never saw him take them off. We started calling him "Shades." I couldn't see his eyes, so I couldn't tell if Shades was as engaged as the other jurors.

Andres continued by talking about the email from Hedrick to Milford that said they needed to get the deal with Mesa papered up quickly because they were recompleting the Colt well the next day. The email said that they didn't want good results from that well operation to influence Pickens' decision about selling. "Ladies and gentlemen, the evidence is going to show they were actively hiding information from Mesa so that we wouldn't know what's going on," Andres said.

Then, he explained how Strickling had set up Delaware Basin Resources as a completely new and unknown company and how it wound up with Mesa's 15 percent interest in the Red Bull, along with all of Baytech's. He wrapped up by reminding the jurors that they would see a lot of documents from the defendants as that side made their arguments. "The one thing they're not going to be able to show you is a piece of paper where Mr. Pickens signed agreeing to get out of the deal." Finished, he turned and headed back toward our table. He had brought the entire argument back to the point that Bill had made during jury selection—paperwork. I was proud of Andres and my decision to trust him. He had mastered everything in the lawsuit that we had spent the past two years building. He delivered it all in a powerful opening statement.

As he sat down, I realized I'd been holding my breath for most of the time he'd been speaking, Now, it was my turn. I may not have acting experience, but I figure that over my career, I've spent at least a year of my life in trial. It was time to call upon that experience.

Chapter 14

MY TURN

I had two jobs in my part of the opening argument. First, I had to explain the damages that Pickens should receive, based on our calculations (adjusted for Judge Swanson's "guidances"). I also wanted to introduce the jury to Pickens himself, in the way I had come to know him. If our trial had been taking place in the 1980s, or even the 1990s, the courthouse would have been packed with reporters and Pickens would have been splashed across TV screens and magazine covers nationwide. But today, Pickens didn't command headlines like he once did. He was no longer rattling the boardrooms of corporate America with his takeover bids. In the previous decade, he'd made more money than ever, but he'd done it by trading and investing, far quieter activities that don't usually draw the spotlight. Most of the jurors were young enough that they probably had little idea who he was. They saw an old man who would struggle to hear or read documents, and I wanted to make sure they understood that despite my client's age, he was as mentally sharp as when he tried to take over Gulf Oil and Unocal.

Pickens sat stoically at the lawyers' table with the rest of the team as I introduced him. I told them that in my time working for Pickens, I had come to consider him a friend. We had our differences, but I respected him. I told them he was eighty-eight years old and warned them that his impairments could come up in testimony if he were asked to read a document or if a lawyer didn't speak loudly enough. I emphasized that Pickens still went to work every day, just like most of them did. Even though he was making most of his money trading on the markets by then, he still loved geology and the excitement of the oil business. That's why he invested in oil on the side. But deals like the Red Bull weren't his full-time job.

"He does not have a staff of landmen," I said. "He does not have oil and gas revenue accountants who can scrub through all the bills. He doesn't have geologists who are looking at every well. He doesn't have petroleum engineers who are going to the Railroad Commission," checking the records.

Pickens looked directly at the jurors as I spoke, not staring but appraising them, and they were looking at him. They were sizing each other up, taking the measure of each other's integrity. Pickens was wearing his high-tech listening device, a pair of earphones connected to an iPad. It amplified everything that was said. Sometimes, it made the audio in the courtroom emit a high-pitched whine.

I wanted the jury to believe that Mesa and Pickens weren't simply ignoring the Red Bull deal, to persuade them to keep an open mind and to not conclude that Pickens should have known from other sources that he had been cut out of the deal. We needed the jurors to understand that Pickens had been kept in the dark and that the defendants had a duty to tell him what was going on.

I walked over to my other star witness, a blown-up map of the Red Bull acreage. Officially known as Exhibit 53, the map had color-coded sections for the Red Bull leasing efforts. The rendering started with the original prospect around the Lyda well and continued with each expansion after that, all detailed in a different hue. The colors corresponded to other documents and would serve as a constant visual reminder of what Mesa believed it was owed and what we claimed in damages. I planned to refer to it with every witness. As the trial progressed, I intended to carry the display around the courtroom like a sandwich board. Repetition helps when you're introducing new information.

I showed them the areas in which we claimed Mesa already owned its 15 percent: the original Lyda well and surrounding acreage in red; the Colt well and surrounding section in yellow; the Hardin Simmons section in blue; the La Escalera, sixteen sections colored in orange; and the Lloyd section in pink. Then, I reminded them that Mesa had elected to participate in these sections and had begun paying for the interests. I added that Baytech and J. Cleo had broken their promises to give Mesa its 15 percent and—I emphasized this next part—*"they kept the money."*

I pointed to Exhibit 53 again. I'd put it back on its tripod in the corner, but it was also projected on a big screen across from the jury box. "The Hardin-Simmons lease is here in blue, and the Colt lease in yellow," I said. "And the Colt lease is where the Colt well was, and that is when Mesa said, 'Yes, we are in. We want our 15 percent.' Instead of giving us our share, that's when they hid the results of the Colt well."

I pointed to other sections: The orange La Escalera lease, which covered sixteen square miles. The pink-tinted Lloyd lease. The jurors would know those colors by heart by the time this was over.

"They took everything else on this map for themselves, all this land and all the wells that got drilled on it later," I said, passing my hand over the display. "There have been seventy-six wells drilled on this, and they haven't given Mesa its share of any of them.

"Mesa is only asking you, ladies and gentlemen of the jury, for its fair share of the Red Bull, what the deal was, what it signed up for, and what the defendants promised to give it. Mesa's going to bring evidence into this case that shows Mesa's share of the Red Bull is worth about $300 million." I swallowed the fact that we felt it was really worth $1 billion, based on the value of all of the reserves and the lost production from the wells to that point. With the judge's latest rulings, delivered right before opening statements, we had been forced to reduce our claim by about $700 million. "But I want you to keep in mind that they're keeping the rest of the pie, and the rest of the pie is worth more than a billion. That's what the evidence is going to show."

I had worked on that piece over and over again, almost from the first month I had the case. How could I convince a jury that we should get $300 million on what was a $515,000 investment back in 2009, when Mesa was eliminated from the deal? It seemed like a windfall, and it was—but that is how the oil industry works. Besides, I believed that this amount was significantly less than what Pickens was owed.

As I was sitting in the offices at the war room just a few days before, talking to David Coale, it suddenly hit me: talk about it as if it were a pizza or a pie. Sure, our piece was worth a lot, but the defendants were getting to keep their five-sixths of the pie. We were only asking for our fair share. I drew a picture of a pie up on the whiteboard in the war room and left it up to remind everyone on the team that what was fair was fair.

The jury seemed to be following me, but now I had to get them through the hardest part—explaining how we knew the property was worth that much. It had to do with what is known in the business as "reserves accounting," which is how companies value the oil in the ground. Reserves refer to oil that's reasonably likely to be produced over time. To determine its value, accountants tally all of those potential barrels and assign a dollar value to them. Fortunately, we had DBR's own reserves reports to use, the same ones they had submitted to their lenders. They would have difficulty arguing against the values they'd assigned to their own properties when they sought financing.

Our damages model didn't just put a price on the oil, it also took into account the market value of the land. Like residential real estate, when a market becomes hot, prices for oil properties soar. Nothing has changed about the fundamentals—whether it's the amount of oil or the number of bedrooms in the house—the only variable is how much the buyer is willing to pay. That drives up prices. And we were in a price boom that I thought might help us get top dollars from the jury. They would know the property was worth a lot, just from living in the county. When oil prices are rising, land values in places like Pecos shoot up with them. Fracking had revitalized the Permian Basin, and touched off a land rush in Pecos and the surrounding communities.

That's why the defendants were fighting so hard over the date on which we were measuring the value of the property. Raw land isn't worth much before you know there's oil on it. It's worth a fortune right after you prove there is. The defendants were intent on holding us to the value of the land before everyone knew how much it was worth. This position would come up over and over again during the trial. It was their main defense, besides the argument that Pickens just said he didn't want it anymore, which I thought the jury would find silly. Unlike the "opt out," the valuation issue was their most threatening argument.

Ricardo Garza, our expert petroleum engineer, would walk jurors through the arcane process of counting the barrels of oil classified as reserves. The discipline involves engineering, statistics, financial modeling, and a host of other concepts that are complex and mind-numbingly boring if not presented correctly. For now, I told jurors an essential point I wanted them to remember about the reserves: the oil has been there a very long time, and the Colt well workover in 2009 was the key discovery that told them that the Red Bull lands held vast reserves.

I put a picture on the screen showing the layers of the earth by age, going all the way down to the core. The newest layer, the crust, was on the top. The layers got successively deeper and older and were labeled with their geologic names. The Permian was deposited almost three hundred million years ago, and the artist had imbedded dinosaurs and fossils in the layers. It was colorful, informative, and interesting to look at. Ricardo had supplied it.

"Most of you have probably heard that the Permian was underwater a very long time ago and that these layers of rock and sediment and animals and plants, all came together, layer by layer, over time, and the time and heat and pressure created oil," I said. "That's why there's so much oil here. You can see from this drawing that it has been here for millions and millions of years. And the defendants are going to try to stand up and tell you that in 2009, they didn't know it was there." I let the point sink in for a few seconds, then I told them that we would show that in 2009, when the Colt well came in, Baytech and J. Cleo knew the Red Bull "was worth millions and millions and millions of dollars."

It was time to wrap things up, but I wanted to remind them of the themes of our case, which we'd been reinforcing since *voir dire*. "I'm going to sit down in just a minute and defendants are going to stand up," I said. "I want you to keep in mind, the minute they rise to speak, three questions:

"First question is where's the paperwork? Where is the paperwork that got Mesa out of the deal? Where is the paperwork in which Mr. Pickens said, 'you can have it back?' It doesn't exist. They're not going to be able to show it to you."

"Number two. Have they acted in good faith?" The Red Bull contracts helpfully required the defendant to have acted in good faith, a requirement that the defense could not get tossed on summary judgment. "Are they going to bring to you evidence that they've actually acted in good faith? And can they say that, when they took Mesa's interest without the paperwork that they knew they needed to get and they reaped hundreds of millions of dollars from taking Mesa's interest, that was in good faith?"

"And the third thing, ladies and gentlemen of the jury, that I'm going to ask you to consider is whether you hear the slightest, tiniest bit of remorse, or whether what you're going to hear is an attempt to avoid their promises and shift blame onto the eighty-eight-year-old man they took property from."

Okay, I admit it. I was laying it on a little thick with that last bit. After all, when I introduced Pickens, I'd portrayed him as a shrewd businessman, not a feeble geriatric victim. But I did find it outrageous that the defendants were essentially blaming Pickens for their mistake. If I played on the jury's emotions a bit to drive home that point, so be it. That's the business of being a trial lawyer.

I sat down, exhausted from the effort. I could tell Pickens wanted to talk with me, but I'd warned him not to speak out loud in open court. His eyes and his body language, though, told me he was satisfied with how I'd done. The jury seemed to be following us, and Andres and I had made the points we needed to. I still had to convince the members of the jury for whom $515,000 was an unbelievable sum of money that he deserved to be awarded hundreds of millions for investing that amount, and that a payout of that magnitude was fair. But we were off to a good start. Far from being a judicial hell hole, Pecos might just prove to be a godsend for my famous client.

Chapter 15

GROWING FRUSTRATION

We ate lunch across the street from the courthouse at Bill Weinacht's offices, which also served as our daytime war room. Over the course of the trial, this would become our daily routine—a brief interlude from the proceedings where we could discuss strategy or just talk about something else. Sometimes, Mike Lynn or Pickens would entertain us with war stories on a host of subjects, oil-related and not. Pecos didn't have a lot of restaurants in 2016, and the few it did have were usually jammed with oilfield workers at lunchtime. So, one of the paralegals would order food, and we'd all share pizza or Subway sandwiches.

Pickens could be remarkably unpretentious for a billionaire. He may have been accustomed to private jets and multi-million-dollar houses, but he never complained about eating fast-food takeout or staying at a Best Western hotel. I never got the sense any of it bothered him. In fact, he'd almost always insist that we stop by the local Dairy Queen to get his favorite treat, a Blizzard soft-serve dessert, usually with Butterfinger pieces blended in. It was my favorite, too.

After lunch, we made our way back to the courtroom and settled into our respective places. It was time for the defense to present their opening statements. Tim McConn, the lawyer representing Baytech and DBR, stood up. McConn was in his mid-forties, tall and thin with dark hair.

"My clients are here in the courtroom today to defend not just their company but themselves, their honor, their integrity," he said. "These men don't come into court today lightly. They come in here today because they have been accused, as you heard in opening statements, of doing some very bad things. They have been accused of cheating, lying, stealing, hiding things. We are here for the next two weeks to help these men clear their good names. We are going to ask you to clear the good names of Delaware Basin Resources, Baytech, and more importantly, the good people who work for those companies and who have worked so hard over the years to turn those companies and the asset—the Red Bull Prospect that we're talking about in this trial—into something valuable."

I was stunned by McConn's opening premise. He hadn't yet handed the jury a single fact or reason to like his clients, let alone believe them, but he was already telling the jurors that they needed to clear his clients' reputations. In the movie *Contact*, Jodie Foster's character gets some advice from her father: "aim small, miss small." McConn had just aimed really, really big. I sure hoped by the end of this, he missed really big as well.

"You're going to hear that back in 2009, the Red Bull wasn't a really big deal," he continued. "It wasn't at the time Pickens decided to quit it. And that's what you're going to hear about, how Pickens decided to quit this deal. And then you'll be asked to make a decision. Did we cheat them? Did we lie to them? Did we hide things from them? Or does the preponderance of the evidence show that he quit the deal? Did he walk away, get his money back, and never look back for five years?"

Internally, I agreed that was exactly the choice that the jury was going to have to face. Not all cases present that kind of all-or-nothing decision, but this one did.

McConn reminded the jury that the deal came together in 2007 and that oil and gas projects are inherently risky. I was pleased that he was echoing one of our themes—that oil investments were risky, that the stakes were high, but you did it because you expected an outsized reward when you won.

McConn then covered the 2008 market drop and the decline of oil prices from $130 a barrel to $40 a barrel. He told jurors that Pickens' net worth plummeted at the same time and how the defendants rode out the downturn, but Pickens didn't—he got out of the Red Bull. He pointed out to jurors that Pickens had abandoned other energy projects about the same time. He'd planned to build a massive wind farm in the Panhandle but scrapped the idea in November 2008 after falling energy prices killed the economics. And then, almost five years later, after Baytech and J. Cleo hit the jackpot with the Red Bull, Pickens came calling, McConn said.

McConn admitted that his clients needed to bring in other investors about the same time they took over Mesa's 15 percent of the Red Bull, but that wasn't unusual. That's how the business works. It costs money to drill wells, buy leases, and operate rigs.

McConn talked about the failed negotiations with Pickens, reinforcing the defense's contention that the negotiations were for the Lyda alone. "It didn't go through because Pickens wanted too much money for the Lyda, which wasn't a good well," he said. "You don't buy a lottery ticket, scratch it off to see if you won, then try to get your money back when you don't."

McConn covered how, in the defendants' minds, Mesa hadn't paid for the other Red Bull properties, which meant Pickens didn't have a right to the valuable Red Bull acreage. McConn was in the middle of trying to explain a few more details when the judge told him he had run out of time. We were only allowed ninety minutes per side. Swanson wanted to keep things moving, and if you don't give time limits, some lawyers will drone on all day.

McConn sat down and Geoff Bracken stood up to speak for J. Cleo. "We've been in this part of the world since the 1950s," he said. "We're an operator that I like to think has a very good reputation not only in Reeves County but throughout West Texas.

"Plaintiff's counsel got up in front of you and there was a lot of talk about 'they did this.' Well, there's two tables over there and two separate defendants. The plaintiff has to prove that my client, J. Cleo, did something."

It was an interesting way to start. Bracken had always maintained that we should be suing Baytech rather than J. Cleo, because it was Baytech that took Mesa's 15 percent. In his view, J. Cleo got nothing when Mesa was cut out of the deal. To me, the argument signaled that Bracken, who was the most experienced lawyer on the other side, thought Baytech and DBR might be in for a rocky trial.

Bracken discussed the two Red Bull contracts, which I knew he was doing to distinguish between the obligations of J. Cleo and the other defendants. It reinforced his view that J. Cleo wasn't responsible for the taking of Mesa's interest. He covered how Mesa hadn't fully paid for everything in the Red Bull and brought up the mysterious "current adjustment" credit that J. Cleo had placed on the bills. While it was true that Mesa hadn't fully paid for its 15 percent of everything we claimed it was owed, that was because the defendants hadn't billed it for all of the costs. I contended Mesa couldn't be expected to pay for what it didn't know it owed. Now, the defense seemed to be arguing that the "current adjustment," combined with the alleged "opt out" request, covered those unbilled costs and took Mesa out of ownership of everything but the Lyda well.

Bracken then called us out directly. "Remember when the plaintiff's attorney said, 'we had no idea what these credits were for?' I want you to remember that. Because we are going to show you that they knew exactly what those credits were for, and they booked them in their own books and records just like they were supposed to be booked."

Challenge accepted, I thought. No one beats this former mathlete at an arithmetic game. As Bracken wrapped up, Pickens looked at me and started to ask me something. I waved him off. I'd already told him several times we couldn't talk at the counsel table. Besides, because of his hearing loss, he had no concept whispering, and he wouldn't have been able to hear my response. Whatever he wanted would have to wait until the next break.

The end of opening arguments is a natural break point, but Swanson forged ahead. He told me to call our first witness. I didn't mind. I wanted to get the case moving. The first week was almost over—it was already Friday afternoon—and we hadn't presented any evidence to the jury. We weren't off to a rocketing start.

We called Ben Strickling, the CEO of Baytech and DBR. He was a petroleum engineer from Texas Tech. Although he had been in business for decades, the Red Bull was the first really big find that his companies had hit. When I deposed Strickling the year before, I'd found that he didn't know much about what had happened, either because he wasn't in the loop to begin with or because he'd forgotten, which would make cross-examination difficult. I knew that he probably would not answer a lot of the questions we would ask him, but his companies' documents were smoking guns.

I'd spent a long time before the trial discussing with Mike the best order for witnesses, and we'd settled on Strickling first. Calling an adverse witness—a witness for the other side—was an unusual way to begin, but we felt it showed our confidence in the strength of our case. We also felt that the documents were strong enough that even if all Strickling did was read them from the stand, we'd prove our points. Besides, no one at Mesa had personal knowledge of what had happened, so we really didn't have much choice.

The other reason was team management. I not only had to make sure our case was on track, I had to make sure my team was with me. I knew that Mike was still smarting after getting squeezed out of opening statements. Since I was going to take on the technical witnesses that came later, I suggested he tackle the task of putting Strickling on the stand and getting the concessions we would need.

Mike scored a few points early: Strickling had read the contracts. He knew he had to abide by the agreements he made. He agreed that Pickens had never signed an amendment of the contract and that the words "opt out" weren't in the agreement. He agreed that one of the two Red Bull contracts required the parties to act in good faith in their dealings with each other.

Strickling sat stiffly in the witness chair. His demeanor suggested he was determined to endure the process, even though he clearly was uncomfortable and wanted to be somewhere else. He was cooperative, but he showed little interest in connecting with the jury. That was fine with me. The style of his testimony would create a stark contrast with Pickens, whom I knew would relish the spotlight.

From there, though, the procedure broke down. Strickling insisted he didn't know what the contracts and legal instruments meant because he left that to his lawyer, Rick Montgomery. Every question Mike would ask, Strickling would answer by saying he should ask Montgomery. The other problem was Strickling had no knowledge of Mesa's decision to exit the deal. He was relying completely on Jimmy Thompson's claim that Pickens said he wanted out. He testified that he assumed Thompson had taken care of removing Pickens; Strickling himself wasn't involved.

A dead man seemed to control our fate. We were not going to be able to prove much through Strickling if the judge allowed him to keep avoiding our questions.

Mike parried and probed, trying different lines of questioning to break through Strickling's intransigence. He pressed Strickling on how he, as Baytech's CEO, should have known that he couldn't take Mesa's interest without Pickens' written consent. It was like chipping away at a boulder with a toothpick. The defense attorneys kept interrupting with objections, and time and again, the judge would call us to the bench to discuss these matters out of the jury's earshot.

"Law and Order" never shows the endless bench conferences between attorneys and judges in a business trial. Jurors can get confused by the countless arguments and objections, and they may not realize that certain things the lawyers are saying fall outside a jury's purview. Even worse, sometimes jurors can be swayed by what's said, even if they're not supposed to be. That's why these conferences are held at the bench, in what is known as a "sidebar" conference.

I dreaded these front-of-the-room huddles, and not just because they disrupted our presentation. As many as a dozen of us would squeeze shoulder to shoulder next to the bench, whispering to the judge about our arguments. Some of the male attorneys—I couldn't say which ones—had worn their wool suits repeatedly between dry cleanings. Even though it was November, temperatures were still in the eighties in the early days of the trial. We were in a courtroom built before the advent of modern ventilation and even at five feet seven inches, I was shorter than most of the men packed in around me. Men can get away with wearing the same suits day after day, but when those days are spent in a stuffy courtroom in the heat of a Texas autumn, every conference meant me squeezing into a scrum of odiferous suits, struggling to hear *sotto voce* discussions about legal minutiae.

During one gathering, as I leaned in to hear the argument that Stuart Hollimon was making in his soft, deliberate way of speaking, a loud cracking sound echoed through the courtroom. Alarmed, I bolted upright, but before I even turned around to look where the noise came from, I knew what had happened. Pickens was grinning like a mischievous child, and several of the jurors were smiling.

I'd seen him pull this stunt before, though never in open court. When no one was watching, he would slip an empty water bottle under his collar. Then, he pretended to have neck problems. He'd grab the back of his neck with one hand and put the other on the top of his head, pulling his head to one side, as if he were popping his neck. As he did so, he'd crunch the plastic bottle.

It always got a laugh—including from me the first couple of times I saw it—but this time I was mortified. Swanson already seemed to be ruling against us, and most judges don't take kindly to shenanigans in their courtroom. I'd warned Pickens to be on his best behavior, to the point that I sounded like I was lecturing my sons when they were in junior high school. But he was incapable of following directions that ran counter to his instincts. For decades, he'd faced business partners, lawyers, irate shareholders, intransigent managers, and people on the other side of deals. He could tell when to use humor to lighten the mood and when to be serious. As he sat there, watching us whisper among ourselves, he realized that the jurors were getting tired of the constant calls to the bench. He decided to use his little neck cracking stunt to ease their frustration and at the same time, develop a bond with them. He saw them as bored kids sitting in the back of the classroom, and Pickens was the class clown. I would never have condoned such a tactic, but of course, this was T. Boone Pickens. He wasn't used to asking permission. I just hoped he hadn't miscalculated.

Throughout the afternoon, Mike kept chipping away at Strickling, but between the constant objections and Strickling's failure to recall anything of consequence, Mike's frustration was growing. He gained some ground by having Strickling read from the documents that Baytech had authored. They were good documents, and witnesses, no matter how wily, can't run away from the words written on the page.

Mike honed in on one of the key ones—the email from the summer of 2008 in which Strickling said that "we want all of the interest if possible." He wanted to bring in additional funding for the Red Bull, and he needed a bigger piece of the pie to make the investment attractive to investors. Shortly thereafter, the idea that Pickens wanted to exit the deal started showing up in emails written by the defendants. Late that year, the frequency and intensity of those communications increased.

Pickens had testified in his deposition that he never used email, and I believed him. We had searched and never found any computer correspondence from him. I saw him write appointments and phone numbers in a pocket organizer he kept in his suit coat, even though he wrote in such a tiny font that I doubted he could actually read it. His longtime assistant, Sally Geymuller, kept track of everything for him.

Mike pointed to exhibits showing the discussions between Pickens' employee Alex Szewczyk and Baytech's Mike Hedrick. These also showed no proof Mesa had ever sold its Red Bull stake. He also produced an email that Hedrick wrote to Strickling in early March 2009 indicating that although Mesa said it wanted to sell, "their price is telling a different story." That's when Rick Montgomery wrote the now infamous "opt out" letter.

"And you admit you never bought the interest from Mesa?" Mike demanded.

"The only interest that Mesa had to sell was the Lyda well, and we did not buy that," Strickling replied.

Mike hammered him on the fact that the documents showed that Mesa had elected into and had begun paying for its share of the other acreage and wells. Strickling said he believed that J. Cleo had credited back those payments to Mesa on the next set of bills, but said he had no knowledge about the credit. He told Mike to ask someone else about it.

Mike continued, seemingly undeterred, but I could tell the objections were wearing on him. "And you never received a signed written agreement from Pickens transferring the Mesa interest to Baytech?"

"We didn't think we needed a signed written agreement," Strickling said. "They exited the deal."

Mike kept going. "It is clear from Hedrick's notes on the March 20 conversation that Alex was talking about Mesa having an interest in the Red Bull properties generally, not just the Lyda, correct?"

"I relied on Jimmy Thompson to clear that all up," Strickling said. "We thought Mesa was getting a credit for those costs." Again, someone else was the one to ask, Strickling insisted.

As long as Mike kept focusing on the words on the pages of the exhibits that he was also displaying to the jury, the jury was getting the point. But Mike's frustration kept mounting each time the judge sustained the objections the defense lodged. We weren't making much progress.

Court ended with Strickling still on the stand. We'd continue with him the following Monday, but as we left the room, I could see Mike was wound up and frustrated. I had a growing worry that I had miscalculated on a number of decisions. Maybe leading with Strickling had been a mistake. We weren't telling the story through him in a logical fashion that the jury could understand, even if they were getting snippets of the picture. I also was worried about Mike's frustration with the judge's rulings. He had at least a decade more trial experience than I had, yet I was the calm one. And then there was Pickens. He'd been trying to tell me things all day. He obviously didn't like what he'd seen, and I couldn't blame him.

Everyone's frustration level was high as we left the courthouse and returned to the Swiss Chalet. By the time I'd dropped things off in my room, stepped off the elevator into the lobby, and headed toward the conference room, tempers were boiling over.

Chapter 16

"WE ARE ZOMBIES"

My tense moments in the conference room with Pickens the evening before, ending in his "don't pay her" command, lingered as our team gathered in the war room the next morning. Pickens and I had seemed to patch things up and had, in his words, parted as friends. I was still employed as his lead lawyer. And we still had a trial to win. But about fifteen people had witnessed my argument with him the previous evening, and I knew they weren't completely reassured by our mutual apologies. As we met on that Saturday, November 5, the rest of the team was still undeniably down.

"We are like *The Walking Dead*," Mike said, referring to the popular television drama. "We are zombies, and any day now the judge is going to shoot us in the head and end the case. He's already lopped off a few limbs." He was referring to Swanson's decisions that cut our damages from $1 billion to $300 million or so. We'd entered the trial thinking we would be able to ask for a billion dollars. When Swanson tossed out most of our claims, our potential damages instantly dropped to about $700 million. Then, he limited the amount of land acquisitions we could claim—both in time and geography—which lopped off another $400 million. And Swanson wasn't showing signs that he was done ruling against us. The defense had attacked our damage calculations at every turn, whacking off bits such that Mike's zombie analogy was a good one. The defense team would undoubtedly try again before the few experts we had left took the stand. It was their main strategy at this point, now that we had a jury trial underway. We were standing at about $300 million now and I knew they wouldn't rest until they had whittled us down to almost nothing, or, even worse, at last succeeded in convincing the judge to throw out our experts' opinions entirely.

Debbie, my associate, shared Mike's zombie assessment. I noticed that since the trial started, she seemed to pick up on his moods and amplify them. I tried not to get annoyed, but I didn't need the negativity.

I wasn't as pessimistic as the others. I knew our case inside and out. I had a firm handle on both the legal principles and how we had counted everything we were owed. I had selected our experts and given them the strictures through which their opinions would have to pass, knowing that they'd be challenged. We had discussed, vetted, reworked, and considered every number—from dates and acreage, to oil prices and damages. The experts' work had cost more than a million dollars, and its quality lived up to its price. We'd had some setbacks, but I still liked and believed in our chances. Far from getting "shot in the head," I was optimistic we'd see the case through to a favorable verdict.

Still, there was plenty to worry about. If Swanson threw out the rest of our damage calculations, we were finished. Even if we prevailed on the merits of the case, it would be a Pyrrhic victory if Pickens just got his money back. He would have spent millions to recover a relative pittance. But those are the odds that plaintiffs face. In civil cases, the defense prevails more than half the time. Outside of legal circles, most people don't realize that fact, because only the sensational verdicts make the headlines. You never hear about all the defense wins. Pickens, however, certainly knew the odds. He'd made and lost fortunes over less risky moves than this trial.

As I took the tenor of the room that morning, I realized I had a bigger problem. Pickens was a bit anxious and angry at the judge too. That was unusual. He'd described the Red Bull as "biggest oil and gas play of my life," and his attitude so far had reflected that. He'd shown remarkable stamina and even-temperedness. From time to time, he would get irate at something or someone—including me—but he quickly recovered his equilibrium. I had seen him occasionally snap at Jay Rosser, his communications director, but aside from his blowup the night before, our disagreements had been minor squabbles or friendly ribbing. We had heated debates over politics, but neither of us took it personally. After all, I ran for Congress as a Democrat. Pickens was one of the staunchest Republicans— and one of the biggest Republican donors—in a state full of staunch Republicans. He routinely rubbed elbows with governors, senators, ex-presidents, and candidates. While I found his views on matters such as Hillary Clinton and the infallibility of the Republican party unattractive, we managed to discuss politics occasionally without animosity or derision. Of course, neither of us was changing each other's mind.

So, I'd seen him agitated, and I'd seen flashes of anger, but I'd never seen him morose. Heck, usually when things looked bleakest, it was Pickens who told me to soldier on, to keep the faith. Throughout all the buildup and the first week of the trial, he'd been upbeat. He'd been unwavering in his support for me and his confidence that we would prevail. He would sometimes tell me not to get anxious about settling the case because we might get more money after trial. Now his mood presented another worry. He would be testifying next week. I needed him to be in all his folksy, water-bottle-crunching glory, not some sad sack who looked like he'd given up.

It was time to jump into cheerleader mode again. I really needed to rally our team spirit. Everyone had weeks of work ahead of them, and I needed them to perform at their absolute best. "Guys, we can do this," I encouraged them. "We can get past these rulings. The judge is not going to pour us out of court. Stop the pessimism and get back to work, because we are going to win!" No one started cheering, but they did seem to perk up a bit as they headed back to their desks to resume their preparations. Whether it showed at that moment or not, it was critical that we keep a positive mindset. Where the mind goes, the body will follow.

By Monday morning, everyone's mood had improved. A couple of days away from court seemed to help. Pickens, along with his closest aides, Ron and Jay, had taken a day trip to the Fort Davis observatory. They found a local watering hole to sit and chew the fat with the patrons. We still had an uphill battle in this trial, but the team was feeling better about our chances. Strickling was still on the stand, and now it was the defendants' turn to question him.

The back-and-forth went more smoothly with his own attorneys posing the questions. They got Strickling to explain why things had transpired the way they had. He explained why it was okay for Baytech and DBR to take Mesa's piece of the pie, why it was okay for J. Cleo to have kept Mesa's money, and why Mesa should have figured out what was going on. In his view, the "opt out" conversation was the key to the whole Red Bull outcome.

When they finished, Mike Lynn tried again. The results were much the same. Did anyone notify Mesa of acquisitions after March 2009? "That would be a question better asked of Rick Montgomery." Was Strickling accountable for the contracts and letters he had signed? "The documents were drafted by our legal department, and I reviewed and signed them."

Once again, Strickling answered question after question in the same detached manner, referring most of them to Rick Montgomery. While it might keep Strickling from saying something he shouldn't, I didn't think it looked good for a CEO to appear so uninvolved in a project with hundreds of millions of dollars at stake.

We clearly weren't going to get anything more from Strickling. During a brief conference, I asked Mike to at least have the Baytech CEO walk through Exhibit 53, the color-coded map of the Red Bull. Mike obliged, calling out each of the properties and wells that were acquired by their colors and names.

At least the jury would be clear on how the colors pertained to the Red Bull lands and wells. We would turn back to the rules learned in kindergarten later in the trial. It was time to move on.

Part Three

PICKENS TAKES THE STAND

Chapter 17

"THE BIGGEST PROSPECT EVER"

I woke up earlier than usual on the morning of Tuesday, November 8. It was the day we had scheduled for Pickens to testify, and his habitual resistance to my attempts to prepare him made me uneasy.

I knew that he was smart and wily. He could compose his thoughts well and say what he meant. But he was the most important witness in the most important case of my life, and I felt less ready than I had for almost any other witness I'd ever put on the stand. I was lucky I'd gotten any sleep at all.

I also had to worry about the judge. Would he let Pickens testify the way that Pickens was inclined to do—saying what *he* thought was important? Or instead, would Swanson carve out certain topics and keep Pickens from saying what was on his mind?

I kept reminding myself that it was Swanson's first trial. Many judges never see a proceeding of this size, with so many lawyers and witnesses and so much money at stake. An experienced judge would have found it a challenging case to preside over. But one thing I'd learned about Swanson after the first week: he was deliberate. I might not agree with his decisions, but he took time to reflect carefully before making them. Judges must consider a wide range of factors in deciding how a jury trial should be conducted. What is the law? Is it clear or is it murky? Have all the facts been disclosed? Is the witness testifying from personal knowledge or an opinion grounded in facts and science? Is the witness saying the same thing over and over, or speculating about answers? Are the questions any good? There's an even longer list to consider when ruling on objections.

Even though I'd gained some insights into how Swanson ran his courtroom, I had no idea how he would handle my star witness. All I could do was put Pickens up there, and hope.

I called Pickens, and he stood up from the table, walked past the jury box and up the two steps to the witness stand with the spryness of someone decades younger. All those years of maintaining a steady fitness regimen paid off. Besides, this was the moment he'd been waiting for—the chance to tell his story. He'd been looking forward to it long before the trial started. I only hoped that he would stay with me, covering the points that we had to make to win.

Just in case, I decided to lead with the most important point. Whatever else might break down, at least I'd get Pickens to underscore the themes of our case.

"Mr. Pickens, did Mesa ever elect to opt out of the Red Bull?" I asked.

"No."

I paused. There was something else I wanted to put to rest right away, before Pickens answered any more questions about the deal. I knew at least some of the jurors had to wonder if an eighty-eight-year-old could even remember what he'd done a decade before.

"Now, is it possible," I asked, "that you've just forgotten that Mesa opted out?"

"No."

"How do you know?"

"Never had a conversation with Jimmy Thompson about the Red Bull. Never in my life have I given away property without someone paying me money and me signing over a deed. I wouldn't do that. I can't imagine anyone would say that I just gave the property away."

So far, so good. All the jurors, including Shades, were paying attention. Some of the older ladies were nodding. We were coming back to the points we'd hit on during jury selection, hammering home another theme of our case: you can't get a property without a signed piece of paper. I was betting the jury would remember what Bill Weinacht said.

I knew the defense would start objecting any minute. The longer they sat there, allowing me to continue uninterrupted, the more they'd begin to feel they were losing control. After seeing how they'd peppered Mike with objections during Strickling's testimony, I expected them to start in with Pickens. The more they could frustrate him, the greater the chance he'd lose his temper and embarrass himself in front of the jury.

Objecting to testimony can backfire. Jurors might pay extra attention to the evidence drawing the objection. If the interruptions were too persistent, they might start to feel sorry for Pickens, who couldn't tell his story. Speaking of which, Pickens had behaved himself so far, and it was time to let him run a bit. Now, if the defense objected, they would be picking directly on Pickens, not me.

I asked Pickens to go back to early 2007 and explain why he decided to invest in the Red Bull property in the first place. He launched into his explanation just like we'd rehearsed. That part, at least, he'd paid attention to. He had wanted to be a passive investor in the deal because he didn't have the extensive staff required to run the show like he did when he owned a large public company.

"It had the potential to be a big deal," he said. "It's a lot bigger than I ever thought it was going to be. To have all of that open acreage and the experience of what happened in the Midland Basin—could that be the same thing that happened in the Delaware Basin? The Red Bull was in the Delaware Basin. Geologists always like to have what's called a look-alike, and the Delaware Basin was a look-alike to the Midland Basin."

I would have to make sure the jurors understood that both the Midland and Delaware were actually sub-basins of the Permian. I also would have to remind them that the current boom started in the Midland Basin and was expanding into the Delaware, but since they lived in the area, most of them probably knew that. Besides, Pickens was doing great. He was speaking clearly, with a sense of authority. He was basing his testimony on his deep knowledge of the geology. His extensive background and experience, combined with his command of the facts, might help the jury get over any suspicion that this elderly gentleman may have gotten confused about what happened.

Pickens kept going, explaining his rationale for investing. He had seen the Red Bull maps and the geology of the initial Lyda well. This material showed that the whole area had the potential to produce oil. It was sitting atop deep layers of oil shales—called benches—in the Wolfcamp formation of the Delaware Basin. He knew that there was plenty of land to buy up around the initial Lyda well because no one had "proved" the area yet. In the oil world, there was a possibility of making a vast fortune from a cheap investment, but first you had to prove the oil was where you thought it was. Of course, that also meant trusting your partners.

I wanted Pickens to stress that his role was passive because the defense would argue that he should have figured out long before he did that they were leasing acres and drilling wells without him. They would argue that he should have inspected public records and sued them years earlier. They claimed he waited to see how the project turned out before he spoke up. The euphemism is that he was "drilling for oil at the courthouse." The phrase has been the rallying cry of defendants who believe themselves wrongly accused ever since people started investing in oil.

In this case, it was one of the defendants' stronger arguments. And, to people unfamiliar with the case, it seemed logical. How could a famous oil tycoon, who'd been doing oil deals since the 1950s, not notice that he was being swindled? I wanted to bury that argument quickly, so I cut into Pickens' monologue.

"Mr. Pickens," I asked, "do you have any landmen on staff now?" If he'd had a landman, he or she could spend all day looking at public records to see what was going on in the area, like the folks working at the folding tables in the lobby below us. I knew the jurors had to walk past them in the morning just like we did.

"No, and I shouldn't have to do that," Pickens replied. "There is stuff filed with the Railroad Commission and it's available if I wanted to see it. But I was a non-operator and the operator was supposed to do all that." Pickens said he didn't have engineers or even geologists other than himself. In other words, his company wasn't in a position to operate wells or to verify that the operator was doing its job. The whole point of being a non-operating partner was that you hired someone else to do the work. "It was a service they provided, and we paid for," Pickens said.

Bracken, the J. Cleo lawyer, stood up in the middle of the answer to object that it was non-responsive. This was what I'd been worried about. Non-responsive means that the answer doesn't match the question. Earlier, I'd asked Pickens if he had any landmen, and he'd gone into an explanation of operating agreements. He probably should have just said "no," as he did to my earlier questions, but I was happy for the jury to hear the broader context.

I had to be careful, though. If I asked open-ended questions that allowed him to give long explanations, he might miss crucial details. But if I asked specific questions that would remind him of the points we needed to make, I'd draw endless objections that I was leading the witness.

The judge called us up to the bench, and I explained that I needed some latitude because Pickens couldn't see or hear well. "He's explaining as best he can," I said. I was walking a tightrope. I wanted the jury to see Pickens as sharp-minded and alert, but I wasn't beyond playing the helpless old man card with the judge. And both things were true, in alternate measures.

Swanson told me to stick to the question-and-answer format. This meant that Pickens could only answer what I asked, not give long narratives. I'd known this was likely to happen, and it would make the testimony more difficult from here on out, but I'd at least gotten this far. Pickens' words were resonating with the jury, and he'd gotten to tell a lot of the story the way he wanted.

Still, Pickens had his own way of putting the story together, and it varied every time. I couldn't control what he said, even if the judge wanted me to.

We went on to cover the basics. Pickens had dealt only with J. Cleo, the operator, regarding the Red Bull deal. He'd never spoken directly to Jimmy Thompson about getting out of the deal after he signed the paperwork. All he knew about Baytech was that it was another passive investor that had brought the prospect to J. Cleo, and he only knew that because he'd seen the company's name in the paperwork. Only later did he learn that Baytech had taken his 15 percent interest, but that wasn't until late in 2015, after we had filed the lawsuit.

I moved on to the question of the additional acreage. "Mr. Pickens, did you intend to participate in additional acreage that was acquired?"

"We participated in everything the operator asked us to," Pickens said. "The strategy was the Lyda well would be reentered. If it showed more oil to go get, then we would buy additional acreage. And when we saw the oil recovered—that was the key here. If you could establish oil in the vertical hole of the Lyda well, then you could come back with horizontals and your recovery would be so much greater than just the vertical."

Pickens knew exactly what he was talking about. He had done thousands of deals like this and could cut to the chase and tell you what really mattered to him. Trouble was, the jurors couldn't follow it. I wouldn't be able to guide Pickens through all of the background details to bring them into a full understanding. Fortunately, I had Ricardo Garza waiting in the wings to explain it later. The trick now was to not let Pickens get so far down in the weeds that the jury got confused and stopped paying attention. And he was still talking.

"So, when we looked at the Lyda and it had the oil," he continued, "Thompson's office notified us that they were ready to buy more acreage. and we immediately said 'okay, buy it.'" Exhibit 53 was still sitting on the easel. I knew that his testimony would reinforce with the jury the importance of the colored parcels on that map.

Bracken stood up again, raising the same objection about non-responsiveness. The judge turned to Pickens. "Mr. Pickens, I'm going to ask you to be careful to listen to the questions," he said.

"Are my answers too long?" Pickens asked, with just a dash of meekness and bewilderment.

Swanson hesitated. He had difficulty making direct statements himself, as we'd seen with his "guidances" at the start of the trial. "Well, what I want you to do is just listen to the question, meet it head-on, and then stop," he said. "And if the lawyers have more information they want from you, they're going to need to ask another question."

I plowed ahead. Since Swanson sustained the objection, I needed to go over what Pickens had just said, one question and answer at a time, while cutting out the extraneous issues that Ricardo, the geology expert, would cover later. Bracken was savvy enough to know that his success on the objection would cause me to repeat the same questions. The jury would hear it twice, reinforcing the evidence's importance. I hoped they might get annoyed at Bracken for wasting their time. Bracken, meanwhile, was probably hoping that Pickens would falter on the second try.

I put a document up on the monitor screen and read it aloud: "Baytech has continued its leasing efforts in the prospect and has secured leases covering the remaining 50 percent interest in the original contract area. The total cost of this effort will be approximately $1,458,000." This referred to the La Escalera purchase, the orange sections of Exhibit 53. Mesa had chosen to participate in sixteen contiguous square miles saturated with oil reserves. Pickens recognized his signature at the bottom. Then I showed the documents for the Colt well, which he had also signed. I was reiterating that each time Pickens had received a notice of election, he had returned it with his signature and that when the bills came, he paid them.

"To your knowledge, was Mesa ever presented with any notice of election that it did not agree to participate in?" I asked.

"No," Pickens said. "We participated in everything that was offered to us."

We needed more to combat the key defense claims that Pickens had opted out of future acquisitions and wells in a phone call with Jimmy Thompson and that Pickens was out of money in 2008, when his net worth plunged by two-thirds from the market crash.

"If you had been offered the right to participate in additional purchases, would you have done so?" I asked.

"We would have followed the same practice—we would have participated," he said.

I asked him about the defense contention that he couldn't pay the bills, given his losses. Despite his reluctance to rehearse, we had managed to cover this question, so he knew it was coming. But when he heard it in open court, in front of strangers, he looked indignant. He shifted in his seat before answering, clearly uncomfortable with the notion that he refused to pay.

"That's just not true," he said. "We paid our bills. We always paid our bills."

I asked if anyone else could have decided not to pay for the acquisitions.

"No," he said. "I made the decisions on spending money." No one would challenge that he was in charge.

I was feeling pretty good about Pickens' testimony so far, despite our improvisation. He'd explained the basics of the deal and rebutted important points the defendants wanted to make. Now, it was time for some color. "Mr. Pickens, let's turn to why the Red Bull was attractive to you as a geologist. Can you tell the jury about your work as a geologist?"

While the judge had forbidden Pickens to testify about his expert opinions based on geological knowledge, I could still ask him about his background as a geologist. The jury would be able to draw their own conclusions about Pickens' expertise. Anyone could Google Pickens and find anything they wanted to know about his past, including how notorious a person he'd been in the 1980s and 1990s. But the jurors had sworn an oath they wouldn't do that, and they didn't know about him, so I wanted to fill them in.

"I was born in Oklahoma as an only child during the Depression, in 1928," Pickens said. "That was when families they just had one kid, because they couldn't afford to have any more. My dad and mother both had a job. My mother worked for the government and my dad was a landman in the oil business.

"We moved to Texas in 1944, and I graduated from high school in Amarillo. I went one year to Texas A&M and transferred to Oklahoma A&M, now Oklahoma State. Graduated with a degree in geology in 1951. Went to work for Phillips Petroleum for four years, then went out on my own."

He'd told this story a lot, and it was in all three versions of his autobiography, but I enjoyed hearing him recount it. I figured the jury would, too.

"I'll never forget the day I came home and told my wife that I had left Phillips. She said, 'What are we going to do? We have two children, I'm pregnant, and you don't have a job.' And I said, 'On top of that, I don't have a car.' I had to use her car. We had to trade back and forth until I had enough money to buy one for myself. But I did have fifteen hundred dollars I had saved at Phillips in the retirement plan. Didn't tell her that. I was making five hundred dollars a month at Phillips. So, the fifteen hundred was there. And I figured I had three months to do something. And I did. I never had to use the fifteen hundred.

So, I got to work and bought a car about six months later. And that's my story. And then I retired."

The jury laughed, knowing from what they already heard that he had left out a few things. Shades adjusted his sunglasses slightly to get a better look at Pickens. It was exactly the reaction I was hoping for, because even though we hadn't practiced this part of the testimony, Pickens loved telling the story, and he always told it just like that.

We still had several hours to go before the day was done, but Pickens appeared to be holding up well and even enjoying himself. We covered other details of his career. We noted that he'd personally operated more than two thousand wells and had held interests in more than a thousand others as a non-operating partner, the same type of interest he held in the Red Bull. Then I asked him what he expected the operator to do in a play like the Red Bull, based on his experience.

"The non-operating partners pay the operator for its services," he said. "The operator is supposed to provide all of the information about what is going on to the non-operators. Wherever you are, you tell that non-operating partner all about the well. And it's—I always thought of it as a fiduciary responsibility that I had when I operated—"

Judge Swanson cut him off. He'd already ruled against our fiduciary arguments, and he wasn't going to let Pickens open that door. He instructed the jury to disregard the testimony on fiduciary duty. Without being asked the next question, Pickens followed his next instinct, which was to play the sympathy card.

"I don't understand what I said wrong," he offered rather meekly. I tried to move things along.

"Can we talk about the Colt well?" I asked.

"I'm almost afraid to," he replied. I knew he was trying to keep the jury with him even if the judge wasn't. He wanted them to know he was trying to follow the rules, but he was implicitly asking them to excuse him from violating them. Now was the time for him to really show his stuff. He knew all about the Colt well reentry. It interested him and he could explain all of the details.

"What was the plan for reentering the Colt well?"

"Well, the Colt well had been completed in the Devonian formation. Now, we were going to reenter the well and plug off the Devonian and perforate the Wolfcamp and the Bone Springs"—two benches of the Delaware Basin—"which we did. And we got more oil —wait, am I going on too long?"

And that's why T. Boone Pickens made a formidable witness and opponent. He just told the jury about his deep knowledge of the various layers of oil formations below the land we were suing over. He told them he was paying attention to every detail in the deal. And that he was also trying to follow the judge's rules and make the defense objections seem silly and pointless, all in a matter of a few sentences. The jury probably didn't follow all the geological terms, but it didn't matter. To put it in movie terms, he was our version of Marisa Tomei in *My Cousin Vinny,* the most brilliant legal movie of all time. I guess that made me Joe Pesci.

I asked him to tell the jurors about the results of re-drilling the Colt well.

"I know now that they reentered and got a big confirmation of five thousand feet of oil-saturated thickness in the Colt well," he said. Then he added: "I did not know about it at the time, because they didn't tell me. But they knew right then that they had a major discovery."

Pickens had covered an essential plot point. We believed the defendants were contractually bound to tell Pickens about the results of the operation on the Colt well, which he had agreed to participate in and pay for. They didn't, and that was the discovery that made all of their later efforts in the Red Bull pay off. And in our view, that's why they wanted Mesa out before the Colt well was drilled, because it revealed that the Red Bull was a monster find.

"We had bought acreage as well, and had signed up for the Colt well, but all they were offering was to buy my interest in the Lyda well. Now if I can offer my speculation at this point..."

All the lawyers at the defense tables jumped to their feet to object.

"Mr. Pickens, you are not to speculate," Swanson cautioned.

"Okay, but I forewarned it." Outwardly, I remained stoic, but I was chuckling to myself. He'd just done it again. He'd known exactly what he was doing when he uttered the word "speculation." The way he'd phrased it allowed them time to object, and now he once again appeared compliant. But he had taken control of the proceedings. He was calling the shots, taunting the defense to object, and you could feel that the jury was with him.

"So, anyway," Pickens continued, "we returned and counter-offered three weeks later. I told Alex...that if they wanted it, they could pay back the $515,000. And then we didn't hear back from them for about four years."

Mesa had paid in $515,738, to be exact, by March 2009. The money had gone to finance not only the original sections of land and the Lyda well, but also a portion of all of the other acreage purchased on Exhibit 53. Pickens wasn't going to give up those additional lands for only $160,000. If he was going to sell, he wanted all of his money back. But Baytech never offered that sum and no sale ever took place.

Now was a perfect opportunity to get into those mysterious "current adjustment" credits. I asked him if he'd ever agreed to accept credits in exchange for giving Mesa's interest to Baytech.

He said he hadn't, and then I asked him his reaction to the opt out letter.

"I didn't know what they were talking about," he said. "I never heard of an opt out before this case. I didn't understand why another non-operator—Baytech—would be telling me that I'd opted out of anything. How would they know? And why were they trying to buy me out if I had already opted out?"

Pickens pointed this out to us. It was obvious, but we'd all missed it. J. Cleo, as operator, should have been the one calling the shots about who owned what, not Baytech. If Mesa actually had relinquished its interest, the operator, J. Cleo—should have sent the documentation.

We were making good progress. I was checking off a lot of key points with minimal objections from the other side. I didn't know how long it would last, but I wasn't about to slow down. I asked Pickens if he had agreed to sell Baytech his interest for $515,738 because he needed the money.

"I needed my money back?" He was again indignant. "They make comments that I didn't have enough money to do the project. At the time, I had hit a high-water mark of $4 billion in net worth, and I gave away $1 billion, lost $2 billion and still had a billion left." He noted that he'd supported a number of charities and hospitals, including the M.D. Anderson Cancer Center in Houston. "I could have financed this whole deal if they wanted me to, if they'd just sat down with me and talked to me, asked me about it."

On the trial team, we had been struggling with how to portray a man who the jury might dislike simply because he was wealthy. Between our jury consultant and Mike Lynn, they came up with the idea to let jurors know how generous he had been to so many people. Pickens focused on the hospitals in his answer, but there were countless other organizations, colleges, and schools we could have named. I'd taken a picture of the photograph that hung on the wall at the T. Boone Pickens YMCA in downtown Dallas showing him as a young basketball player, which had been put up after he financed a renovation of the facility. I was closing out my direct questioning of Pickens, and as I did a quick mental survey all of the high points, I realized I had one left.

"Mr. Pickens, in your experience over sixty-two years as a geologist and someone who passionately loves the oil and gas industry, how does the Red Bull compare to the other plays you've been in?"

"Interesting question," he said. "I had drilled wells in Africa, Australia, and the North Sea. And I had been an operator in the Gulf of Mexico, partners with Pennzoil. And of all the wells I drilled, this actually turned out to be the biggest prospect that I've ever been involved in. I was involved in one in the Gulf that was over a billion barrels. What you've got here is over three billion barrels."

I asked him how it felt to be treated the way he had been treated in the Red Bull deal. Again, he shifted in the witness chair uncomfortably. In my experience, titans of industry don't like to admit emotional involvement. He took a deep breath, and then he said, somewhat more quietly: "Well, that didn't make me feel very good. The biggest deal I was ever in, and I had it taken away from me."

"Your Honor, I'll pass the witness," I said. Now it was my turn to take a deep breath—and a sigh of relief. Pickens had made a powerful witness. I was so proud of him, and he must have felt that. He had held up to the strain of trial at age eighty-eight and had proved his formidable expertise. But the most difficult part was yet to come.

Chapter 18

FROM HELL TO BREAKFAST

We broke for the day and headed back to the hotel. I was feeling good about Pickens' performance on the witness stand, but I knew the bigger challenge was prepping for what the defense would pepper him with in the morning. We ate a quick meal at the Alpine Lodge, the restaurant adjoining the Swiss Chalet. It wasn't fancy. It was the kind of place that if you ordered a steak they'd ask if you wanted it chopped or chicken fried. We'd eaten there most nights because it was convenient, and there were few other options. After dinner, I went straight to my room. I still had a lot of documents to review so I could be sure I was ready for the next day. The defense would be questioning Pickens, but in this scenario, I was his protector. My objections could save him from endless badgering or unfair questioning from the other side, but I had to use them with discretion.

I'd almost forgotten that it was Election Day in 2016. I'd voted early, before the trial started. I was counting on Hillary Clinton to break the "highest, hardest glass ceiling" in the world that evening, but I wouldn't have time to watch the returns.

It would be an historic moment, seeing America elect its first woman president. Despite my excitement, I would have to view the recap on the morning news.

I wasn't worried. The polls showed Clinton had a comfortable margin, and no one thought Donald Trump was a serious candidate. I frankly hadn't paid that much attention to his candidacy, except his creepy invasion of Clinton's personal space during one of their debates. Mostly, I was too caught up in the pretrial preparations to notice.

Holed up in my room, surrounded by notes, transcripts of depositions, and myriad other documents and pieces of evidence, I let the election pass from my mind. I concentrated on the trial, drifting off to sleep about 10:30 p.m.

I woke up at 4:00 the next morning, as I usually did, and flipped on the TV. I stared at the election results in a state of disbelief. Was this a nightmare? Was I still asleep? The news outlets not only hadn't declared a winner, but some were even saying it appeared Trump had won. I kept listening as I got dressed, but I felt like I was moving through a thick fog. How could Hillary have lost? What would this mean for the country? It seemed as if I'd gone to sleep in the world I'd always known and awakened in an upside-down universe. (Years later, I'd discover there's an internet meme that says an explosion in 2016 at the Large Hadron Collider in Switzerland had actually altered the space-time continuum. Maybe it did. It sure felt like it that morning.)

I forced myself to wall off the maelstrom of emotions churning through me. I had to focus on the case—I *had* to. Even if I felt as if the unbelievable had happened, as if the America I loved might be entering its final days and democracy itself might crumble under the leadership of a clearly unqualified president, I still had to win this case.

And then the worst realization of all hit me. None of those things was going to be as difficult as just getting through breakfast that morning. The case I could manage. Donald Trump as leader of the Free World? Still couldn't fathom it. But breakfast would be unbearable. I was representing one of the most hard-bitten Republicans on the planet, and he had a cadre of similarly-minded followers—some of them right here with him in the hotel. Most days, I tried not to think about how odious I found his politics, but there was no denying that Pickens was as red as the Oklahoma dirt of his birth.

His entourage—Ron, Jay and even Ricardo—shared his views. I was about to endure the most excruciating plate of chilaquiles and refritos ever eaten. Actually, my stomach turned, and I knew I wouldn't eat at all.

I stepped into the elevator, and for an instant, I hoped maybe Pickens wouldn't mention it. Maybe he was so concerned about the trial, he wouldn't want to distract me. I almost laughed out loud. Of course, he'd mention it—hell, he was going to *gloat*. Pickens loved politics. He'd once planned to run for Texas governor himself. He'd probably spent the night watching the returns and chatting with his Republican buddies across the state while I scoured musty law books looking for ways to win his case.

Up to this point, my Democratic Party membership and views on politics were the stuff of sport for them. They teased me about it when we needed to blow off some steam. But it was all friendly banter. For all his devoted partisanship, Pickens also knew, liked, and worked with plenty of liberals and Democrats. The "Pickens Plan" that he rolled out in 2008 called for expanding wind energy. He had generated an entirely new following among environmentalists who either didn't know his politics or assumed he'd had a change of heart. Many of them were still among the millions who actively followed him on social media.

But as the elevator slowly descended, I knew that this morning would be different. No matter how nonchalantly I poured my coffee and sat down, Pickens would have already planned a way to draw me out. Worse, he would do it not just in front of his loyalists, but the entire breakfast room full of West Texas oilfield roughnecks, landmen, and the rest of the "Make America Great Again" hangers-on who would be milling about.

And then, as the elevator lurched to a stop, another worry flashed into my mind. I'm not superstitious, but what if Clinton's loss foreshadowed the outcome of my trial? I was a woman up against a bunch of men from three of the top corporate law firms in the country. Mike kept telling me we were losing and that the judge at any point was going to "shoot us dead"—legally and metaphorically. I'd been fighting to keep us alive, but what if it wasn't enough? What if I wound up being as stunned by the verdict as Clinton had been about last night's returns? I had felt like we could win this case from the moment I first started looking at it, but then again, I'd been equally sure that Clinton would prevail on Election Night. What if I was misreading our chances?

The doors opened. I headed to the coffee pot, poured myself a cup, took a deep breath, and walked over to the table where Pickens and Ron were sitting.

Pickens started right in: "Chrysta, can you believe that Hillary lost?"

It was actually a softer opening than I'd expected. I thought I might even have detected a touch of sympathy in his tone. My face probably revealed that I was crestfallen. Pickens knew I'd been a big supporter—donations, yard signs, the whole bit.

I had a picture of Clinton and me on my phone that had been taken at one of her fundraisers.

"No, Mr. Pickens," I said slowly. "I can't believe it. I cannot believe that Donald Trump is going to be our next president." I almost choked on the words. It was as if in that moment, the weight of the election came crashing down on me. I stared into the deep, dark abyss of my coffee cup in a desperate attempt to find solace. I braced for the next comment, the jokes, the badgering that I was sure would come.

But then—nothing.

He didn't say anything more about it. He turned to Ron and started discussing the trial and his second day on the stand. Maybe he didn't want to distract me in the middle of the case, or maybe he didn't want to distract himself. I knew Pickens was not the strongest devotee of Trump. At one point, I recalled that he had preferred other primary candidates. I assumed Pickens must have met Trump at some point. Perhaps Trump's business record, with a string of bankruptcy filings, and his belligerent, New York-style manner hadn't set well with Pickens. But I'm sure he would have rather gouged his own eyes out right there at the breakfast table than to vote for Clinton. Regardless, I was grateful for the chance to pull my mind back from politics and, as if their conversation were pulling me forward, to begin to focus on the case once more. We recapped the highlights of Pickens' testimony the day before, and I reminded him of what we would cover in the day ahead.

In the face of the biggest political disappointment in my life—bigger, in fact, than when I'd lost my own race for office because the national stakes were so much more important—I welcomed the chance to wrap myself in the mundane details of the trial.

At 7:30 a.m., we rolled out for court. I rode in the car with Cathy, my sister and legal assistant. I used the safe space, away from my Republican clients, to vent during the fifteen-minute drive. "I cannot believe it!" I ranted to no one in particular. "It's incredible that a man as perverse as Donald Trump is now president of the United States, and that Hillary helped him get there!" The sense of disbelief had started to fade, and I realized I was angry at Clinton—angry that she had missed when we couldn't afford her to miss, angry at the idea that her own foibles might have been the cause of her loss, angry that seemingly only a perfect woman candidate might succeed even though no such woman existed, and angry at the sexism of other women in particular.

As grateful as I was that Pickens had gone easy on me, I wasn't sure I'd be so lucky with Debbie Eberts, my associate from Dallas. Debbie may have been more right-wing than Pickens, if that were possible. She was deeply religious and had told me in the past that she believed that women should not take leadership positions over men in the church. She was fervently pro-life and pro-gun. While I liked her personally and we worked together well, she was unwavering in her political views. Thankfully, Debbie, like Pickens, seemed uninterested in talking about the election. In fact, she seemed a bit shocked by the election results, too, and we quickly moved on to business.

I was relying on Debbie for feedback about Pickens' performance on the stand. She also prepared a detailed trial report about the prior day's events that I sent to Pickens and his lieutenants each morning. Even though they were sitting through the proceedings most days, the reports served as a handy reference of what was happening and what we might need to revisit later in the trial or on appeal. Like Mike, Debbie wasn't optimistic about our chances of winning, and was in a down mood that morning.

I told her to stay positive. After all, we didn't know how things would turn out. I believe that mental energy helps to shape your future. But secretly, I was worried by her reaction to the trial. Along with Mike's repeated warnings that we were losing and Clinton's defeat, Debbie's gloom seemed to settle ominously over the case. Maybe the grind of the trial was taking its toll. Despite Pickens' masterful testimony the day before, I was becoming more worried. What if, after everything we had done, we wound up losing this damn thing?

Chapter 19

PICKENS VERSUS THE DEFENSE

By the time we reached the courthouse, I'd tried to bury my anger at the election outcome and my insecurities that Clinton's loss was an omen for our case. Walking through the front doors seemed to have a cleansing effect, blocking out my worries. As I settled in at the plaintiff's counsel table, I was glad I hadn't watched the results the night before and had instead spent it reviewing what the defense was likely to bring up on its cross-examination of Pickens.

As Pickens walked toward the stand, I thought I detected a slight wobble in his step. It was subtle, but he didn't have quite the same confident gait that he'd had the day before. Maybe he was tired from the previous session. After all, I'd questioned him for a couple of hours, and then the defense started in. I'd barely gotten the words "pass the witness" out when Tim McConn, the attorney for Baytech, jumped up to begin the cross-examination. The rest of the afternoon had been a tedious journey through documents, most of which Pickens knew little about.

Pickens had held up well during that first round. McConn's best shot of the day had been grilling Pickens on why he or his staff didn't notice he wasn't getting regular production reports from the Colt well. I wished, once again, that Pickens had realized much sooner that the Red Bull was still out there. We would have been able to claim more damages, and the defense would have had a harder time portraying him as oblivious or even careless. Still, for all McConn's efforts the day before, he hadn't accomplished much. His most effective tactic may have been simply tiring out an old man on the witness stand.

Now, McConn was at it again. He asked a series of questions intended to catch Pickens in a lie. "Are you a man of integrity?" "Your word is your bond?" "People can rely on you?" "People can trust what you tell them?" Pickens answered "yes" to each one, then added: "but I can make a mistake." He was insulating himself in case McConn pointed out inconsistencies in his testimony. Again, I had to marvel at Pickens' agility on the stand. McConn asked about his trustworthiness again, then added: "and Jimmy Thompson could trust what you said in 2008?"

"Didn't talk to him," Pickens shot back. "Didn't talk to any of them in 2008."

This exposed the fundamental problem with the defense's case: they were relying on the word of a dead man against Pickens, who was convincing the jury that he was reliable and could be trusted, thanks in part to McConn's own tactics.

Then, McConn's questioning took an even more bizarre turn. He referenced a statement Pickens had made the day before about Baytech and J. Cleo. "Now, at the end of yesterday, you used the word 'crook' to describe my clients...and said that they had hidden the interest from you?"

"Yes."

Where could he possibly be going with the notion of rein-forcing that theme? I wondered if McConn was also operating on the "aim small, miss small" maxim. Perhaps he thought he would win by showing that Pickens had aimed too big in calling his clients crooks, that the jury wouldn't agree with that label, and they'd vote against us. It was a risky strategy. If it worked, we would lose on every claim and walk away with nothing but legal bills. But if it didn't, McConn would be helping our case.

He pulled out another document that I had worried the jury might find troubling. Baytech and J. Cleo had filed a deed with the property records clerk directly below us in the courthouse, assigning some of their rights in the Red Bull properties to the other participants besides Mesa. Conspicuously absent from the filing was any mention of Mesa's 15 percent. McConn wondered why, if Pickens really thought he owned something, he didn't ask for a similar assignment for his interest in those properties? Why, when the assignment was filed and didn't mention Mesa, hadn't anyone asked any questions?

A new wave of worry washed over me. Listening to your client under cross examination is like sitting on the beach during a tropical storm. Concerns rise up, crash ashore, then almost as quickly slide away to be replaced by new ones. There's no shelter. You just have to sit there and get battered. In this case, the defense had a big problem because they didn't have a signed document from Pickens giving away his interest. But I had reviewed all their documents—several again just the night before, in fact—and I knew they also had quite a few that implied that Pickens simply didn't care about what had happened to his Red Bull interest. The lack of questions or concerns about things like the deed assignment could be seen as evidence of his disinterest.

McConn was linking this document to another point he'd raised the day before: that for more than four years, Pickens hadn't mentioned the Red Bull in his daily investment committee meetings at BP Capital. Would the jury think he was simply trying to get back in now that the Red Bull was profitable?

I had one more card to play to counteract this notion, but it would have to wait for my chance to question Pickens again after the defense lawyers were done. In the meantime, Pickens was weathering the pounding from McConn as best he could.

"...based on your sixty-two years of experience, it's your understanding that, because you're not listed as an owner here, that you don't have an interest in the properties, correct?"

Pickens sidestepped and tried to score a few points. "I don't understand why you don't tell me what happened to my property." The judge leaned over and reminded him to answer the question that was asked.

"I'm sorry, your honor, this is hard to take," he said.

McConn tried again, pointing to the assignment document: "you see that you are not listed as an owner of these properties?"

"Yes," Pickens replied. "I'm not saying I agree with you, only that I see what you are reading."

McConn went in for the kill: "and J. Cleo Thompson...is telling that to the whole world by filing this record in Reeves County?"

"That I'm not an owner?" Pickens looked a little befuddled.

"Yes, sir."

"I understand that, yes. That's why I call him a crook."

"A crook who's telling all the world what he is doing?" McConn sounded incredulous.

"Yes."

"But you knew and trusted Mr. Thompson? You believed he was a good operator who would deal fairly with Mesa?"

"Yes."

I found myself wishing that Pickens had been a bit more combative in his answers, like he had been earlier. McConn next turned to his "financial incentive" argument. He used this strategy to bolster the idea that Pickens had decided to get out because oil prices had dropped. Prices *had* dropped at the same time that Baytech and J. Cleo claimed Pickens had "opted out." Even worse, I knew that McConn was going to drill down on something that many business executives would find tough to stomach.

"Mr. Pickens, during the last three months of 2008, the value of your hedge fund went from $1.2 billion to $40 million?" He showed financial reports that BP Capital had filed with the U.S. Securities and Exchange Commission that year. Pickens acknowledged that his hedge fund had indeed lost 97 percent of its value at the same time that the defendants were saying he allegedly exited the Red Bull deal. Pickens also agreed that he had 20 percent of his personal wealth in the fund. McConn showed statements on Pickens' net worth from the same time period. "Your own net worth dropped from $3 billion to $1 billion?"

Pickens, looking uncomfortable, admitted that it had.

"Mr. Pickens, you and your team were cutting costs across the board at this time?"

"Costs had already been cut," Pickens replied. "And having a billion dollars still allows you to do a lot of things."

There it was. With one quick quip, Pickens turned the momentum against the defense. As a trial lawyer, there's an art to letting the jury make their inferences. Too often, I see lawyers asking one question too many, just to make sure that the jury draws the inference that they want them to draw. But people want to make up their own minds. You can lead them to the evidence, but you can't force them to adopt your desired conclusions from it. Instead, the best lawyers empower jurors to think for themselves and let them figure things out based on the evidence presented.

McConn wasn't wrong. Pickens and his team *had* been canceling projects. He'd had plans, for example, for the billion-dollar Panhandle wind farm on his ranch, but declining natural gas prices meant that high-priced wind power was no longer competitive. None of these projects had anything to do with Mesa's oil deals, but Swanson still allowed the defense to enter them as evidence.

Next, McConn turned back to whether Mesa paid its share of the costs. This was a theme that I fretted over most nights, and many mornings, too. The unexplained credit, the "current adjustment" notation and a handwritten note on Mesa's copy of one bill that said "pay only Lyda charges per Alex" all tended to support the assertion that Mesa wanted out of the Red Bull. Pickens didn't know anything about the accounting, and he wouldn't be asked to provide the details, but I worried how the jury might see it if we didn't explain it. I didn't have a witness who could do that, because all of the details were in the defendants' long-lost accounting records.

McConn had saved what I knew he considered his best shot for last: in early 2012, Pickens' in-house lawyer, Sandy Campbell, emailed another company asking if it wanted to buy Mesa's interest in the Red Bull. This was three years after Baytech's offer to purchase Mesa's interest fell through, and three years since Mesa had heard from the defendants about the Red Bull. Campbell indicated there might be additional acreage available from other investors as well that hadn't been offered to Mesa. "If you see some acreage that you think might be attractive, we could begin a dialogue with J. Cleo to see why we weren't included and perhaps work our way back into the acreage. *If not, we can let sleeping dogs lie.*"

There were at least two ways to read the email. One was that as late as 2012—long after the supposed "opt out"—Pickens' own lawyer doesn't know why J. Cleo hadn't been sending notices to Mesa of the additional leases that were taken in the Red Bull. On the other hand, Campbell said Mesa was willing to "let sleeping dogs lie" instead of confronting J. Cleo about the missing notices, which the email acknowledges Mesa might have suspected were missing. The document could easily be read to support Baytech's argument that Mesa really didn't want to participate further and that the "opt out" conversation had happened. Rather than asking Pickens for an explanation, McConn simply displayed the email and highlighted the last sentence. I wished he had continued his habit of asking one too many questions, but this time, he didn't. He just left the image on the screen for the jury to study, and then he sat down.

The cross-examination wasn't over, though. Now Pickens had to face J. Cleo's lawyer, Geoff Bracken, who was a more experienced litigator than McConn. Bracken stood up and took a few steps toward the witness stand.

"Mr. Pickens, are you okay to continue? Are you doing okay?" he asked.

Pickens didn't miss a beat. "Yes, Geoff, I'm fine, but I'm a little worried about you."

The jurors chuckled. I grinned a bit myself. We could all see that Bracken was winded and sweating as he paced the floor. He seemed to be nervous, which I thought unusual for someone who'd tried as many cases as he had. He started off with the issue of Mesa's missing Red Bull payments.

"Mr. Pickens, you would expect that if there were a payment made by Mesa, there'd be a canceled check or a wire transfer advice?" Pickens agreed, saying that his CFO, Dick Grant, "doesn't pay hundreds of thousands in cash." The jury chuckled again. They clearly liked Pickens.

Bracken focused on many of the points that McConn had covered about the accounting, including whether checks had been sent back and forth, and so on. Then, he returned to the issue of how Pickens' net worth had declined in 2008. He noted that Pickens had agreed to pay for the Red Bull acreage before the drop in his net worth, implying that Pickens hadn't paid because he didn't have the money.

"And if you didn't pay for it, you didn't earn an interest in it?" Bracken asked, turning away from Pickens to look toward the jury. He tended to make this move when he thought he was scoring a point.

I saw a flash of anger cross Pickens' face. "Look at me when you ask me," he demanded.

I realized instantly that he couldn't hear Bracken when the lawyer turned toward the jury. Bracken turned back, asked the question again, and Pickens conceded that he had to pay for things to fully earn his interest in the Red Bull. Of all the issues Bracken raised, this was the most problematic. I didn't agree that the law required Mesa to pay for things when the defense had refused to bill it for all of the costs. In my mind, this argument put too much power in the hands of the defendants to undo the written contracts that they'd signed.

"Mr. Pickens, one last question," Bracken continued, picking up where McConn left off with the idea that J. Cleo had given Pickens his money back. Referring to a check that J. Cleo had mailed Mesa in 2009 to clear a credit balance, he asked, "Have you ever known a crook to try and give you your money back?" Pickens didn't miss a beat.

"I haven't had a lot of dealings with crooks," Pickens said. "Not as many as you have probably." I almost laughed out loud. Another score for Pickens.

We hadn't just survived Pickens' time on the stand, we'd scored some important points and deflected their cross examination. My eighty-eight-year-old star had again pulled off his part in the dance.

Chapter 20

"DON'T RUSH
THE MONKEY"

To win a lawsuit, you must prove that the defendants did something wrong and show how much money would compensate you for what they did to you. That doesn't mean, though, that you can go into court and name whatever damages you want. Judges will throw out any claims they deem "unscientific" or too speculative to present to the jury. The defense had already moved to limit our experts' testimony on damages, before the trial began and nearly every day since, and I knew our numbers would come under attack again and again until we were through the trial.

But I had an ace in the hole that you don't usually get in a lawsuit like this.

Delaware Basin Resources had used its own reserves report to get loans, and we had used that same reserves report to calculate Mesa's share of the Red Bull. This move was only logical, because DBR now held Mesa's 15 percent share. It would be hard for the defense to disclaim the reserves report as unscientific when it had used it to borrow money. It seemed to me that

DBR would have a hard time arguing it had one number for the banks but another, much lower, number for the jury.

But just as I felt our momentum was building, Judge Swanson once again wielded his pen and put our damages in doubt yet again. He decided that we could claim damages only for properties and wells acquired in the Red Bull from December 2010 through January 2012—just fourteen months of a ten-year string of acquisitions. He accepted the defendants' argument that the original Red Bull deal ended by its own terms in January 2012 and that we could not claim damages for the additional Red Bull acquisitions beyond that time, even though the defendants had amended the deal to continue into 2018. The judge also ruled that we could not seek damages for properties taken before December 2010 because that was more than four years before we had filed suit. In doing so, he rejected my arguments based on the Texas Supreme Court case I had discovered in the stacks of the SMU law library.

Once again, we needed to recalculate and regroup, and we were already weeks into the trial. Damage claims have to be based on evidence, but the ground rules matter enormously. The judge had just moved the goal posts on us—again.

Pickens had already spent almost $1 million on experts who had precisely calculated the engineering and financial implications of our claims. Garza and Sowards had carefully separated the reserves attributable to Pickens' portion of the Red Bull from other data. They'd tested and retested their assumptions, until they were comfortable testifying under oath that the basis for their work complied with the scientific principles applicable to their fields. Now, with the stroke of a pen, all those calculations were worthless. The computations would all have to be done again. This was highly unusual. In more than twenty-five years of practice, I'd never seen a trial ruling like this one.

Swanson hadn't questioned the soundness of their work; he'd essentially stopped time. He'd carved out a specific number of years and properties and instructed us to ignore everything that happened after that. It was a little like trying to sell a home and being told you couldn't base the price on the kitchen remodel you just put in or the pool you installed ten years ago.

We'd spent months getting ready for a different trial than the one we now faced, and we'd have to essentially retool overnight. Most of our original claims were now gone—we were down to a couple of counts for breach of contract—and our potential damages had been slashed by two-thirds to a maximum of what we thought would be about $300 million. And, now we were going to have to recalculate again to show how that $300 million fit within the judge's "guidances." The defendants had scored a big win.

As soon as we took a break, I explained to Pickens what had just happened. He wanted to know the bottom line, of course, and I told him we'd been whacked down from asking for about $1 billion to some $300 million or so based on the first set of rulings. Now, the $300 million we sought was in doubt unless we could show how it precisely fit into the rulings.

Our experts, Ricardo and Rodney, would have to redo all their calculations. Watching the proceedings from the back of the courtroom, Ricardo didn't seem too impressed with Swanson's handling of the issue, but he knew what he had to do. Rodney had come to Pecos to testify in the pretrial hearing challenging his work but hadn't returned yet. We had to call him and explain how he had to rework most of his team's numbers. Neither of them was happy. They were in for a lightning round of number crunching.

Pickens, meanwhile, was furious. As he saw it, the judge was cutting him out of the deal a second and third time. Pickens thought the judge was favoring the defense at every turn, and that Swanson didn't understand the case. Then Pickens went off on a rant about the geology before noting that Swanson had been nominated by Greg Abbott, Texas' Republican governor. You had to watch out for GOP judges when you were seeking damages, he said, failing to observe the irony of his statement.

I'd told him about the potential impact of conservative judges on our case many times before trial, but I was surprised to hear him echo those sentiments, Republican stalwart that he was. Yes, it was true that conservative appellate judges generally hate big verdicts, but we weren't even through the trial yet. We were still a long way from a big verdict. I tried to calm him down. I needed to focus on our next move, and I couldn't do that until I got my client under control. I told Pickens that when the trial was over, he'd have the right to appeal the things that we thought were wrongly decided. I also explained that it might take five years or more to sort it out. I couldn't help but think that at his age, the saying "justice delayed is justice denied" takes on greater significance. I put that thought out of my head.

Pickens actually settled down more quickly than I expected. Crucially, he remained steadfast in his belief in me. "Chrysta," he said finally, "they cut me out of the deal. The jury's going to see that if we just get them the case. You're tough. Go get 'em."

Now that the judge had ruled against us on so many issues, tossing out dozens of claims and whittling our damages to a sliver of what we'd asked for, Rick Montgomery, the Baytech lawyer, proposed settling out of court. We'd held a day-long mediation two months before the trial but got nowhere. Pickens wanted two hundred times what the defense was willing to offer. I didn't think he'd changed his mind even now. If anything, the judge's rulings seemed to have made him more determined. But I never turn down a chance to talk about a settlement. Trials are inherently risky and nearly every lawsuit is settled out of court at some point.

I tried to anticipate the settlement discussion driving back to the hotel. I figured Rick would raise his offer a bit from the mediation we had held but I knew Pickens was unlikely to take it unless the defense was adding a couple of zeroes to the end of their prior offer. Pickens wasn't one to leave money on the table if he thought there would be more at some point.

Despite being on opposing sides of the case, I felt that Rick and I got along pretty well. I thought his legal position was nonsense, but he was likable enough. He came over to the Swiss Chalet, and he, Mike Lynn and I met in the lobby amid the decorative beer steins, painted plates and other Alpine tchotchkes. Mike and I sat on a couch facing Rick, who took the chair across from us. This was a discussion among lawyers, and none of our clients—not even Pickens—joined us.

"Guys, the judge is ruling against you," Rick said. "It looks like it would be a very good time to try to get this resolved. I might be able to double our offer from the mediation."

I ran through the numbers in my head.[1] Their proposal was still a hundred times less than what Pickens wanted. I knew he wouldn't even want to respond. He realized what the property was worth—whether the judge let us talk about it.

I told Rick we'd discuss the offer with Pickens, but I also warned him that the fundamentals of our case had not really changed from our perspective. While we had lost a significant portion of our claims and damages, I still believed the jury was going to go our way and that we would win many times what he was offering. Despite everything that had happened, I knew deep in my soul that we would prevail, even if no one else on my team besides Pickens believed me.

Pickens shot the offer down immediately, just as I expected. He had a saying that he repeated every time we discussed settlement: "Don't rush the monkey. If you wait awhile, you'll see a better show." The expression referred to old-time street musicians, called organ grinders, who cranked barrel organs while their trained primates performed tricks to draw an audience. Pickens' expression—one of his favorite Booneisms—meant that if you let the monkey take its time, you'll see all its tricks for the same money. It was his folksy way of saying our case was far from over and we should wait for the culmination.

I didn't know it at the time, but Rick's meeting was just a formality. While he was sitting with us at the Swiss Chalet, the defense lawyers were discussing how they believed Judge Swanson, given all his rulings against us, was about to pour us out of court entirely. They thought that the most they could lose was $5 million, according to their emails that we obtained after the case was over. Apparently, everyone but Pickens and me believed the zombie theory. What they didn't understand, but we knew, was that the monkey was still warming up.

Chapter 21

"YOUR'RE GOING TO GET YOURS!"

With settlement nowhere in sight, we headed back to court. We still had several witnesses to call before we rested our case. One was Alex Szewczyk, Pickens' point person for dealing with the Red Bull issues. Alex reviewed and approved all the bills Mesa received for the Red Bull. It was no small task. The bills often ran twenty or thirty pages, depending on how many project expenditures had been made.

Even worse, the tallies were full of errors. J. Cleo had no regular accounting department. Cliff Milford was supposed to keep it all straight. The company didn't have a land department that tracked which properties were leased for a project. That, too, fell to Milford. And it wasn't just the Red Bull. Mesa had other projects with J. Cleo at the same time, and sometimes charges were assigned to the wrong projects. That was a big problem because each one had different investors. Sometimes Mesa got charged for a payment it had already made instead of earning a credit, doubling the size of the error. It could take months to unravel it all.

That's why a Mesa accountant had scribbled a note on one of the bills to "pay only Lyda charges per Alex." The defendants said it proved Mesa knew its interest was limited only to the Lyda well and that it proved Mesa had wanted to get out of everything else.

I knew that as a witness Alex wouldn't recall a lot of the details. When we first got the case, Debbie and I met with him for several days, going over the documents. Even looking straight at them, he didn't remember much about them. His lack of recollection would be an issue for us. It meant we'd have to prove our case through adverse witnesses like Strickling and Hedrick.

Pickens expected his people to be ready with the answers for any question he asked, sometimes out of the blue. Alex wasn't that type of guy and he probably grew to resent it. Some Pickens deputies over the years definitely did. Before I filed the Red Bull lawsuit, Alex had left to start his own energy-focused investment company with a couple of former Pickens colleagues. But he'd agreed to come to Pecos ready to testify. I decided to let Andres Correa present him. We still had a long time to go in this trial, and the jury would appreciate seeing another lawyer take the helm for a while.

The questioning went smoothly. Alex covered the basics, holding firm on the issue that mattered: only Pickens himself could authorize Mesa getting out of the Red Bull, and only Pickens could sign the paperwork. That hadn't happened. Alex insisted he never agreed to opt out or to sell the Mesa interest on Pickens' behalf.

As Andres wrapped up, I had one more question I wanted him to address. "Have you faced any obstacles to come here and testify to this jury?" Andres asked Alex. It seemed like a routine formality, but it wasn't.

A few days earlier, during a break in the court proceedings, Alex had been sitting on the bench in the hallway outside the courtroom door when a man in a suit approached him, clearly angry. The man's face was red, and veins were bulging at his temples. "You're going to get yours!" he said, pointing at Alex. Alex was stunned. He thought the man might take a swing at him, but he had no idea who he was. He'd seen the man in the back of the gallery earlier. "Do I know you?" Alex asked. "You're going to find out who I am!" the man shot back. "You're going to get yours!"

Alex, clearly shaken, returned to the courtroom and told us what had happened. By then, the man had taken a seat at the back of the room. Alex pointed him out to us. It's possible my jaw fell open. I couldn't believe it, but I also wasn't going to let such an outburst go unnoticed.

Alex recounted the story for the jury, then he added, "he's actually sitting right out there," pointing toward the back of the gallery.

"Is that the gentleman that's sitting back here in the court-house with the yellow tie?" Andres asked.

"Yes, that's him," Alex replied. He identified the man as Frank Peterman, J. Cleo's chief operating officer.

"Did you see Mr. Peterman again after that?" Andres asked. Alex said Peterman had walked past him at the Midland airport, and Alex had said to him, "I didn't appreciate you threatening me." Peterman, according to Alex, looked at him and said again, "you're going to get yours."

It was an astounding encounter, and we were not going to ignore it. As shocking as the Peterman exchange had been, I was even more surprised when the judge didn't halt the trial to investigate. A defense witness had threatened a witness for the plaintiff, but apparently, west of the Pecos, this was okay.

Swanson seemed unfazed by the testimony. At least the jury heard about the incident, I thought.

We broke for lunch and headed over to Bill Weinacht's office. Pickens was already there. Sometimes he went to lunch early, especially if we were involved in bench discussions with the judge. He'd gotten away with the water bottle trick, but I didn't want him pressing his luck, so I had Cathy make sure his food was ready early for him. That day, we had Subway sandwiches, as we did many days, given the lack of choices around town for restaurants equipped to deliver lunch for twenty. Pickens had been in the courtroom long enough to hear Alex's testimony about Peterman. Pickens said the executive was known to be a hothead.

"Looks like they think we're getting the better of them, Chrysta!" Pickens exclaimed. "I can't believe that no one told Peterman to at least wait to threaten violence until after Alex was done testifying!"

I smiled at that. I was pretty sure I would never have to tell a witness or client not to physically threaten the other side, but if I ever needed to do it, I'd be sure to get the sequence right.

Chapter 22

"BLINDERS ON"

I hoped Pickens was right and we really were getting under the skin of the defense. Even so, we still had to get our experts' damages testimony in front of the jury. The judge had ruled a few days earlier that before we could do so, we had to get their new calculations cleared by him first. The experts had worked around the clock, and at the eleventh hour, produced new figures that we hoped had met his latest guidances.

Ricardo Garza, our petroleum engineer, would have to explain those calculations that day. I'd known Ricardo for about fifteen years and had used him as an expert in several cases. He was six feet four inches tall and held dual Mexican and American citizenship. (He had a twin brother to boot.) You don't find a lot of towering Hispanic petroleum engineers who can testify in jury trials. He'd graduated from Texas A&M, a land-grant school halfway between Waco and Houston where Pickens had spent his freshman year. A&M was more than a hundred years old and until the 1960s, it had been all-military and all male. Ricardo joined the officer training program, known as the Corps of Cadets. After getting his engineering degree, he signed up for officer school in the Navy and later served four years on a nuclear submarine. I asked him once how he'd tolerated living on a sub, given his height. Claustrophobia, he'd said, was better than bullet holes. His only other choice during the Vietnam era was to join the Army as an infantryman.

Ricardo was the expert who had quantified the number of barrels of oil that lie under the Red Bull waiting to be produced by current and future wells. His testimony on how many of those barrels of oil were attributable to Mesa's 15 percent was the key to our damages claim. If we couldn't prove that number, we couldn't prove our damages, and our case would fail.

Ricardo had stayed in town throughout the trial. He'd come to Pecos when the rest of our team moved into the Swiss Chalet. Rather than flying, he drove his Ford F-350 from Houston, hauling all manner of gadgets and exhibits he would bring out to entertain the jury when—we hoped—he finally would be permitted to testify. He repurposed everyday items to explain complicated concepts about petroleum engineering and shopped at Home Depot and sporting goods stores for his homemade science projects. He was the courtroom version of Bill Nye the Science Guy.

For this trial, Ricardo had constructed a series of demonstrations about how operators drill horizontal wells, frack the shales, and extract oil. He had bought and painted twenty clay pigeons that normally would have been used as targets for skeet shooting, like the hundreds Pickens kept at the Mesa Vista Ranch for target practice when quail weren't in season. Ricardo had painted his set with different primary colors to show the benches of oil under the Red Bull. Those layers had different names like the Wolfcamp A, the Wolfcamp A2, the Wolfcamp B, and so on. And, the colors he used matched the ones on Exhibit 53, the map of the Red Bull acreage.

Ricardo was special because he wasn't just an expert witness, he was also a jury consultant. Sitting in the back of the courtroom, he evaluated how the jurors responded to everything they heard. He had terrific feedback on how witnesses presented themselves and what points weren't making sense.

One of Ricardo's most valuable roles was talking to Pickens about geology every day. He and Pickens would discuss the different oil benches under the Red Bull. They would go through which ones were currently productive, how many more were available, and how much oil Pickens should have for his share. They'd cover the same topics over and over again. Pickens never grew tired of the scientific discussions, and he and Ricardo grew close during the trial. When Pickens got frustrated with the rest of us because he didn't think we were listening to his geological monologues, Ricardo was always standing by, ready to run through it one more time.

Because of Swanson's guidances, Ricardo had worked and reworked his calculations every night. He'd use his retractable pencil to write in his clear handwriting the digits that made up the numbers of barrels of oil in each section of Exhibit 53. He'd created a chart, colored like Exhibit 53, of how many barrels were attributable to each area.

I'd met with him the night before to go over his computations one last time before he testified. We ran through his science demonstrations. We believed we had exhausted all of the defense objections to his calculations and that he would finally be able to testify before the jury.

Not so fast. That morning, when I'd announced that we'd be calling him to the stand, Peter Scaff, one of the defense lawyers, objected again. He proclaimed that Garza's testimony was based on a reserves report that contained data that wasn't available in 2012. He asked Swanson to call Garza back to the stand so they could show that Ricardo's new calculations violated the judge's latest guidance. Scaff wanted to keep our damages claims out of the case entirely, which he would be able to do if they did not meet the judge's requirements. I knew it was their best chance at avoiding a big loss at trial. This was their goal line stand.

The defendants had challenged our experts' work so many times, and Swanson had given so many guidances, that it was hard to keep it all straight. First, we had to limit our claims to only the original Red Bull territories shown on the Exhibit 53 map, even though the defendants had expanded the Red Bull to three times that acreage after Mesa was cut out of the deal. Then, we were further limited to damages relating to only those properties that were acquired between December 2010 and January 2012. Finally, in their latest attempts to cut back our damages claims, the defense lawyers had convinced Swanson that Mesa's damages could be based only on what was known about the value of the Red Bull by January 2012, the end of the original Red Bull deal.

Scaff had convinced the judge of this latest requirement using his "blinders on" argument—meaning that our experts would need to blind themselves to any evidence not available in 2012. The experts could cite nothing after that time. Each time Scaff brought it up, he would put both palms to the temples of his bald head with his fingers splayed out like antlers, to imitate blinders like a horse might wear. Except, he looked more like a reindeer. The stunt was starting to get on my nerves.

Now, this morning, Scaff's final attack was to argue that horizontal drilling wasn't known in 2012 and that our damages model was based on much more recent information from 2016. According to Scaff, we shouldn't be allowed to base our damages on the incredible amount of drilling that had taken place in the Permian after 2012 that had proved exactly how valuable the Red Bull was.

What doesn't kill you makes you stronger, as the saying goes. In this case, it made Ricardo and me determined to beat the opposition.

After the judge had accepted Scaff's "blinders on" argument, Ricardo and I had spent half the night combing through documents and data to prove that the defendants did in fact know in 2012 that the Red Bull had a lot more oil than they were letting on. This case had generated more than a million pages of documents in pretrial discovery, and I and my team had read most of them over the past two years. None provided what we needed to show right now. Trying one last shot before he gave up, Garza scoured a thumb drive that another expert, Russell K. Hall, had produced at his deposition months earlier.

Hall, who lives in Midland, was the reserves engineer that Delaware Basin Resources had hired to quantify the value of its own Red Bull reserves. Hall has written extensively about reserves analysis in "resource plays," which are fundamentally different from "conventional" oil and gas reservoirs. Conventional reservoirs are like upside-down mixing bowls deep within the earth. The oil pools under the bowls. When a drill bit punctures one of them, the accumulated pressure of the reservoir forces the oil to the surface. If the drill bit misses the bowl, though, or if there's a dividing line known as a fault, no oil comes out.

Resource plays are more like a layer cake. You know there's frosting between each of the layers and all you need to do is find it. Once you know how deep the frosting is, you can poke a straw into it and pull it out. There's a much greater chance you'll hit oil in the frosting layers or benches of a resource play. More important, your odds go up with the more wells you drill.

Horizontal drilling is the straw that gets you the frosting. Once the drill bit digs deep enough to find the oil bench, the driller turns the well bore horizontally to travel along the layer of oil. Then, the pipe is perforated with holes to access the oil. But unless we could prove that the horizontal drilling techniques were available in the Permian by 2012, we wouldn't be able to claim that the reserves under the Red Bull were accessible by that date. Our damages model would fall apart.

Russell K. Hall had literally written the book on using statistics to figure out the amount of oil in a resource play. I read it before I took his deposition. Hall and I hit it off when I questioned him. I always like talking to fellow engineers, and statistics are something I understand fairly well and enjoy. But there was a mix up with the documents the defense team was supposed to share in advance of his deposition. As a concession, they had Hall give me a thumb drive of all of his work for them. I was miffed at the time because I didn't get to review the documents prior to the deposition and ask questions about them.

Ricardo had calculated that Pickens would have been entitled to 28 million barrels of oil for his 15 percent share of the Red Bull, after applying all of the limitations the judge had imposed. He had used the reserves report on the Red Bull that Hall had prepared for Delaware Basin Resources in 2016 as the basis for that calculation. But the defense had succeeded in convincing the judge that I couldn't rely on something created as late as 2016. The only thing that would count was a reserves report created in 2012 or before. We didn't have one—or so we thought.

The night before his testimony, Ricardo sorted through the material on Hall's thumb drive out of sheer desperation. His last-ditch search turned up something remarkable. The defense, of course, had no idea we were about to use their own thumb drive against them.

Scaff asked Ricardo if he had based his count of the 28 million barrels attributable to Mesa's 15 percent on a reserves report that was dated in 2016, four years later than the judge's guidance. Garza said he had.

"Your honor, J. Cleo moves to strike Ricardo Garza's expert opinions and exclude them from this trial," Scaff said. "They are not based on the court's guidance on how Mesa must calculate its damages." McConn, the DBR lawyer, joined the objection. It was a full court press, so to speak.

Now I rose. "Permission to question the witness, your honor?" The judge let me proceed.

"Mr. Garza, do you have evidence that the defendants themselves knew that all of the barrels of oil in the 2016 reserves report were also known to be present under the Red Bull in January of 2012?"

"I do," Ricardo replied. Scaff looked perplexed at the response while the defense table started to scramble.

"Please describe it."

"After your honor instructed that my reserves calculations must be based on information that was known in 2012," Ricardo began, addressing the judge directly, "I set about to investigate the state of knowledge at that time. I looked generally at information that was known about this area of the Permian in 2012, including information that was known by other operators. I found that many operators had been drilling horizontal wells as early as 2009 and 2010 so the technique was known that allowed this to be classified as a resource play.

"Once it was classified as a resource play, which Russell K. Hall's work on the Red Bull clearly did as early as 2010, it is a simple matter of plotting out the locations where you will be drilling the wells. From that, you can easily get to the number of barrels of oil that you are likely to recover."

Scaff rose to object. "Your honor, that is the point exactly. No one had done that in 2012. In 2012, Hall's reports say that he only calculated a small number of barrels of oil that could be claimed as reserves for the Red Bull."

"Ms. Castañeda, your response?" the judge asked.

"If your honor will permit me to continue my questioning, I'm sure we can clear up the matter in a manner that will be satisfactory to Mr. Scaff." I knew no amount of clarification would be satisfactory to him, but I allowed myself the satisfaction of saying it anyway.

"Mr. Garza, would you please focus solely on what the defendants actually knew in 2012? Did you find any evidence on that point?"

Ricardo smiled. He was a feisty witness when confronted, letting his indignation rise to the fore when he felt the defense was falsely attacking his work. When he was pleased, though, his natural love of his job shone through. This was undoubtedly one of those times.

"When the Court instructed that we had to base our information on what the defendants actually knew in 2012, I went back to the Russell K. Hall files I had been given a copy of at his deposition," he said. "On his thumb drive, I found a map with proposed well locations for the Red Bull in 2012."

"And how many proposed well locations were there?"

"Over five hundred."

Five hundred wells, all that were proposed to be horizontally drilled in 2012. As many as were scheduled in the 2016 reserves report.

I displayed on the overhead screen the 2012 map from the thumb drive that Ricardo had found and handed a copy to the judge and opposing counsel. They immediately objected that we hadn't made this a trial exhibit, that we hadn't put it on our list of materials that we would use. I knew that those objections would fail. The judge would have to let us use it. After all, we were following his guidance—issued after the start of trial—and we were using the defendants' own documents. Ricardo showed the vast oil deposits beneath the Red Bull had been known for a long time. The judge was satisfied, even if Scaff and his colleagues weren't. Swanson finally agreed to let Ricardo testify in front of the jury, and as I returned to my seat, I resisted the urge to turn to Scaff and make his antler sign.

The rest of that afternoon was enjoyable. Testifying before the jury, Ricardo constructed makeshift tables in front of the jury box from cardboard cartons and plywood and covered them with a cheap tablecloth. Pickens leaned forward in his seat to watch intently. Ricardo placed all of his science projects on the tables to explain how oil is contained in shale rock, how you frack it, and how wells are drilled and produced. He used marbles and sand in jars to substitute for the pores in shale and poured a blue liquid over them to simulate how oil became wedged in the rock.

Ricardo connected with the jurors by referencing the highways and county roads they all knew to explain exactly where the Red Bull was. He told them the prospect was about eighty square miles (it was much larger, but the judge had limited the territory we could claim). This was still a lot of land, even in terrain of vast distances and vacant landscapes.

Ricardo talked about how J. Cleo had worked over the Colt well in 2009. He explained what the defendants were looking to find by doing that, and what we believed they were trying to hide from Mesa when they got results that showed significant quantities of oil.

"The Lyda well was tested in 2007 in that first workover. Then, the Colt, which at this point in time was in May of 2009, it had its first workover when the thousand feet of the Wolfcamp had been perforated and tested. Those are the leads to say that we think we really have something here and this is what our proposal is. Let's go get all this open acreage," Ricardo testified, as he gestured at a map of the open territory between the Lyda and the Colt. He explained that you need a strong showing of oil in at least two wells to establish that the territory in between is a good place to drill. Once the Colt results came in, the Red Bull partners knew they were on to something really big.

I again thanked the universe for the day that Cathy turned up the Colt well recompletion documents after reviewing thousands of others in discovery. If she hadn't focused on the workover, then Ricardo and I wouldn't have either, and a key piece of evidence in the lawsuit might have been missed. Thankfully it wasn't, and we had proof that they were trying to keep an important discovery from us—the information about the Colt well workover—just as Baytech was negotiating to buy Mesa's Red Bull interests. It wasn't an attractive picture for the defense.

When it came time for his opinion of how many barrels of oil were under the Red Bull, and how many were therefore Pickens' share, Ricardo set up his stack of clay pigeons, or skeet, on the corner of my table. His display was right in front of Pickens and the jury. We listened to him describe how each colored set of those pigeons represented a layer of oil shale, or "bench." The ten benches of oil under the Red Bull, represented by twenty painted skeets, rose about ten inches high. He then put a four-skeet stack next to it and said that was the thickness of the Eagle Ford Shale in South Texas. Another three-pigeon stack represented the Bakken Shale in North Dakota. Using these stacks of skeet, he brought home an essential truth: the jurors were living in a county covering the largest oil play in the history of the world, one that was many times thicker than the next biggest fields in the United States. And, he told the jury that ownership of 28 million barrels of the oil represented by those skeet was what Mesa had signed up for and what had been taken from it when the defendants breached their Red Bull contracts.

I could see a little swell of pride in the jurors as Ricardo described the importance of Reeves County to the world. Their esteem was no doubt amplified by the fact that someone who looked like many of them was lifting up the significance of their community. Reeves County didn't get a lot of appreciation from the outside world, but Ricardo was showing these jurors that their home mattered. As far as energy was concerned, Reeves County was the center of the universe. And it was certainly the center of theirs.

Ricardo did something even more powerful. By telling the jurors how essential their home was to the world's energy supply, he underscored the critical nature of their work on the jury. They, as small-town citizens, would sit in judgment over oil giants with their billions of dollars—the companies who were taking over their homeland like an invading swarm. It was up to Pecos to stand up for what was right.

Chapter 23

"YOUR CLIENT IS NOT WELL"

O ur case was winding down, and most of the remaining testimony consisted of clips from videotaped depositions of witnesses who weren't in court. After nearly three weeks of live testimony, ten or fifteen minutes of video—without objections —would seem like a breath of fresh air to the jurors.

The first one we played was Cliff Milford, the J. Cleo CFO. Oddly, the defendants weren't planning to call him as a witness, but Mike and I had each taken his deposition. A few video clips from my deposition of him backed up everything we'd been claiming—Mesa had opted to participate in every Red Bull acquisition it was notified of; Mesa hadn't gotten any money back from Baytech when it took over Mesa's share; Mesa had never signed anything saying it was out of the deal. There was no documentation transferring Mesa's interest to Baytech, not even paperwork between J. Cleo and Baytech. He also admitted he'd forgotten to bill Mesa for some of the acquisitions, which helped us explain why Mesa hadn't fully paid for the properties. He agreed that if he hadn't billed Mesa, the company wouldn't have known it was supposed to pay. We had clipped those bits of his deposition testimony into a fairly short video, along with Mike's question to him about whether he would show up and testify at trial. Milford enthusiastically agreed that he planned to attend, yet the defense didn't bring him. I knew Mike would point out in our closing arguments that his absence was tantamount to an admission by the defendants that his testimony hurt their side.

We were close to resting our case, but there was one more expert witness we had to get on the stand. Once again, the defense was trying to block him, just as they had tried to shut out Ricardo. Rodney Sowards, our accountant, had calculated the exact dollar amounts that Pickens had lost when the defendants took the Red Bull interests. Ricardo had quantified the barrels of oil we claimed, but Rodney had to put dollar figures on those barrels. The defense lawyers made one last stand to keep him from testifying. Scaff again led the charge.

The judge asked Rodney to take the stand so that Scaff could question him about his revised calculations without the jury present. The issues never changed: the defendants were intent on establishing that Rodney had used information that wasn't known in 2012, defying the rule the judge had established a few days earlier. Rodney had to endure another two or three grueling hours of grilling over the fine details that underpinned his calculations. I knew that he could cite every one of those details from memory. That's why I hired him. Like me, he wouldn't leave the details to others. And, the more than twenty binders of calculations that Pickens had paid him hundreds of thousands of dollars to perform were a real demonstrative, sitting around him on the witness stand, showing both the judge and eventually the jury how much thought had gone into those details.

Afterwards, the judge made additional rulings about Rodney's calculations. He wanted Rodney to sort his numbers into two sets, or "buckets," of damages. These buckets related to the two agreements Mesa had signed when it invested in the Red Bull. One would be for damages associated with breach of the Participation Agreement. This was the main agreement requiring the defendants to notify Mesa of the properties they had taken in the Red Bull so that Mesa could claim its 15 percent ownership in exchange for paying 15 percent of the costs. The first bucket would value the damages for defendants having failed to give those Participation Agreement notices. The other set of numbers was for breach of the Joint Operating Agreement. This contract required the defendants to notify Mesa when it was drilling the wells, for the same purpose of allowing Mesa to claim its 15 percent.

We had that night to sort all of the numbers into those two buckets. Once again, Rodney pulled an all-nighter, recalculating to meet the judge's newest guidances. The next morning at breakfast, concerned that the defense would challenge us again for not sorting the "buckets" the right way, we went through everything he'd done. I asked him if he could make one tweak to it, to re-sort some of the properties from one bucket to the other. Rodney flatly told me no, he was done. There simply wasn't time to run the numbers again.

In court, the defense predictably insisted on cross examining Rodney before he could explain his math to the jury. I knew they were determined to keep the jury from hearing about the hundreds of millions of dollars we claimed for our damages.

I'd had enough, and Rodney clearly had too. I pressed the judge to let Rodney testify about our $300 million claim. I told him that what had previously been in the Joint Operating Agreement bucket was now going to be in the Participation

Agreement bucket. I told him that while his latest rulings told us to sort the properties into the two buckets differently, we were still going to claim all of the money we had been claiming since the attacks on our damages started. I knew what I wanted to do was legally correct, but I also could tell the judge disagreed with me. He just hadn't said so explicitly.

At this point, I needed clear instruction from the judge on the record telling me that I was prohibited from doing what I wanted to do. I needed to hear him say that I could not introduce evidence supporting the whole $300 million in damages. We could then take that ruling to the court of appeals and complain about it, but only if the ruling was clear. My only other option was to plow ahead in front of the jury and present the whole $300 million. I worried that if I did so, the judge would stop me after it was too late, and there would be a high likelihood of a mistrial. It would likely mean we would have to start the whole trial all over again, months or years later. We couldn't afford that. Pickens might not live to see the retrial, and we couldn't put on the case without him.

I needed the judge to speak his mind clearly. Now.

"Your honor, let me be as clear as I can," I said. "Sowards is going to move some properties from the Joint Operating Agreement bucket and they will now be in the Participation Agreement bucket. Same calculations, different buckets. Defendants have cross examined him on these numbers and we are ready to go."

"Ms. Castañeda, I don't want us to miss each other here," the judge replied. I knew he was warning me against doing what I intended to do, but he hadn't yet clearly said that I couldn't. I had to press him again.

"I don't want us too, either," I responded. We continued back and forth, the judge and I, circling around the issue as I pressed for a specific statement of his rulings.

The team could feel the tension between us, and they were getting nervous. It's always dangerous to challenge a judge. Mike Lynn tried to intervene, asking for a moment because "our client has called us right now." Pickens had left the courtroom early for lunch, but I knew he hadn't called us, Mike just wanted to extract me from the confrontation.

I ignored him, and the judge did too.

"Let me say two sentences before the break," Swanson said. "If the Joint Operating Agreement numbers are being shifted into the Participation Agreement bucket, that's a new damage calculation. And that's the point."

We were finally getting closer to a direct statement. I reiterated that I needed a clear ruling. "Okay, that's the clearest instructions I needed to understand. So, the court is saying that whatever we presented yesterday cannot be shifted to the other bucket. That's what the court's ruling is?"

Sternly, he replied, "And that was the court's ruling yesterday evening." I internally disagreed that he had been clear the previous evening, but at least it was clear now.

The judge released us for the break Mike had requested. I walked to the back of the courtroom and my team surrounded me. Debbie grabbed both of my upper arms with her hands, looked me in the eye, and said, "You've got to calm down or I'm going to have to get a straight-jacket." David Coale looked concerned, too.

I was calm, I reassured them. But I wanted to make crystal clear what the judge was telling us, without inference or equivocation. The judge had just made indisputable that we once again had to cut our damages model—this time from more than $300 million to about $129 million. There would be no further calculations. He had simply lopped off damages from more than half of the properties. Because we couldn't shift properties from one bucket to the other, we had to give up on them entirely.

We might have been zombies, we might have been like the Black Knight in *Monty Python and the Holy Grail,* fighting defiantly while missing all four limbs, but we weren't done yet. We still had a claim for $129 million. And we were finally going to get to tell the jury about it.

Rodney finally took the stand later that day. For all the buildup, challenges, guidances, and recalculations, his testimony was remarkably short. He said that Mesa had suffered almost $129 million in damages, $117 million for breaches of the Participation Agreement and $12.5 for breaches of the Joint Operating Agreement. Thank God, I thought, this part of the trial was nearing a close.

We were almost finished with Rodney when Swanson interrupted us and called us to the bench. I bolted to attention. Andres had been questioning Rodney, and I'd zoned out after the final wrestling match with the judge.

"What now," I thought. In that moment, I feared that Mike's Zombie theory was true and that we were now officially dead. If our damages model was wrong this time, there was nothing more I could do.

When we got to the bench, Swanson leaned over and said to me, "Your client is not well. His face just flushed." I turned around and looked at Pickens. I hadn't noticed, but he did look a little red in the face. We took a break, and Pickens got a drink of water before returning to his seat at the front of the courtroom. He assured me he was fine. I assumed he was just tired. After all, we had been in Pecos for weeks, and we'd spent the whole day arguing over arcane—but crucial—accounting practices. The trial was taking a toll on us all.

Chapter 24

THE POWER OF A PENNY

With Rodney's testimony, we wrapped up our side of the case. Now, the course of the trial would shift, and our job would be to attack the evidence that the defense would bring forward. I'd been wrestling with how to handle the other side's witnesses. The only way to cross examine them effectively would be to dig into the facts underlying their testimony. The questioning required a deep understanding of the minutiae of accounting notations, land acquisition processes and documentation, and general all-out knowledge of the oil industry. We wouldn't get by on sound bites and high concepts. We had to dig in and prove we knew the details and the defense did not.

I decided I needed to question almost all of the defendants' witnesses myself. It might kill me, and we might lose, but I didn't really see any way around it. Mesa had paid me to become an expert on every aspect of its case and it was time to use that expertise. My team members didn't have the knowledge of the details that I'd gained through study and sweat over the past two years. It was up to me.

Surprisingly, the defense first called the executive of another oil company that had invested in the Red Bull. The company signed the same sort of documents that Pickens had signed. He'd also done a number of deals with Jimmy Thompson over the years. When it came to the Red Bull, he testified that Thompson had told him in one of their meetings, "I talked to Boone. Mesa's out." Once again, we had someone else recounting what a dead man had supposedly said and no documents to support it. Mike Lynn cross-examined him on that point, and he conceded that a signed document was required for Mesa to have exited the Red Bull deal.

Next, the defense called Paul Rudnicki, a young man who had risen quickly through the oil and gas ranks. After Cliff Milford left the company in 2012, J. Cleo hired Rudnicki as chief financial officer and told him to make sure the company's financial records were in order. He had no first-hand knowledge of the issues in our case, but he had studied J. Cleo's books. I doubted that when he was hired, he expected to wind up in court a few years later to explain the murky accounting records he'd inherited. Yet his job was to tell the jury that Mesa was wrong, and that Pickens had in fact gotten all his Red Bull money back because J. Cleo had credited Mesa's account.

The "current adjustment" credit that showed up on the bills that Mesa got from J. Cleo was a thorny problem from the beginning. I knew Rudnicki's testimony would come down to these key issues: if Mesa didn't want out of the deal, why did it take its money back in the form of a credit? Mesa not only didn't complain about the credit, it even asked J. Cleo to cut it a check for the balance that was left in its account at year's end after the credit was issued. And why did Mesa write on its own copy of one of the Red Bull bills, "pay only Lyda well charges per Alex?" These were major hurdles to our case, and as I got ready to cross examine Rudnicki at trial, I still had no irrefutable proof that the defense spin on these issues was wrong.

Pickens and others had testified that they never understood what the "current adjustment" credit was for. We had showed it might have been issued for erroneous charges. But I knew we needed to conclusively explain it away, rather than just say we didn't understand it. To win, we needed something —anything—that would directly disprove the idea that the credit took Pickens out of the deal and left him with only the Lyda well. The Lyda well was a crap well, and I thought the defendants were more than willing to let him keep 15 percent of it because it kept him on the hook for part of the costs. The true value of the Red Bull came from the other wells and the reserves, starting with the reworked Colt.

J. Cleo's defense lawyer, Geoff Bracken, questioned Rudnicki first. Bracken had him acknowledge errors in the first bill Mesa received because of J. Cleo's mix up of some accounting for other investments with the Red Bull accounts. He went through other incorrect entries for which J. Cleo had made errors and fixed mistakes. In each case, Bracken asked whether Mesa's notes showed that it understood what J. Cleo had done. Rudnicki said they did. I lodged some objections about him speculating, which the judge overruled. I was objecting occasionally, but mostly I was focused on what I was going to do when I stood up to ask questions. We desperately needed something substantial for my cross examination.

Bracken moved on to how the bills were structured. In the Red Bull account, J. Cleo had four subaccounts: one for the Lyda well, shown in red on Exhibit 53; one for two sections of land taken early in the deal, shown in red; one for the Colt well, in yellow; and one for the new acreage purchased by J. Cleo and Baytech, including all of the La Escalera sections shown in orange. Most of our damages were associated with the Colt well and the new acreage subaccounts.

I was following along as Bracken asked his questions, but I was having trouble focusing. I was nearing exhaustion from day after day in the courtroom, late nights of trial preparations, and managing both the presentation of our case and a large team of people. I was feeling the effects of too much mental strain and too little sleep.

Staring at the exhibits for the umpteenth time, I suddenly noticed a detail I hadn't seen before, thanks to Bracken's questions. Was the explanation of the credit buried in the arcane subaccount descriptions Bracken had just reviewed? Was it possible that the "current adjustment" credit had been recorded to the original two sections of land and the Lyda well—the least valuable accounts—rather than the two that pertained to the new acreage and the Colt well—the ones associated with all of the reserves that supported our damages?

Suddenly, my mind was racing. I began formulating new questions to unpack my idea, even as I kept listening to the rest of the testimony. Rudnicki claimed that, based on the records, Mesa hadn't made payments on the Colt well subaccount but did make some payments on additional acreage in the last subaccount. He said that J. Cleo put the $307,000 "current adjustment" credit on Mesa's account and Mesa didn't complain. Because he joined the company after the adjustment had been issued, he had no personal knowledge about what it was for. Mesa asked for a check to be cut to it for about $40,000 in late 2009 after the credit had been applied.

Rudnicki had created a spreadsheet of the payments Mesa had made for the Red Bull and a running tally of the costs. It resembled a checkbook ledger. I immediately noticed that the balances didn't add up to what we had constructed ourselves—and it hid a critical fact that Rudnicki seemed to be conveniently overlooking.

During a short break after Bracken finished, I scratched out a few notes to help organize my thoughts. As I began my cross, I pulled up on the screen in the courtroom Exhibit 53, the colored map I'd been using throughout the trial. It was the only way I knew to reinforce the complicated facts of what leases we believed were taken from Pickens, when they were taken, and what they were called. By now the jurors understood that the Lyda well and surrounding acreage was in red; the sections attributable to the subaccount called "Red Bull Prospect" were in red; the Colt well was yellow; and orange was for the valuable sections containing most of the reserves, the La Escalera Ranch. These sections were the key to decoding both the ledger subaccounts and the meaning of the "current adjustment."

I'd carried that Exhibit 53, blown up and mounted on foam board, around the courtroom for weeks. As I pulled it out again, Cathy later told me that someone on the defense side—she couldn't tell who—muttered under his breath, "not that fucking Exhibit 53 again."

Matching the bills to the areas on the map, I could show that Mesa had indeed been billed for purchases of the valuable La Escalera and Colt sections. Rudnicki conceded that Mesa had paid some of those costs. I asked Rudnicki to find the account in which he'd placed that $307,000 credit for Mesa's stake. At the same time, I displayed that page in front of the jury on the overhead screen. Leaving nothing to chance, I'd also blown it up and placed the enlarged copy right next to the map.

I pointed to the single page that contained the accounting entry. "Mr. Rudnicki, is this the only mention of the $307,000 credit?" He agreed.

"And its only description is 'Current Adjustment?' It doesn't say it reverses the Colt charges? It doesn't say that it reverses La Escalera charges?" Again, he agreed.

"And the account you used for the $307,000 credit is the one that says, "Red Bull Prospect?" He said it was, but he spoke a little more slowly, and I could see by the look on his face that he was beginning to see what was coming.

"Now, Mr. Rudnicki, please tell the jurors what colors of Exhibit 53 the Red Bull Prospect covers?"

"Red."

"Those red sections are not the Colt well section, are they?"

Reluctantly, he said they weren't. He also agreed that they weren't the valuable new La Escalera acreage shown in orange, either.

"In fact, you'd have to agree that this credit does not apply to the Colt well?" I wanted to reinforce we hadn't gotten out of the key discovery well, the Colt well.

He agreed.

"And the same is true for the orange La Escalera sections that Pickens elected to participate in? No credit took him out of those sections?" I asked, pointing to Exhibit 53. "But he said he wanted out," Rudnicki protested.

I ignored him. He'd walked right into this, and I wasn't about to let him out. "There is no credit giving Pickens his money back on those sections, is there?" I said. I was going a bit brain dead by then but was mentally replaying the scene in *My Cousin Vinny* in which Joe Pesci cross-examines the automotive expert hired by the prosecution. Pesci gets the expert to concede that everything he'd previously said on the stand was completely wrong. Pesci's line: "You can go ahead and say it. They know already." I really wanted to say exactly that, but I didn't.

Rudnicki conceded that the credit was not issued for the valuable La Escalera sections.

I turned to my last point: an error in his ledger of Mesa's bills and payments. Even after the credit, even after he applied all of it to the red section sub-account, J. Cleo had failed to give Mesa back more than $27,000 for the acreage and wells it had elected to participate in and began paying for. The operator, J. Cleo, was still holding Mesa's money.

"Can you point me to a credit in Mesa's bills?" I asked. He had been sifting through thick notebooks full of accounting information. "In all that paper, can you show me a single correction that relates to the $27,000 of Mesa's money for the Red Bull acquisitions that J. Cleo still holds?"

He couldn't.

"Mr. Rudnicki, has Mesa gotten its money back on the Red Bull from Day One?" I was invoking Milford's language from his deposition. He'd been clear that getting its money back from Day One had been Mesa's requirement for selling its interest in the project.

"They have not been paid back 100 percent of what they spent."

I felt that the only conclusion the jury could reach from his testimony was even more damning: the credit on Mesa's bill related to the original sections, not the valuable parts of the Red Bull. Further, J. Cleo still held $27,000 of Mesa's money. It hadn't gotten its money back from Day One, and Mesa therefore still had an interest in the Red Bull. I was done. I passed the witness.

We broke for lunch and headed over to Bill Weinacht's office. Ricardo turned to Cathy, who hadn't been in court during most of my questioning. "Where were you? Your sister shot, skinned, gutted and field dressed Rudnicki. She's one of the best lawyers

I have ever seen try a case." I gulped. Ricardo had been a witness in hundreds of jury trials, and he'd been there every day of this one. He wasn't just an expert in petroleum engineering, he was an authority on Texas jury trials. His stamp of approval was the highest professional compliment I could have earned.

We were almost done with the trial. After lunch, the defense called Wayman Gore, an engineer and seasoned expert witness whom I had hired myself in other oil and gas cases. I usually found him to be careful and accurate, but in this case, I felt his calculations were intellectually dishonest. I was upset that he was trying to get away with what appeared to me to be an obvious deception. The defense wanted Gore to value damages based on the few leasing bonuses that had been paid to landowners between December 2010 and January 2012—the timeline prescribed by the judge—and to claim they were the "true" measure of Mesa's damages. His opinions had evolved during the trial because of the judge's incremental rulings about damages. In fact, I'd just received his calculations the night before he took the stand.

Gore was measuring the value of the Red Bull leases by a completely different standard than we were. We based our damages on the future profits Mesa would have recouped, while Gore was going to say that the value of the lease to Mesa should be the same price per acre that Baytech had paid to the landowners. His total allowance for Mesa's 15 percent was just over $102,000 even though the defendants received billions for their share of the same properties. We clearly were not cutting up the same pie. They were keeping eight thousand times as much for themselves as they were going to allow Pickens to recover—and that was only if the jury first found them liable.

I knew the jurors had some familiarity with business in the Oil Patch. Many of them had either been approached about leasing their land to oil companies or they knew someone who had. The landowner typically not only gets a bonus payment up front based on the number of acres leased, but also would receive a 25 percent royalty from the value from the oil and gas as it was produced in the future. Those royalties could be substantial—in the tens of millions of dollars or more—depending on how much land the owner leased, and how much oil was there.

Gore wanted to give us damages based only the first part, the bonus. He contended that it was the best measure of what a willing buyer would pay for an oil lease.

Stuart Hollimon, the lead counsel for Baytech and DBR, walked Gore through his direct testimony. Gore had found that the defendants had taken more than thirty leases before 2012. He had gone through Baytech's records to determine the value of the lease bonuses. Mesa's interest in those leases should be valued the same way as the landowners', he said.

Thing was, Mesa's interest was nothing like a lease between a landowner and the oil company. The jury knew that the oil companies were getting the better end of the deal. Mesa was supposed to be treated as a partial owner of the operator's side of the deal, not as a landowner.

At this point in the trial, late on a Saturday after four full weeks, I was operating on instinct and sparse notes rather than my usual detailed preparation. I'd taken back-to-back witnesses with nothing but a lunch break between them.

What I did have was Ricardo Garza. He and Pickens always thought in terms of barrels of oil and the price of a barrel when it came to calculating damages. He made the passing observation that at forty dollars a barrel, the defendants were really only conceding that our share of the reserves was about 3,500 barrels, not 28 million.

That had given me an idea. What if I compared the value of what they were saying we owned with the value of what they were keeping, in the simplest of terms? I fished four twenty-dollar bills and a penny out of my purse and put them in my jacket pockets before I stood up to cross-examine Gore.

I started by challenging a few of his assumptions.

"Mr. Gore, you've seen the testimony that Mesa paid $515,738 to the defendants prior to being kicked out of the deal?" I asked.

"Yes."

"And on your analysis, defendants wouldn't even have to give Mesa its money back? They'd just give us $102,000?"

"Yes."

"So, in your analysis, defendants keep all of the reserves that are attributable to a 15 percent interest in the Red Bull, and Mesa gets $102,000 if it proves its case. Is that your testimony?"

"I don't think, at the relevant time period, reserves had been established. So, I didn't take that into account."

It was the same tired argument the defense had made throughout the trial—that they didn't know what the reserves were in 2012.

"So, you didn't take into account Mr. Garza's 28 million barrels of oil?"

"No ma'am, I considered it, but it's not relevant to my opinions." His face was starting to flush a little bit under cross examination.

"Mr. Gore, can you buy 28 million barrels for $102,000?" I was holding onto the twenties and the penny in my pocket, making sure they were still there.

"Not today."

"If that were the exchange rate, do you realize that a barrel of oil would be worth less than half a cent each? So, a penny would buy about two barrels of oil?"

"I haven't done the math."

"What is the price of oil today?"

"I haven't looked recently, but it's probably somewhere in the mid-forties."

"Let's just call it forty dollars per barrel, shall we?"

He agreed.

"So, in your opinion, Pickens' barrels of oil are priced at half a cent each, while defendants' barrels of oil are valued at forty dollars. For every two barrels of reserves, you want to give Pickens a single penny and the defendants get to keep eighty dollars' worth of oil?"

No answer. I pressed again.

"Is that what you're asking this jury to do?"

"Absolutely, because that's all Mesa was entitled to."

I walked back and placed forty dollars on each of the two defense tables, then walked closer to the jury and placed a single penny, with deliberate action, on the top of the stack of clay pigeons that Ricardo Garza had used to show rich oil deposits under the Red Bull. The display was still on the corner of the plaintiff's table, right in front of Pickens and next to the jury box, where it had been throughout the trial.

Gore's face was now deep red. Perhaps he realized that they had overreached in claiming eight thousand times for themselves what they would allow for Pickens' 15 percent. Perhaps the thought even crossed his mind that the defense might be in deep trouble. I passed the witness.

The defense took a stab at redirecting him, and I zoned out. I knew there was nothing more to ask him and that I had left it all on the field in my original cross examination. I declined to ask any more questions, and he left the stand.

I was exhausted but also exhilarated to be done with those opposing witnesses. That evening, we had a little celebration at the Swiss Chalet to mark the end of four full weeks of trial. Cathy and my other legal assistant, Kara Guillot, were both excellent cooks and had offered to make a home-cooked meal. We hadn't had one in weeks. They bought crockpots and made chicken tortilla soup and chicken and dumplings—real Texas fare—with cornbread on the side. The hotel had a full kitchen with a patio area, which we appropriated for our party. Ricardo brought beer, and we watched the Texas Longhorns play the University of Kansas Jayhawks in football. Kansas won for the first time since 1938—twenty-four to twenty-one—in overtime. Cathy was ecstatic as a former KU student would be. I focused on the fact that the underdog victory might be a good omen.

Pickens looked completely happy as we sat around talking and enjoying the meal. The fatigue that appeared to weigh on him in court, the lethargy and flushed face that had caused Swanson to express concern about Pickens' health, seemed to have passed. He had a bowl of homemade soup and a beer and I thought he must be loving life. He'd waited on that monkey, and he was getting a better show as a result.

The next day, Sunday, I decided we all needed a break. Pickens and most of his team departed for his ranch. Kara returned to Dallas for Thanksgiving, her tasks over. Cathy, Debbie, and I drove to Balmorhea, a small town about forty-five miles away. It's famous for its enormous spring-fed swimming pool that sits atop a giant aquifer. All the drilling in the area is starting to intrude upon this oasis in the high desert. Fracking oil wells takes millions of gallons of water, threatening Balmorhea's supply. I wanted to enjoy the pool again, because someday it may be gone.

We drove down the two-lane road from Pecos, admiring the cactus and other scrubby native plants as we shot by. To the southwest, we could see the tops of the Chisos Mountains in

Big Bend. I was starting to feel at home in this endless expanse of dirt and blue sky.

We drove to the pool and hiked around the park that surrounds it. It was a cool, crisp day that makes late fall a special time in Texas. Walking in the sun for a few hours was a welcome gift after spending weeks sequestered indoors. We watched the crystal-clear water move ever so slowly as a big school of small fish swam with the gentle flow.

Momentarily refreshed, we headed back to Pecos. It was time to make one final push towards a verdict, and hopefully, victory.

Chapter 25

"NO AMENDMENT REQUIRED"

Stuart Hollimon, the senior lawyer for Baytech and Delaware Basin Resources, had extensive expertise in oil and gas matters. He'd gone to law school with Mike Lynn at SMU, more than a decade before I did, but he wasn't primarily known as a trial lawyer. He's one of the most deliberate lawyers I've ever met, carefully considering every statement before making it. Most lawyers are cautious people. Stuart took caution to the extreme: he seemed obsessed with certainty and control. One of his former paralegals told me once that he ate the same exact thing—a Subway turkey sandwich—every day for lunch, regardless of whether he was with clients or working at his desk. I knew that when faced with the unknown, he became agitated. I thought perhaps this trait might play to our advantage. No matter how much you prepare, a trial takes a certain amount of improvisation and risk taking. You never know what a witness is going to say, and you have to adapt quickly. If that makes you anxious, you're going to struggle.

Stuart was questioning Rick Montgomery, the in-house lawyer for Baytech and DBR. Montgomery also was a part owner of DBR, which meant he had a financial stake in the litigation. Based on my interactions with Rick up until this point, I was pretty sure that he was certain of victory and awaiting the day that the jury returned a verdict in favor of Baytech and DBR. As he climbed into the witness stand, he exuded a confidence that I thought was premature.

I had taken Montgomery's deposition. Mike had also deposed him briefly, but he hadn't gotten much out of him. Most of his questions were blocked by the defense lawyers' assertions that the information was protected by attorney-client privilege. That didn't leave me a lot to work with. But Mike's questioning did give me one tidbit: the sense that Montgomery held a strange view that the Red Bull agreement didn't require a written amendment to take Mesa out of the deal. We didn't know any details, because the lawyers blocked further questions, so I would have to do some improv when I cross-examined Montgomery. That wasn't all bad. If I didn't know my questions, Hollimon couldn't prepare his witness to answer them, which would take him and his witness off their stride.

Hollimon turned first to Montgomery's 2014 meetings with Alex Szewczyk. Montgomery said that Alex knew what had happened to Mesa's interest. "I thought we owned a little more than the Lyda," Montgomery recalled Alex saying. Montgomery worked through his memory and told Alex, "No, you only own that." I objected that this out-of-court discussion was hearsay, but the judge overruled my objection.

"That may be fine, but part of my responsibilities in investigating this for Mr. Pickens is to find the piece of paper that says that," Montgomery said Alex had replied. Montgomery had been annoyed by the length of time that had passed since hearing from Mesa, and told Alex during the meeting, "Look, you and I know that Mesa got out of the deal." He testified that Alex replied, "I know, but Mr. Pickens has required me to find that piece of paper." Only Montgomery claimed that Alex had made the admission; I never heard that directly from Alex.

Montgomery testified that after his first meeting with Alex, he went back to his office and began combing through emails and computer files to find paperwork relating to the opt out. They found a lot of documents, but nothing signed by Pickens.

Of course they didn't, I thought. I was firm in my conviction that this was all that really mattered. It didn't matter that *they* wrote a bunch of emails and documents telling Mesa that Mesa had opted out; there had to be a paper with a signature from Mesa agreeing that it had left the deal. Pickens would have had to sign it himself.

Montgomery said he flew to Dallas in the fall of 2014 to meet with Alex and Sandy Campbell, Pickens' in-house counsel, and testified that he had tossed the March 2, 2009, "opt out" letter on the table. He told them "Mesa opted out" and emphasized that no one wrote back after that March 2, 2009 letter for more than five years. Montgomery testified that Campbell was unimpressed; he thought the letter raised more questions than it answered. Montgomery said he left the meeting feeling apprehensive, strongly suspecting that Mesa was going to sue.

Montgomery acknowledged that the agreement had no opt-out provision. But he said something I hadn't heard before: "If someone is getting out of an agreement, you don't amend the agreement. You don't need a signed piece of paper saying they're getting out. You're not really changing the agreement; you're just taking part of the pie and giving it to someone else."

I was stunned. The contract couldn't have been clearer. It had the same language all contracts did: all amendments had to be in writing and signed by both parties. I'd just heard the inexplicable position that Mike Lynn's deposition of Montgomery had hinted at.

In fact, Montgomery never even asked Mesa for a signed opt out document. He'd trusted the word of Jimmy Thompson because Thompson had brought Mesa into the deal. In Montgomery's experience, handshake deals got done all the time.

As I stood up to question Montgomery, I felt a wave of anger welling up inside of me. He was a lawyer. I thought he should know better. I'd never, in more than twenty-five years of practice, heard anyone try to get around an "all amendments must be in writing" clause the way Montgomery just had.

I started my cross-examination by recounting the original exchange between Montgomery and Alex. "So, Alex came to you asking the same question that Mesa is here asking today: where's the paperwork?" He tried to avoid answering that question directly, but after three attempts, he said yes.

"And you went and combed through your files, and did you find a piece of paper saying that Mesa, Mr. T. Boone Pickens, gave up the rights in the Red Bull?"

"We didn't find that piece of paper, no," he replied.

"What does an amendment mean? Does it mean a change?"

"No, not necessarily," he said. "It means a rewriting of the agreement." After several more attempts, he conceded that an amendment was, indeed, a change to the agreement. This wasn't going to be easy, but the fight sometimes just reinforces key concepts for the jury.

I forced him to read the language of the agreement, which I also put up on the large viewing screen for the jury to read. "It says, 'no amendment hereto shall be binding unless mutually agreed to in a written document specifically referring to this Participation Agreement.' Do you have that kind of document?"

"An amendment? No, there was no amendment required."

Again, Montgomery repeated the concept that the plain words of the contract did not mean what they said. I turned to some background details that I hoped would prove I was right. Operators set up what they call "division of interest" decks to show who owns what part of every well and lease. It tells them how to distribute revenues and assign expenses. I knew that Mesa had been listed as an owner at one time in everything that was shown on Exhibit 53, including the all-important Colt well and the La Escalera Ranch sections. I knew this because I'd carefully examined J. Cleo's division of interest decks, and before February 2009, Mesa was listed as a 15 percent owner. After that date, Mesa's interest had disappeared from all but the Lyda deck.

I confronted him with those documents. He agreed that at one point, J. Cleo had set Mesa up as an owner. However, after February 2009, J. Cleo had transferred those ownership interests to Baytech.

He conceded that after Baytech set up DBR, it reassigned both its own rights and Mesa's 15 percent to the new company. He further agreed that Mesa had never signed off on the changes. *That was it.* He used the word "change." A few minutes earlier, he'd admitted an amendment means a change, and nobody at Mesa signed an amendment.

I was starting to feel energized again. Montgomery's key contention, that the contracts didn't require a document signed by Pickens for Mesa to have gotten out of the deal was now toast, in my opinion. There'd been changes to the ownership of the Red Bull. A change is an amendment, and no one had gotten a signed agreement from Pickens to make those changes.

I turned to the next subject. I had learned in his deposition that the reason Baytech and DBR hadn't bought out Mesa in

2009 was because Montgomery had decided not to pay the money Mesa wanted. Montgomery had told me that the Lyda well was all Mesa owned, and it wasn't worth more than the $160,000 that they had offered. They could have bought everything from Pickens for $515,738 and put all doubt to rest, but Montgomery didn't want to pay. I had confronted him with that issue before the trial, asking out of court, "Rick, aren't you sorry you didn't pay Mesa the $515,738 when you could have bought it out?" Refusing to admit he had made a mistake, Rick had told me at the time that the original purchase, the Lyda, wasn't worth the $515,738, so no, he wasn't sorry, even though Baytech had gone on to spend millions on the lawsuit. He insisted that Pickens shouldn't get his money back.

I hit him with those questions again under oath on the stand. No, he hadn't wanted for Baytech to buy Mesa's interest in the Lyda. He didn't want to pay for it because it was a bad well. Because he didn't want to pay the $515,738, Baytech didn't buy it and Mesa didn't sell it. He agreed that it was true that Mesa did not get its money back, either.

I wanted to press one final issue: Montgomery's pride in his legal work. He had written all the contracts and documents, and he couldn't admit that they didn't cover the position Baytech was now taking at the trial. I asked him on the stand whether he knew what malpractice was. I didn't explain what malpractice was or imply whether he might have committed it. I figured the jury knew enough about the topic to get the point: he had a vested interest in defending his work.

Baytech actually had received lengthy legal documents called title opinions written by other lawyers. The point of a title opinion is to ensure that you own what you think you own before you go and invest millions in drilling wells. The defendants had obtained title opinions that contained "exceptions," a list of items that had to be addressed to ensure the title was clear. Those exceptions told Baytech that it needed to make sure Mesa had received its notices of election for lands that were purchased after 2009. When I asked him why he didn't follow the advice of the title opinion attorneys, Montgomery said it would cost too much to clean up the "exceptions."

Montgomery hadn't wanted to pay a title attorney to fix the mess and straighten out the documents, just like he didn't want to pay Mesa the $515,738 it had asked for to sell its Red Bull interests. And because he hadn't done either, Mesa had never sold out and now stood to recover more than $100 million.

It came down to money. It almost always does.

Chapter 26

CLOSING ARGUMENTS

It was the Monday before Thanksgiving, and it was time to end this thing. We needed to hammer home the points of our case one last time in closing arguments: Mesa had valid written agreements that required the defendants to send it notices of its right to participate in each lease and well for a 15 percent interest. After 2009, the defendants hadn't sent any of those notices. Before then, Mesa had elected to participate in everything for which it was notified, and it had paid $515,738 on those notices by the time Baytech offered to buy Mesa's interest. When those negotiations fell through, Baytech worked with J. Cleo to transfer Mesa's interest to itself in February 2009 and then later to DBR. No one told Mesa about it. Baytech had needed to bring in investors, and it needed Mesa's share to make the deal more attractive to them. Never had Pickens signed anything agreeing to give up Mesa's interest.

I was relieved to be near the conclusion. I had started the case confident that we would prevail. Now, after more than four weeks of toil, mental strain, and what seemed like endless rulings against us by the judge, I hoped I was right. Regardless, we were all ready for the verdict, one way or another. Everyone on my team was exhausted. I was glad that I was physically fit, at least when the trial had begun a month earlier. My training as a distance runner had paid off; I just had to get us across the finish line. I knew that closing arguments would be mentally and physically difficult, especially after weeks and weeks of stress, lack of sleep, poor food, and being away from home.

As I did most days, I checked in by a short phone call with my husband. I would recount some of the high points or low points of the day, and he'd offer supportive comments. He wasn't above giving his own probing thoughts about what was happening, but most of the time, he was simply supportive, and it was good to hear from him.

Pickens had left Pecos on Sunday morning. When I'd talked to him by phone later that day, he hadn't seemed like himself. Cathy's homemade soup had perked him up at our dinner, but now he sounded fatigued. When the judge had pointed out that Pickens looked ill in the courtroom, I dismissed it as a possible blood sugar issue. I wasn't too concerned. But when we talked, he kept repeating himself. This wasn't like him. He knew he wasn't making sense, and he told me that he was tired.

By Monday, he and his team were back in court, ready to hear the closing arguments. He'd sat through every day of the trial, a remarkable feat for a client of any age. But Pickens still seemed a little off. Despite my concern, I had to focus on closing—and winning—the case.

The jurors were hard to read. They'd been emotionless during the trial, and I couldn't tell how closely they were following all the testimony—especially with the seemingly incessant objections. It had been hard to build any momentum. The only time I got a sense that they were with us was during Ricardo's demonstrations. I didn't blame them: the case was complicated, and it hinged on arcane clauses in contracts, difficult engineering concepts, and even more dense accounting details. They had sat through seemingly endless objections. Ricardo's models were like Friday show-and-tell in the middle of algebra class.

At least we had stayed true to the themes of our case throughout the proceeding. It went back to what Bill Weinacht had told the panel during *voir dire*: no one would believe that someone got out of a big oil deal merely by saying they wanted to get out—especially to a man who was now dead and couldn't confirm the conversation. It took more than words, as the jurors knew from their own personal lives. *No paperwork,* I thought.

We had one last chance to imprint our case on the minds of the jury. We needed closing arguments that would cement the key concepts, but we also needed an interesting presentation that would keep them engaged. The best way to do that, I decided, would be to split up closing arguments four ways.

Real closing arguments aren't something you see on television. The TV version is usually a stunning but brief monologue, like Gregory Peck's in *To Kill a Mockingbird* or Jeff Bridges' in *Tucker: The Man and His Dream.* In reality, preparation for effective and compelling closing arguments takes weeks. In some ways, you start long before the trial even begins. You have to know how you'll structure your presentation to highlight the best evidence and deal with the worst. You need a theme that the jury will remember. You need to shape your review of the witness testimony and documents to fit that theme. Then, after deciding all of that, you need graphics, PowerPoints, and pictures that amplify your words. Each requires a lot of time to prepare. To top it off, you must make it all seem logical and unassailable by exuding confidence, mastery, stamina, and righteous indignation in equal measures when necessary.

In other words, you don't just stand up, open your mouth and say something brilliant that no one has ever thought of before.

I don't particularly like closing arguments. I'd much rather give opening statements, when the evidence is fresh and no one is tired of hearing the same things ten times. Once the trial begins, I'm usually preoccupied with examining witnesses right up until the end. I always feel as if I'm rushing to slap together a closing argument. I also don't like making a spectacle with grandiose words and accusations of how the other side has done us wrong. This Kansas-raised girl would rather the jurors see the evidence and come to their own commonsense conclusions—which, of course, meant recognizing we were right and had the evidence to prove it. But closing arguments are critical. They would give us one last chance to remind the jurors why we were right. We needed a powerful close to the case.

We would split the argument between Mike, Andres, Bill—who'd made it back from Peru—and me. The judge had given us enough speaking time that we wouldn't have to rush through our presentations. I'd been so busy with the cross examinations that I hadn't had time to perfect our entire argument, and I wanted to hedge our bets in terms of which lawyer the jury might trust most. I knew that Mike lived for this part of the case. Unlike me, he loved closing arguments and I knew he would spend days perfecting his part. Andres, the former actor, knew how to play to an audience, so he was in. I wanted Bill to reinforce the paperwork idea he'd started in *voir dire* and that we had harped on ever since. I was still convinced those arguments would win the case.

In a civil trial, the plaintiff gets to make closing arguments first, the defense gets its turn, and then the plaintiff gets another shot—essentially a rebuttal that serves as the final word. I understood all the pesky details of the evidence and testimony. If the defendants hit on any of them during their remarks, I would have the easiest time refuting them, so I decided to take the rebuttal argument.

It would have been easier to let others handle the close entirely, but I had another reason for not ceding this final moment in the spotlight. It didn't pertain to the case, but it had hung over my entire career. The only way a woman gets to do what I have gotten to do as a lawyer is to take every opportunity that comes up, even if it scares the shit out of her. The tests start early. You get asked to take that deposition of a seemingly meaningless witness that no one wants to prepare for, and they ask you at the eleventh hour because no one wanted to deal with it beforehand. You do it in hopes of burnishing your reputation as someone who can be trusted to come through in a pinch, someone who will make sure the client's interests are protected.

You stand up and take the hard motions at hearings that the judge is going to deny and hate. You stay up all night studying for a witness exam so you can kill it the next day in the shortest time possible. You tell your senior partners that you will take every opportunity that comes your way, even if it means you have to write briefs while on your beach vacation with your children. It sucks at the time, but it also means that you get to take those children to Europe because you eventually earn the money and the right to do it.

I remembered the advice I'd received early in my career about getting out on the skinny branches. You might fall, but taking the risk is the only way to work your way up. I was not going to miss my role in closing the biggest case I might ever get the chance to try.

And, I owed it to Pickens. He'd counted on me from the start to see this through and to win it. He believed in me, and I in him. I wanted to do the best I could with the last opportunity I would have to win the biggest case of his life.

With four lawyers, it seemed logical to have two take the first round of arguments and two take the rebuttal, but in what order should they go? Bill wouldn't know what he was going to say until he said it. His argument might be brilliant, but we wouldn't know what it was beforehand. Mike, on the other hand, was meticulous in his preparation. He liked having PowerPoint slides to speak from, illustrated with visually stunning graphics that our team of artists working remotely would whip up.

We decided Mike should go first, followed by Andres. Mike would drive home the more compelling "they done him wrong" arguments about how Pickens had been treated, while Andres would cover the damages Mesa had sustained. Bill and I would take the rebuttal argument, our final chance to persuade the jury. I would bat clean up. My job would be to keep the jury focused on what mattered most, and I wanted to do that right before they retired to deliberate.

The judge wasn't done throwing a monkey wrench into our plans. He had just ruled that we could not mention in our closing arguments the ten benches of oil waiting to be produced, the deep pockets of reserves that everyone knew were there. We could present the final claim for damages but couldn't argue about those ten benches, even though they had already been admitted into evidence. We wanted to bring it up because it made us look inherently reasonable: our damages calculations were based on the value of just one of those benches—not all ten. We were all annoyed. Cathy joked with Andres that he should start his closing with, "There are ten things I want you to remember about this case…" and point at Ricardo's painted stack of skeet representing those ten benches, still sitting on my table next to the jurors. She has a sarcastic wit.

That day, the Tuesday before Thanksgiving, we were ready to finish the case. The jury settled into their places, stoic as ever, but looking as tired as we felt by that point. I wondered if a month in the courtroom was taking a toll on their lives—it usually does—and how, if at all, that might color their views of the case.

As Mike stood up to begin, I felt strangely calm. I knew he'd done this many times. Recounting our story for the jury was where he was most comfortable. He started by stressing the importance of the case, not to Mesa or our billionaire client, but to Reeves County. He reminded them that their decision would affect how the oil and gas business was conducted in their home. It wasn't just about one rich guy being cut out of the deal; it was about the fairness of the process for everyone.

Then he got down to the particulars: "There are three things I want to focus on in the few minutes we have left before you go to deliberate. The first is, we had a written deal for Pickens to have 15 percent of the Red Bull. That deal was never amended, and Pickens never signed anything saying he wanted out. Second thing is, they wanted us out, but they got us out the wrong way. They had a choice of the wrong way or the right way, and they chose the wrong way."

As Mike spoke, the screen behind him showed a fork in the road. The right-hand branch led to sunny skies and a clear path. The left path led to perdition: bolts of lightning, angry skies, and alligators in a river.

"Thirdly, they did not act in good faith when they dealt with Mesa. The contracts said they bore a duty of good faith in their dealings with each other. They did not act in good faith. They did not act in a manner that is becoming in Reeves County. Rather than follow their promises, they intentionally took what was Mesa's. It was no accident.

"Why? Because there were hundreds of millions of dollars at stake. Ladies and gentlemen, I want you to focus on what I call the North Star when you deliberate. The Red Bull contracts. Those agreements were the Bible."

Now, the screen showed a picture of the Good Book, lit in a shining gold light. Mike liked religious imagery. It might be a risky tactic in many courtrooms, but this was West Texas. He'd frequently talked to me about how his dad, a man about the same age as Pickens, had been a preacher, and Mike had grown up listening to him preach.

"They want you to think that you can do these deals on a handshake. This was too big for a handshake. You know that paperwork is required for every major transaction in your own lives. It was required here as well.

"I want you to recall how Strickling and Hedrick took the stand and I asked them, 'Have you seen an amendment of the Red Bull contracts signed by Pickens?' And rather than admit that there wasn't one, they crawfished." (That is a southern term for duplicity.) "They said they hadn't seen one. But they know one never existed."

I felt shortchanged by the way that Mike focused primarily on the two witnesses he had presented, Hedrick and Strickling, rather than the many witnesses that I had put on the stand, even though their testimony was more compelling. Then it hit me: Mike hadn't even been in the courtroom when I had cross-examined Rudnicki and Gore. He had been off preparing for this closing argument. He didn't watch some of the most critical testimony. I just hoped the jury recalled it.

"You also heard that they never sent any more Red Bull notices to Mesa when they bought the properties, like they were supposed to do. Instead, they made up the opt-out story. For their opt-out story to make sense, you have to believe that

Pickens was giving away his property for nothing. Ask yourself whether that makes any sense. He told you he has never given away his property for free, except to charity. He gets money and signs a contract. That's the way Pickens does it.

"I want you to weigh Pickens' credibility against Cliff Milford. Milford was the guy who said he heard Pickens say he wanted to get out of the Red Bull to Jimmy Thompson. Pickens sat through the whole trial at eighty-eight years old, being cross-examined by good lawyers so that he could tell you the truth from the stand. Milford, even though I asked him to come to trial and he said he would, came nowhere near this courthouse.

"Here's another thing to weigh when you evaluate Pickens' credibility versus the defendants' credibility. Remember that Pickens left Phillips Petroleum with fifteen hundred dollars, a pregnant wife, and a car with no air-conditioning. He would not have been as successful as he was if he wasn't honest. If he wasn't fair."

Mike then covered the smoking gun documents we had introduced as evidence, reminding the jury of their importance. "I call this Evil Bingo," he said, and as he recounted the details a bingo board appeared on the screen behind him.

"Remember, when they couldn't buy Pickens' Red Bull interests, they just took them. I asked the witnesses over and over whether they thought it was right, whether it was fair. There was only one man who was free from sin, Jesus Christ. Well, Hedrick ain't no Jesus. What they did was not right, moral, or fair." A picture of Jesus appeared on the screen behind him. I wasn't sure what the connection was between Hedrick and Jesus, but Mike was in full tilt preacher mode at the moment, heading for his call to the altar.

"I remember when I was a kid and we'd go scuba diving, chasing the squids. Squids put out ink to keep you from catching them. You've got to let the ink settle. The defense attorneys are going to get up here in a moment. As you listen to them, remember to let the ink settle before you decide."

I doubted many of the jurors sitting in the high desert courtroom had scuba-dived on a regular basis. I was certain that no one but Mike had chased squids. I was reminded again of *My Cousin Vinny*, this time of the vignette in which the prosecutor draws blank stares from the African-American jurors upon referencing a legal principle handed down by all "our little ole ancestors in England."

Mike rounded for home. "This is a big case. People need to know that when they do business out here, when they sign up for important deals, they can trust Reeves County to honor their deals. To enforce them in court."

Squid chasing aside, Mike had nailed his part, punctuating his comments with a call to the jurors' civic and religious pride. It was inspiring and effective. He sat, and Andres took the floor.

With his charisma on full display, Andres reviewed much more of our evidence. He gave a thorough recap of everything else we'd presented during the trial. He ended by talking about the damages and offering some perspective on one aspect of them, the bucket for Participation Agreement damages —the damages for the 15 percent of the value of the properties taken between 2010 and 2012. "Those are big numbers," he said, "but remember: if we get $129 million, they get to keep $860 million. You have a choice: buy their excuses or follow the agreements. We think there is just one choice: follow the agreements."

Good job, I thought, and then I recalled how I'd wondered if this might be the biggest case he'd see in his career. I hoped for his sake that it wouldn't be.

After a short break, Tim McConn gave the closing argument for Baytech and DBR. He again claimed that Pickens had opted out of the deal and wanted to blame his partners rather than taking responsibility for making a bad choice.

"This case is about his ego, his embarrassment, and his attempt to shift the blame and not take responsibility for the decision he and his team made," McConn said. He referred to Pickens' testimony. "He told you from the stand himself 'I'm dealing with crooks.'"

Again, with the "crooks" theme. What was he thinking, reinforcing that concept?

"Let me tell you," McConn said, emphatically pointing his finger at his clients, *"I'm proud to represent these crooks."* It reminded me of how lawyers identify a defendant in a criminal trial, and it made me cringe—for him, for what I knew imme- diately was a gross miscalculation. "They're not crooks," he continued. "They're good people." But my short time in public relations had taught me that wouldn't be what would stick in everyone's minds. Sure enough, the reporter who covered the story would condense his closing argument to the pronounce- ment that he was "proud to represent these crooks."

McConn ran through the same arguments the defense had made during the trial. When he eventually sat down, he looked satisfied that he had delivered the closing speech that he'd planned. He was splitting his allotted time with Stuart Hollimon.

"My clients are grateful to you because they are here trying to restore their reputations," Hollimon said as he began his part. "Their honesty and integrity have been challenged in this litigation and it's a very personal thing for them. They've come to this court seeking relief, asking to restore their reputation."

That was another huge risk, in my mind. He was asking the jury to do too much. Restore reputations? Juries can't do that, certainly not in a civil trial like this. *Aim small, miss small.*

They were aiming big, and I hoped it was going to be an even bigger miss.

"They want $129 million from us when the buy-in was only $515,000," Hollimon went on. "Does that strike you as right? They are right that we kept $27,000 that didn't get credited back to them on the acreage. But does it strike you as right that a $27,000 accounting error should get them $129 million?"

Holliman was asking the jury to let his clients keep Pickens' share of the pie. I hoped that my cross of their expert, Wayman Gore, had driven home my "fair share of the pie" theme. Gore's assertion that the defendants could keep eighty dollars of oil for every penny that they were willing to give Pickens seemed ridiculous. As if to underscore the point, the penny for Pickens' share still sat atop the stack of clay pigeons representing the oil reserves, which remained on the corner of my table in plain sight of the jury, a physical rebuttal to Hollimon's closing statement.

When Hollimon sat down, Geoff Bracken stood up to conclude the summation for J. Cleo.

"First, Lynn told you that Milford is a liar. He's a scoundrel. He's a crook. He testified for seven hours by deposition. So, shame on you, Mike!"

He was visibly angry at Mike, which perplexed me. And I didn't understand his point. Was it that Milford didn't need to come to trial? If so, it seemed irrelevant. Surely Bracken had a more compelling point to make.

"Lynn also said that if Thompson was alive, Pickens would likely have called him up and they would have worked this out. Well, that's what they did. Pickens got out and got his money back. And their internal ledgers show that they accounted for the credit. So, shame on them for coming here and saying that the Mesa accountant didn't know how to do her job.

"Szewczyk tried to run from the whole situation. He lacked memory of pretty much everything. But he had the authority to tell the accountant to 'pay only Lyda charges.' It's Pickens' fault for putting him in that position, but he had the authority to do what he did.

"Then Lynn said the written contract was the Bible. Well, I'm here to tell you that it is not the Word of God. The judge has told you what has to be proved, and Pickens didn't need to sign a document to have gotten out." The judge hadn't ruled that way; he'd only allowed them to make the argument that Pickens *could* have orally opted out. But rather than object, we all let the point pass unnoticed. Objections wouldn't help now.

"The judge has also told you that you have to find my client, J. Cleo, grossly negligent or that it had some kind of evil purpose and was engaged in willful misconduct. There is no evidence that J. Cleo did any of that. Look, we made some mistakes in our accounting. Rudnicki admitted it on the stand. That's not an evil purpose. And even if we had sloppy accounting, it doesn't matter, because Mesa knew how to apply the credit, and they haven't been damaged. And the discrepancy was only $27,000. They aren't suing us for $27,000."

I thought saying "the discrepancy was *only* $27,000" was another miscalculation. This was a jury of small-town, hard-working folks, and he characterized twenty-seven grand as chump change. Most of the jurors probably saw it as a large sum of money.

After a few more remarks, Bracken sat down. My turn.

I rose from my chair to start Mesa's rebuttal closing argument. I walked around my counsel table, out in front of the jury. I began the way I hoped I had started, by trying to establish a personal connection with the jurors.

"It's nice to speak to you one last time before you go deliberate. You've been so attentive. You've listened so well. I could tell that you are trying hard to understand everything that's been presented. And it has been a real pleasure.

"While I've been up here trying to tell people to play by the rules and tell the truth, and I've been confronting people here, I'm coming to you with humility and humbleness in my heart because you are the ones who are going to decide. I've only got a short time here, but I want to give you some additional information that I think is going to help you fill out these questions."

I had saved one last surprise for closing—something that the jurors had not heard during the trial. I could get away with it only because the parties had stipulated the document into evidence as an exhibit. I wasn't presenting anything new. It contained one simple thing that I think disproved the whole defense position that we had opted out, that we no longer had rights under the Red Bull contracts. If I had played the card earlier, the defense no doubt would have come up with another explanation. This was the time to use it.

"Let's look at what the defendants filed in the property records in December 2009. That's *after* everything else happened, the 'opt out' and all of their story. Let's look at that document." On the overhead screen, I displayed a simple legal document that assigned rights from Baytech to Mesa in the Lyda well. But there was an important detail buried in the legal lingo, and I zeroed in on it: Baytech recognized Mesa's rights in the Red Bull Participation Agreement and Joint Operating Agreement. Those two contracts gave Mesa rights to 15 percent of the Red Bull and all future acquisitions in it.

"Do you see that?" I asked the jury. "They say right there, in this document, that *Mesa still has rights* in the Red Bull Participation Agreement and Joint Operating Agreement. Those are the same two contracts we've been here talking about the whole time. Look at the stamp in the lower right-hand corner. This is a certified copy of something they filed right here in the courthouse in December 2009.

"And yet they are coming to you here today and saying, 'Disregard what we filed downstairs in the records recognizing Mesa's rights in these contracts.' It's a sleight of hand, and you shouldn't let them get away with it."

Letting that sink in for a moment, I next did something I had never done in closing before. I asked the jurors to take out their jury questionnaires and take notes. I didn't know why lawyers don't do it more often; maybe they don't want to take attention away from themselves and their presentation. I decided to do it differently.

The jury questionnaires list the questions that the judge determines jurors must answer in reaching a verdict. The lawyers prepare the initial drafts and then argue over them for hours until the judge decides what the questions should be. We'd concluded that exercise late the night before.

"Please pull out the questions and flip through the pages with me. You're going to have to go back in the jury room, and you're not going to have a lot of information other than what is in your notes, so I think taking notes will be really helpful to you."

Nearly everyone one of the jurors pulled out their papers and a pencil, listening attentively for what came next.

"Let's pull up Question 1, the first question that you have to answer. It asks, 'Did Baytech and Delaware Basin Resources fail to comply with the Participation Agreement that required them to provide election notices to Mesa?'

"The DBR Defendants jumped right over that one." I actually jumped, not high, but enough to get the jury's attention.

I wanted to wake them up, just like the act of writing might do. Fortunately, I didn't fall as I landed in my high heels. It just occurred to me to do this; I hadn't practiced it. "Why did they jump over that question? Because there is no contrary evidence. They breached it. Their own expert created a map that shows the thirty-five leases that they concede they didn't offer to Mesa. They never gave us notice of those leases. So, you answer Question 1 'yes.'"

The jurors were writing. I frankly was shocked that I was getting away with it, but the judge had told them that they could take notes, and the defense didn't object. So, I decided to help them write down some more important information.

"Next question. 'Did they fail to comply with their agreements, which required them to act in good faith?' Remember when I talked to you about kindergarten rules a few weeks ago? Play fair. Don't take other people's stuff. They took our stuff, they took our money and kept it, and then took our property interest. That's not good faith. So, you answer 'yes' for those questions, one line for the Delaware Basin Resources and Baytech together, and one for J. Cleo.

"Mesa asks that you answer the first three questions 'yes' because those questions ask you whether the defendants breached the two contracts. Mesa then asks you to answer the next three questions 'no.' Mesa didn't waive its rights. You need to answer those 'no' because here's the thing: they all require Mesa to have intentionally given up its rights. Pickens told you he never intended to give up the property. 'I've never given up property that way in my entire life. I sign a document and they pay me money,' he told you. 'We offered to sell; they didn't buy. We never intended to give up the property.'

"And here's another reason you have to answer questions 4, 5, and 6 'no.' Let's focus on what the court is telling you:

that you have to find that it would be unconscionable for Mesa to assert its rights under the contracts. Here's what is unconscionable. It's unconscionable that Mesa paid almost a million dollars to these defendants."

Even after offering to sell for $515,738 in 2009, Mesa had continued to pay its Red Bull bills up until the trial began. From 2007 until that very month, Mesa had continued receiving bills from J. Cleo for the Red Bull. Even though no one had sent it the required notices to indicate when new wells or acreage were purchased, Mesa was still getting billed, suggesting the Red Bull was ongoing. No wonder Mesa had been confused about what had happened to its Red Bull interests.

All told, Mesa's Red Bull payments topped $1 million by the time of trial. "It's unconscionable that they are keeping all the money. It's unconscionable that they are still keeping money for the sections we paid for. It's unconscionable that they filed a deed in the property records downstairs saying Mesa still has rights, but they don't honor those rights. That is what is unconscionable, not Mesa asserting its rights."

I sat down. I still had one small bit to go, but it was Bill Weinacht's turn to help bring this home. Bill stood and began, taking my spot in front of the jury.

"Ladies and gentlemen, we are finishing right where we started. It was about the paperwork from the very beginning. It's still about the paperwork.

"They are here looking for integrity? 'Where's my integrity, they say?' They think you can give them integrity? You don't get integrity by a jury telling you something. You get integrity by following your written agreements.

"Now they are coming in here with all kinds of stuff about repudiations and estoppel and words you never even heard before. Nobody signs an agreement saying I guess you'll get out of it by estoppel. We sign our most important affairs. Our most important affairs are done by deeds, they're done by court papers. In writing.

"These are experienced oil men, every one of them. They did everything in writing. What happened is they wanted him out; he wanted out at one time. They tried to get him out, they didn't do it right and now they are trying to cover for it, and they want you to give them integrity.

"They're looking for it like the Tin Man looking for his heart. 'Where is my integrity? It's gone, it's gone, please give it to me.'"

Bill startled me by crawling halfway under the counsel table, looking for the missing integrity. Perhaps like me he thought a bit of physical action would help. He certainly got my attention.

"How do you keep your integrity? You honor your agreements. You put it in writing. You say, 'We're not changing this unless you give me a signed writing.' Are we being overtaken with greed here? In this community? All of a sudden, below our feet, thousands of feet down, here's this black stuff. Everybody wants it. And they're hungry for it with the biggest greed you ever saw in your lives.

"They say he opted out. That talk is like a poker game out in the backyard. 'Oh, Pickens folded.' Folded! You don't fold out of an oil deal. You sign out.

"They had the winning ticket like in a lottery. They had it and they didn't let him know.

"Is this a house of justice? Or is it a brick building that means nothing? They want you to make it mean nothing. No justice.

"You all are speaking to the other oil people who might come here. I don't know what you do in your regular lives. Maybe you see stuff that is wrong. Maybe you think, 'somebody ought to do something about it, but I can't right now. I'm busy working over here.'

"Well, not today. Today, you decide. You make the rules and say if it is right or wrong. This becomes a house of justice when you say yes, 'you have to follow the rules.' Let's do justice. Let's show people that when they come to Reeves County, they've got to be just, they've got to honor their agreements."

Damn, I thought. That was powerful. I was happy. Time to finish this thing.

I stood up one final time. I would have the last word.

I asked them to look at Question 7 of the jury form; I hoped they'd already written six of the answers as I'd suggested minutes before. Question 7 asked what amount of money would fairly and reasonably compensate Mesa for its damages for breach of the Participation Agreement.

"This is the number: $117,485,615." I called out each digit slowly and asked them to write it down. "That's the answer to Question 7 if you believe the evidence shows they breached the agreement." This was the number Rodney Sowards had calculated after weeks of revisions.

Question 8 was actually four questions that essentially asked them to assign damages for everything else that the defendants had done wrong in breaching the Joint Operating Agreement. "You're going to have to actually fill in four numbers here," I told them. "The good news is, they're all the same: $6,177,506." I waited as most of them wrote the number four times.

Many lawyers don't ask jurors to award specific amounts, thinking that they won't like being told what to do. I don't agree on this point. I figure that if by the end of the case, I've laid out the evidence in a way the jury understands, then my last act of service to them is to make it clear what they are supposed to do with that evidence. I hoped I was helping them in their difficult task of filling out the numbers on the jury form. If only they would go back into the jury room and write those same numbers on the official version, we would hit a home run and claim victory in a case that I'd been toiling over for the past three years.

I waited for the jurors to stop writing, then I looked directly at as many of them as possible and thanked them for their rapt attention and their time. I sat down.

The judge gave them a few more instructions on how they should deliberate. More importantly, for me, he told them to leave their other notes with the court bailiff, but that they could take their copies of the jury questions. Of course, those copies were now full of the notes I'd asked them to take, including key numbers for Mesa's damages that they might otherwise have forgotten. The jurors stood and filed out of the box and into the jury room, each holding the answers I'd prescribed for the questions. I could see some of their handwriting on the forms as they walked out.

You don't often get a chance to ask a jury to take notes. Not every judge even allows it. In Texas state courts, it's up to the individual judges. I can't imagine sitting through a lengthy trial without being able to write anything down. I was grateful that Swanson had done the right thing by allowing it, and I was grateful that he hadn't required them to hand back the notes on the jury forms.

We all exhaled and sat for a moment. As we started to pack up our detritus from five weeks of the trial, a commotion started at the defense tables. The defense lawyers huddled, murmuring among themselves. I wondered what took them so long.

Finally, Bracken spoke up. "Your Honor, the court has taken up the notes from the jurors but has allowed them to keep their copy of the jury questionnaire. Ms. Castañeda asked them to take notes on them and the jurors did it. So, those are notes, and we don't think it is fair for them to keep them."

Mike argued against it for a minute, which I knew was going to be futile, and the judge ruled that the bailiff should go collect those notes too. The jury had been out for a full five minutes at that point. I only hoped it was long enough.

Chapter 27

ALL OR NOTHING

I don't know how other lawyers feel when they wait for a jury to come back. I'm usually pretty calm. I have done all that I can to make the case, and it's really out of my hands. My client's fate is up to others and since there's nothing I can do to change it, I'm at ease. This has been true for me in every case, even if I lose.

The Pickens situation was different from the start, but I was still relaxed while the jury was out. I knew early on, after I was a few months into the case, that I was going to have to go to trial. I had a strong feeling that the defendants wouldn't settle because too much money was at stake. But I had an even stronger feeling I would win. Pickens seemed to share that belief, and he was willing to fight the case to the end. He had stayed by my side until we finished closing arguments. But his fatigue had persisted since the day in court when the judge noticed he looked flushed. With our case wrapped up, he left Pecos to seek medical attention.

I felt badly for him that he wouldn't be there when the jury came back. He would have loved the drama of this moment, waiting to find out if he'd made a big score or drilled a dry hole. I was sad that we wouldn't be able to celebrate the victory together—assuming it came.

The jury had gotten the case on the Tuesday afternoon before Thanksgiving 2016. They deliberated the first day for about an hour before they went home. We came in the next morning, Wednesday, at the usual time. I didn't think they'd be out that long. The jury questionnaire outlining the questions they would have to answer based on the evidence wasn't lengthy. As these things go, it was pretty easy to understand. Plus, I'd given them all the answers to hand us a victory, if only they'd take them.

The verdict was likely to be all one way—either they thought the paperwork mattered, that "a deal is a deal," or they thought Pickens was making the whole thing up just to undo his decision to get out of the arrangement. Unlike the results in some cases, I didn't see how they would split the decision, giving some things to us and some things to the defense. This would be a knockout punch, not a mixed decision.

I wanted to wait at the courthouse while the jury was out that Wednesday morning. Someone at the court would have called the lead attorneys on their cell phones when the jury came back, but I wanted to be there already. I didn't want to waste a single minute in transit. It was, after all, the day before Thanksgiving.

A few of us hung out in the foyer of the courthouse, taking turns telling jokes and talking about nothing. We'd spent so much time together during the past month that we'd pretty much said to each other all that there was to say.

Shortly before lunch, we had a decision. That was a good sign: it meant that the jury didn't have any difficulty reaching a verdict. At least ten of the twelve jurors had to agree to the same answers for all the questions that were posed. The more disagreement, the longer they would have taken. And, if jurors are going to award big damages or, conversely, zero out the plaintiff, they're also going to do so more quickly than if they deliver a mixed decision. Now we'd have to see what we got—all or nothing.

The judge called us back into the courtroom and we took the same spots where we'd already spent hundreds of hours. We rose as the jurors filed in silently, with their heads down and faces expressionless. Perhaps they were trying to hide their emotions, or maybe they didn't want the losing side to feel badly. Then again, they may have just wanted to leave, now that they'd done their duty. They had, after all, been in court every day for more than four weeks and the next day was Thanksgiving.

I thought of Pickens again and how much he wanted to be present for what came next. He would have loved talking to the jurors after they were released, getting their opinions, talking over the case's events and witnesses—and yes, explaining the geology one final time. It was a shame to receive the verdict without him. As the fog of the trial began lifting from my brain, I finally considered the reality of what was coming and grew anxious. It was time for the culmination of the three years of blood, sweat, and tears I'd shed preparing for my client's case. It was the first test of my fledgling law firm. And success in this courtroom could serve to reinforce what I knew deep down: that a woman could compete with men in a high-stakes, high-profile arena and win.

"Jurors, have you rendered your verdict?" the judge asked, jolting me out of my contemplation.

"We have, your honor," Shades stood and said. He'd been elected jury foreman. Surprisingly, the man who had worn his sunglasses during the entire trial, who I couldn't even tell was paying attention, had been chosen as the head juror. I wasn't sure what to make of that.

The bailiff took the signed verdict from him, carried it over to the bench and handed it to the judge. Swanson turned the pages one by one. Part of a judge's job is to read the verdict first to ensure that it makes sense and that jurors followed the instructions. He flipped the pages faster as he read. I wondered if he was unhappy with the result. He turned the verdict over and flipped through it again, more quickly this time. Yep, I was pretty sure he didn't like what it said.

That was the moment I knew we'd won. All the same, I stood there holding my breath, waiting for Swanson to read the verdict aloud. He asked the parties to rise as he announced the answers to each of the questions.

Question 1, which asked if DBR breached the agreements by failing to notify Mesa of the additional areas they'd acquired: "yes."

Mike was standing next to me, and I lightly tapped his forearm in a small, silent act of mutual celebration.

Question 2, which asked if J. Cleo acted with willful misconduct or gross negligence: "yes."

The lawyers for J. Cleo had insisted on including that question, hoping that Swanson would never submit the issue to the jury because it is so difficult to prove. Juries almost never answer yes to a question like that, and their refusal to do so insulates the defendant from liability. But if the jury does answer yes, that defendant is likely in trouble on damages. Gross negligence means the jury didn't like what went on.

Swanson worked his way down the list, eventually coming to what we were all waiting for—the damages.

Question 7, which asked how much DBR owed Mesa for breaching the Participation Agreement: "$117,485,615." The precise number I'd told them.

Question 8, which asked how much DBR and J. Cleo owed Mesa for breaching the operating agreement: "$6,117,506," repeated four times.

They'd written down the numbers exactly as I had asked them to, and they had given us every dollar I'd asked for, even though they'd been allowed to keep their notes for only five minutes. They must have made up their minds quickly. They'd had only minutes to transcribe those numbers into the official version of the questionnaire before the bailiff had snatched their notes up.

And, to put the cherry on the top of the sundae, the verdict was unanimous.

Adding all the damages together, and factoring in our attorney's fees and interest, we'd just won a verdict of more than $164 million. It was the biggest verdict in the history of Reeves County, the oil capital of the world.

When we were allowed to leave, I called Pickens on his cell phone. Jay Rosser, who'd been sitting in the courtroom, had already told him the news. Pickens was happy and proud—and relieved. "Chrysta, I knew you'd do it! You did an amazing job!" He repeated this several times. I was happy and grateful to hear it each time he did. He also asked me several times when they'd have to pay the money. Each time, I repeated how the judge would enter judgment, that there would be appeals, and that the money would only come after all of that had been determined. As if I hadn't spoken, he'd repeat the same question.

Despite our mutual joy at the verdict, something about him was definitely off, changed, different. It showed through even in the midst of his enthusiasm, and it worried me.

We hung up after I wished him a Happy Thanksgiving. I was relieved that he was under watchful eyes with his family at his ranch. Judge Swanson had been right. Pickens indeed wasn't well that day in the courtroom, and eventually the doctors would determine that he'd had a mild stroke. He'd insisted on being present for most of the testimony, even though he'd been ill. He was heavily invested in this case. He'd spent millions on legal and expert fees, of course, but he was also invested to the core of his being. This was the biggest oil and gas play of his life. It was a big deal that capped a lifetime of big deals, and he'd been determined to be there.

A few weeks later, we held a post-trial dinner celebration for the lawyers. Mike and his wife, Barbara Lynn, the presiding federal judge in North Texas, hosted the gathering at the Tower Club atop one of the high-rise buildings in downtown Dallas. All of the lawyers attended with our spouses. As we ate, we toasted our successes but also relived the odd and wonderful moments during trial. Mike and Barbara gave me an expensive watch to commemorate the occasion. Debbie and Dee Janice, Mike's paralegal, put together a memento booklet of Dee's photos from our time in Pecos and a song that Debbie had secretly composed during our darkest moments. She'd called it "The Ballad of the Red Bull." It was meant to be sung to the tune of Marty Robbins' "El Paso," the city where the appeals court over Reeves County sits. It began:

> *Out in the West Texas town of El Paso*
> *I sent my case to be heard on appeal*
> *Judge Swanson in Pecos, he treated me badly*
> *I needed relief from the Court of Appeals.*

I never knew that the team had been so discouraged that Debbie had written a ballad about our inevitable loss. I was thankful for my ignorance because it would have angered me during trial. Fortunately, Debbie's fears were unfounded, and we could all laugh about it now.

A case isn't over when the jury renders a verdict. The judge must still enter judgment based on that verdict. Sometimes, that can take a few weeks or months, because the losing parties will file motions to complain about the result. Not surprisingly, that happened in this case. Baytech, DBR, and J. Cleo reiterated the same challenges to the damages that they had litigated during the trial. J. Cleo argued that it hadn't been grossly negligent, nor had it acted with intentional misconduct, and that it should be let out of the case entirely.

One year later, Swanson finally entered the judgment, but not before we had to go to the state appeals court in El Paso and ask the justices to force his hand. The appeals court ruled that Swanson had had more than enough time to enter the judgment and told him to get it done. He finally did, in December 2017. At this point it had been more than a year since we'd first holed up in Pecos.

Swanson let J. Cleo off the hook, and I still don't understand why. I know the arguments it made, hundreds of pages of them, but I don't know which ones the judge found persuasive. Baytech and DBR, however, still owed us about $136 million plus interest, the amount of the verdict that was left after J. Cleo's share was removed.

During the time that passed as we waited for Swanson to enter the judgment, a tragedy befell our team. Ricardo Garza had been working with a hired hand on his weekend property, clearing brush. The man had been using a Bobcat with giant swirling blades attached to the front to cut brush and small trees. Somehow, the man struck Ricardo with the blades, severing his right leg. He was airlifted to a Houston hospital and died about five hours later. He left behind his wife of four decades, two sons, and nine grandchildren. I had the honor to speak at his memorial service, which was packed with his loved ones, friends and colleagues. I still miss him, and I think of him and his wonderful homemade demonstrations every time I need to discuss a petroleum engineering issue.

A few months after the judgment was entered, we mediated the Red Bull case again. We had set up the mediation before the judge entered the judgment, and even after it was entered, everyone seemed eager to settle rather than endure years of appeals. The defendants seemed more in the mediating mood than when Montgomery had come to the Swiss Chalet during the trial. Even Bracken, on behalf of J. Cleo, seemed willing to settle. This time the parties took two days to mediate, and Mesa reached an agreement with the defendants to settle it all.[1]

I felt like we were holding most of the cards at the mediation exept for the most critical one: after the stroke he suffered during the trial, Pickens' health began to falter. He had several more strokes, and then what he would describe to me as a "Texas-sized fall" in which he hit his head. I knew that even though we'd prevailed in Pecos, the cycle would continue with appeals that stretched through the Texas Supreme Court. This would undoubtedly take years more and Pickens wouldn't live to see the end. The monkey had given him a good show, but it was time to put the case to rest.

We settled for a confidential amount, and most of the team was satisfied. Two of us weren't: Pickens and me. I saw him regularly after that, heading up to his office about once a month for lunch. Every time I did, he asked me if he'd done the right thing. He wondered if he should have appealed the rulings we disagreed with and litigated another trial again after the appeal sorted out the legal points. But in the end, I assured him he'd made the right choice. I believed in my heart that he had. I didn't tell him that I feared he wouldn't live to see a retrial, but I suspected he knew my thoughts. He talked a lot, more than I ever remember, of how he was in the "fourth quarter" of his life. He'd mostly recovered from the stroke, but it served to remind him of his own mortality.

For my part, I wanted to take the case to the Supreme Court to get the law straightened out, to set the record straight on how companies are supposed to treat investors in oil and gas deals like these. I may never get that chance. Cases like the Red Bull just don't come along that often. Nor do clients like T. Boone Pickens.

Chapter 28

"SHOW UP EARLY. WORK HARD. STAY LATE."

Despite his continuing health struggles, Pickens was in high spirits on his ninetieth birthday in May 2018. Held at the ritzy Dallas Country Club, with one of the largest brunch spreads I've ever seen, some five hundred luminaries and dignitaries of all sorts surrounded him. He sat at the center of it all, the brightest sun in a galaxy of admiration. Everyone wore Oklahoma State's signature orange color in his honor. My husband, John, came with me, and every few minutes he'd lean over and whisper, "there's Roger Staubach," "there's Mayor Ron Kirk," "there's Ed 'Too Tall' Jones," "there's Walt Garrison."

Jay Rosser had arranged a video presentation in which celebrities and fellow businessmen wished Pickens well from afar—media mogul Ted Turner, football coach Barry Switzer, fellow corporate raider Carl Icahn, actor Burt Reynolds, investor Warren Buffett, and singer Garth Brooks. All appeared on the giant video screen, sending their regards. The Oklahoma State cheerleaders and dozens of the marching band members showed up in person in full uniform, playing "Ride 'Em Cowboys," the

OSU fight song. Even two of Pickens' five ex-wives—he and Toni had divorced by then—attended.

Pickens loved every minute. At one point, feeling euphoric, he declared that he'd live to be a hundred. In that moment, we all believed him, or at least we wanted to.

Six months later, I was tipped off to a mysterious pleading that J. Cleo's lawyers had filed earlier in the year. I don't even recall how I found it, but I think I'd been searching online records for other information. It alleged that Chief Financial Officer Paul Rudnicki and Chief Operating Officer Frank Peterman had breached their fiduciary duties as executives of J. Cleo.

According to the pleading, Rudnicki and Peterman had told Jimmy Thompson's widow and daughters during our trial that they might "lose everything" as a result of Pickens' suit against J. Cleo. According to the filing, they'd convinced the heirs to distribute to them $100 million each from J. Cleo's coffers, claiming the payments would secure their help in the Mesa litigation and put J. Cleo's assets beyond Pickens' reach.

In response, Rudnicki and Peterman filed an affidavit attaching emails from the J. Cleo lawyers about the advice that Bracken and McConn had given during the trial. It showed that the lawyers believed that even as the trial was proceeding, the judge would soon pour Mesa out of court and that their worst outcome would be a mere $5 million. They filed the materials to countermand the "you might lose everything" contention that J. Cleo was now asserting.

When we received the verdict in November 2016, I remember looking over at the defense counsel and their clients, seeing the shocked expressions on their faces. I knew they had never seen coming the train that hit them. These new emails from the lawyers confirmed that they hadn't.

J. Cleo later settled its suit with Peterman, the pugnacious COO. But in October 2019 the company filed a new pleading that accused Rudnicki of extorting "outlandish" bonuses from the company. Rudnicki said the payments were justified because he sold Red Bull assets the weekend before the Mesa trial started, generating about a billion dollars for the company. According to Rudnicki, J. Cleo sold its portion of the Red Bull assets just as we had started the trial so that Pickens couldn't reclaim his 15 percent even if we won.

The case between J. Cleo and Rudnicki is still pending as of this writing.

I saw Pickens for the last time on August 23, 2019. Every month or so, I'd go to BP Capital for lunch to catch up with him and some of his longtime associates. Jay Rosser, Ron Bassett, and Dick Grant were usually around. I always brought dessert. Despite his stringent health regimen, Pickens had a sweet tooth, and he loved it when I'd bring chocolate covered strawberries, Sprinkles cupcakes, or an assortment of cookies. I regret that I never baked him a peach pie or cobbler, which were his favorites.

Pickens' health continued to decline. He replaced his physical fitness routines with physical therapy to help him regain his balance and speech that the strokes had compromised. He worked with speech and occupational therapists with the same determination with which he'd attacked everything else in his life. I could tell his mind was still sharp, but he couldn't always articulate his thoughts, which frustrated him.

Gradually, he regained most of his capabilities. But an overall decline was clearly taking hold. Even so, he celebrated the small victories for which he fought so hard.

During my last visit, I showed up with cupcakes and greeted him as he came into the huge conference room that was the centerpiece of BP Capital's offices. He'd officially closed the hedge fund by then and claimed to be retired, but the bank of monitors that covered the entire front of the room—probably thirty feet or more of TVs—still flickered with live feeds of CNBC news coverage and screens from Bloomberg terminals depicting real-time market data.

Pickens had presided as the general in this war room since he'd set up the company in the late 1990s. Former presidents, athletes, political candidates, and celebrities had at various times pulled up one of the twenty-two leather armchairs that ringed the twenty-four-foot inlaid wooden table. Pickens still ate lunch there most days while discussing the latest market developments with his traders. By then, many had started their own funds, but still gathered faithfully around the massive central table to share their thoughts with the man who'd given them their start.

Pickens walked in, relying more than he had a year ago on his walker, but still upright and capable of standing without it. At first, he looked at me with confusion, not recognizing me, but then broke into a big smile when he remembered I was his lawyer and we had won the big battle together. I leaned in for him to kiss me on the cheek and gave him a hug. As the end of his life drew closer, he had become affectionate in ways he hadn't been before we won the trial.

We sat down to talk. As usual, he wanted to recap the highlights of the trial. He struggled to join the conversation. He couldn't run through his geological monologue anymore. There'd be no emphatic "swoosh" as he talked about being cut out of the Red Bull. But he followed what we were saying with as much interest as ever, and he delighted in listening as we reminisced about our days in the Pecos courthouse. He wanted to discuss, as he always did, whether I thought he should have settled. I assured him once again that he'd done the right thing. I told him that the prospects of getting more out of the court of appeals or the Texas Supreme Court without retrying the case were slim. Left unspoken was the fact that he was not physically able to give the key testimony in such a trial. Besides, he knew as well as I did that at ninety-one, he was unlikely to see the outcome.

Pickens had lunch brought in for the entire office every day. Sally, his longtime assistant, made him a small plate of food and tried to get him to eat it. He mostly refused. He picked at it a bit before focusing on his favorite strawberry cupcake, which he ate with gusto. I surmised that most of his nutrition was coming from sugar by then. So be it. If I live to ninety-one, I'm damn well going to eat what I want when I get there.

We debated a few political issues for Pickens' benefit. Even though he couldn't really express the thoughts he wanted to say, he enjoyed listening. Ron and Jay took up the conservative mantle (which came naturally for them), debating me and my liberal leanings. I informed Pickens that I was considering a run for a seat on the Texas Railroad Commission, which regulates the state's oil and gas industry (and has nothing to do with railroads). Pickens gave me a wide smile.

"Well, Chrysta," he said, "it's just a short step from there to the presidency!"

I asked him if he'd vote for me for president, reminding him I was a Democrat. He said he just might.

"Now hold on there," Jay good-naturedly interjected. He was ever mindful of Pickens' conservative legacy. I still wonder what Pickens would have done. I'd like to think that maybe, just maybe, he would have gone through with voting for me.

He told us he had an early afternoon doctor's appointment, then made a show of standing up by himself. I complimented him on the effort, and he smiled in appreciation. I gave him a goodbye hug, and he stared at me, then turned and looked at each of the other men in the room.

"I love you all, and I am leaving," he said.

He didn't clarify, forcing us to ponder whether he meant the room, or this life.

As he turned his back to head out, assisted by his walker and his therapist, tears welled in my eyes. It was the first and only time that had happened since I'd known him. I could see the end was drawing near, and I was saddened at the prospect of his passing. I'd never once cried at the possibility of losing the case, or even that he might fire me over one of our heated disagreements. But the thought of losing such a legendary figure, whom I'd come to understand and admire as a friend, was heartbreaking.

For those who didn't know him, Pickens might always be the tough-talking corporate raider, the hardscrabble businessman who didn't suffer fools and who appeared to care about money above all else, but that wasn't the man I knew. By the time we worked together, he had grown closer to his family, his temperament had mellowed, and his generosity had blossomed.

I'd like to think that in his final years, he'd come to understand what really mattered in life. He certainly made me take stock of my own. He was part of the reason I decided to run for public office again in 2020. I don't have billions to give away, but I have found that I can be generous with my experience and desire to make my state a better place.

On Wednesday, September 11, 2019, I was giving a lunchtime presentation at the Dallas Bar Association to a group of paralegals about oil and gas litigation. I always used the Pickens case as an example, because it had some useful lessons and the Pickens name captures people's attention. As I completed my presentation and sat down, my phone flashed an alert from the Dallas Morning News.

"T. Boone Pickens, Legendary Oil Man, Dead at 91."

I froze. While I had anticipated Pickens' death in an inchoate kind of way, I had not prepared myself for the actual moment. I was surprised by the intensity of the grief that washed over me. Right there, sitting on the dais in front of a room full of strangers, I started crying. I can't image what the audience must have thought. My co-presenter finished her talk, oblivious to my tears, but when she ended, I told the audience what had happened.

I left immediately and called Sally and Jay to find out the details of his final moments. He had gone to the ranch the weekend before, seeing his beloved Mesa Vista one final time. He'd returned to his Dallas home Sunday evening and went to bed. The next morning, he woke up unable to stand or to communicate. The T. Boone Pickens everyone knew was already gone. He'd lingered for another day and died the following morning.

I have no doubt that he chose the day that the Twin Towers fell, a day that we mourn as a nation, to leave us.

I was one of about eight hundred people invited to the private ceremony preceding his burial. It was held on a still-hot Texas day at Highland Park United Methodist on the campus of Southern Methodist University. I sat next to my co-author, whom I'd first met a year and a half earlier, during the tour of Pickens' ranch. I brought Debbie Eberts as my guest. She'd spent a lot of time with Pickens, too. The three of us sat together in the middle of the chapel.

While he wasn't particularly religious during most of his life, Pickens had become a Methodist after the trial. According to the pastor who eulogized him, he and Pickens had spent a lot of time together in the months prior to his death. I was glad to hear it and hoped that it had given Pickens some comfort as he faced the ultimate battle.

Pickens' best friend, Alan White, gave a eulogy as well. He focused on the personal details of his friendship with Pickens and some humorous incidents during his life and corny jokes that Pickens would tell. He also took time to proudly expound on how Pickens had helped change the arc of history in his support of the "Swift Boat" campaign that attempted to impugn John Kerry's military record and undermine his presidential candidacy in 2006. I grimaced. I was uncomfortable with that part of Pickens' legacy, and I hoped that reports that he had regretted it later in life were true, despite White's praise.

Jerry Jones, owner of the Dallas Cowboys spoke next. He talked about how he and Pickens had become good friends over the years. Pickens had been one of the first to welcome Jones to Dallas when Jones bought the team in 1989. Jones wasn't particularly well-liked around town at the time because his first decision as owner was to fire legendary (and beloved) head coach Tom Landry. Apparently, Pickens was friendly to Jones nonetheless, and advised him on handling the press. I remembered listening to Jones in 1989, recalling how inexperienced he had been talking to the sports writers who excoriated him. I thought that Jones had come a long way as a public speaker in thirty years.

Jones recounted his days playing for the Arkansas Razorbacks under Frank Broyles, who taught him be a "fourth quarter player."

"In the first quarter, you're ready to go. Your uniform is clean, you're energetic and ready to play your best. By the second quarter, you're still in there fighting, but you've got some mud on your jersey and you've taken a few hits. Then you go into the locker room for halftime. In the third quarter, maybe that rest and pep talk have helped you a little bit, but you are pretty fatigued and banged up. But just wait until that fourth quarter. That fourth quarter is when a player really proves his worth. You're beat up, you're exhausted, you're mentally fatigued. It is the fourth quarter player who can get past all of that and win the game. Boone was a fourth quarter player in life. He gave it his all until the last."

I'd given one of the eulogies at Ricardo Garza's funeral and recall being surprised at how all five speakers had echoed the same themes about Garza's life. I guess that in the end, the truth about a person wins out, because everyone seemed to come to the same conclusion. Jones and I had seen Pickens the same way. Many other people in the chapel that day probably did too.

Pickens had entered the fourth quarter battered and bloodied from a lifetime of winning and losing. But he fought on. At his last trial, seated next to me for a month in Pecos, he continued to fight. And won. Until the final seconds ticked away and lights finally went down, he fought in the fourth quarter as hard as he had in the first.

I will never forget my trial for T. Boone Pickens. Some days, particularly as I write this, I find it hard to believe it all really happened. There were so many funny, absurd, meaningful, and powerful moments during what is likely to have been the biggest trial of my life—and his. After all is said and done, I'm left with this: I was lucky to be in the orbit of a man who was simple enough to enjoy a Dairy Queen Blizzard and complex enough to foresee the future of energy, a man who was complicated and imperfect and vulnerable and human.

EPILOGUE

My years immersed in the last trial of T. Boone Pickens left an indelible imprint on me—and not in the way many people might suspect. Sure, I was pleased with the outcome. And sure, I treasured getting to know one of the energy industry's larger-than-life personalities. But having spent so much time with Pickens digging deep into the dynamics of oil, gas, finance, politics, and the law, I'd gained a unique perspective. It would be a shame to leave that knowledge on the table, to use the metaphor Pickens applied to his own goal of never letting profits go unrealized, either in his personal deals or in those he undertook on behalf of shareholders.

The Texas Democratic Party had been recruiting me for the last couple of election cycles to run for the Texas Railroad Commission. Despite its name, the agency regulates the oil and gas industry in the state and has nothing to do with trains. I'd always had a business reason that led me to say no. But driven by the critical need to address environmental concerns and possessing the expertise to help change things, I decided to throw my hat in the ring.

By December 2019, three months after Pickens' passing, I was actively campaigning for the Democratic nomination on an environmental platform. I made my decision in the summer of 2019 after attending a forum hosted by Bloomberg New Energy Finance. Alex Szewczyk, the Pickens' aide who'd kept tabs on the Red Bull project, invited me to the presentation. Of course, we made time to catch up. Alex had left BP Capital to start a hedge fund, BP Energy Partners, which was also named in Pickens' honor. The fund invests in Mesa Power Solutions— the Mesa name persists—a company that manufactures natural gas generators. The generators turn natural gas that would otherwise be flared from Permian Basin oil wells into electricity right at the well site. This electricity can power the extraction operations, with any excess going into the utility grid.

Many oil wells, especially in the Permian, produce natural gas as a byproduct. Vast quantities of it go unused because there aren't enough pipelines to take it away, let alone at prices that make it worth the trouble. Oil companies find it cheaper to simply set this excess gas ablaze. It's called flaring.

The seminar featured a nighttime satellite image of the Permian. The entire region, much of it among the most sparsely populated in the nation, was lit up like the urban expanse of the Eastern Seaboard. A place that just a few years ago was one of the darkest on earth is now awash in the light from thousands of flames as natural gas is burned away—literally just wasted.

I did a little research and found that the amount of natural gas flared in the Permian in 2018 could have powered Houston—the fourth-largest city in the country—if it had been converted to electricity. Eliminating that flaring would have the same environmental impact as removing almost a million cars from the road. The more I thought about the scale of the waste and the environmental harm, the more determined I became to do something about it. It seems insane that we spend billions of dollars getting fossil fuel from the ground, only to light it on fire.

I'd learned decades ago in law school that the Railroad Commission's first responsibility is to prevent the waste of natural resources. It's written into the state constitution. I also knew that the law allows flaring for only ten days after a well is put into production. After that, operators need an exception permit from the Commission, which has been handing out the permits like Tic-Tacs. I decided to run to correct the issue. With a seat on the Commission, I could work to improve an industry I know well in the state that I love.

I came to realize that the Railroad Commission race is one of the most important—and most overlooked—environmental contests in the country. It sets the policies for energy production and safety in the biggest energy-producing state in the nation. If we're going to find a sustainable solution to supplying power, Texas is where it needs to happen.

Pickens was ahead of the curve on this matter. He had lobbied for his "Pickens Plan" in the mid-2000s, trying unsuccessfully to convince U.S. presidents and other elected officials that it was a blueprint to make the United States energy independent. He pushed for cleaner-burning liquefied natural gas to replace oil for powering heavy machinery, trucks, buses, trains, and other vehicles. (This, of course, also would have boosted the value of his investments in natural gas-related businesses.) The plan, and the social media marketing behind it, turned Pickens into an unlikely environmentalist late in life.

The industry has now about caught up to where Pickens was ten or fifteen years ago. While I never heard him talk about climate change, he was nonetheless moving towards solutions to address the dire forces afflicting our planet. He advocated adopting more wind power as early as 2008 and had proposed a billion-dollar wind farm on his Panhandle ranch. Wind, he argued, would reduce the use of coal, which at the time was the biggest source for generating electricity. (Today, because of fracking, we generate more electricity from natural gas.) In December 2019, the National Petroleum Council acknowledged for the first time that climate change is real, that human activities cause it, and that combatting it must be considered as a part of national and global energy strategies.

Another of Pickens' legacies has gained the spotlight today. He championed shareholder value as far back as the 1980s. His efforts, albeit viewed by some as self-enriching, nonetheless encouraged the pro-business policy group, the Business Roundtable, to adopt his thinking, For four decades, the Roundtable and its CEO members embraced Pickens' philosophy. They recommended that companies view the goal of maximizing profits for investors as the North Star for all business decisions. Then, just a week before Pickens' death, those CEOs officially changed their position. Now they assert that shareholder value is just one factor that directors of public companies should consider when making business choices. Their change of focus frees up companies to look at environmental impact, social concerns, and other issues when making decisions.

Now, three years after the Pickens trial, I see the growing signs that attitudes are changing here in Texas. In December 2019, I went to Midland to campaign. Midland and its sister city, Odessa, don't have many Democratic voters, but the press interest in the race is huge. I was interviewed on TV, the radio, and in the Midland newspaper the same day that the Wildcatters Club was meeting at the Midland Petroleum Club. As the name implies, the Wildcatters celebrate the greatest risk-takers in the energy business, including Pickens. That day, the members were honoring the CEO of ExxonMobil, which at the time was the world's largest publicly traded oil company. Its headquarters, in the Dallas suburb of Irving, lie just a few miles from Pickens' BP Capital office.

ExxonMobil is notable because it has agreed to reduce its flaring and methane emissions worldwide. Most major exploration and production companies have done so, but the current Railroad Commissioners remain steadfastly against even recognizing that such a change is necessary.

I attended the Wildcatters meeting wearing my campaign badge. Introducing myself to the oil men (yes, almost all of them are still men), I announced I was running as a Democrat. I got a few curious looks, and then one attendee gave me a steely stare and asked, "What are you going to do about all this flaring?" He had been an operator in the Permian for decades, and he said he was sick of the pollution and waste. I told him about my plans for alternative solutions to help reduce flaring, and he gave me his business card to contact him again to discuss it.

I took this as a hopeful sign. Much has changed in the past few years, but only November 2020 will tell us exactly how much. Perhaps despite the political divisions nationally, results still matter at the local level. Maybe even in the Permian Basin, where oil continues to reshape the physical and social landscape, we can set aside our politics and work toward common goals that benefit the lives of everyone. After all, Pickens and I were able to see beyond our Republican and Democrat labels to achieve the outcome we desired. I'm reminded of one of his Booneisms:

> *If you never give up, if you push through the resistance and keep driving for what you want, you will ultimately achieve rewards beyond any you had hoped for.*

It worked once. Maybe it will again.

ACKNOWLEDGMENTS

CHRYSTA

I want to thank a thousand people for their help and support but will start with the top candidates. First, I thank T. Boone Pickens for his faith in me and my ability to win the case for him. As I describe in the book, this was not an obvious choice and took some courage. Most men of his vintage and stature would have picked a male partner at a major law firm for a billion-dollar case. I thank his team, Ron Bassett, Jay Rosser, Dick Grant, Sandy Campbell, Alex Szewczyk, Sally Geymuller, Brian Breedlove, and Rob Bartley, both for supporting Pickens' decisions about me and the case, and for providing evidentiary and emotional support along the way.

Of course, this would not have been possible without my trial team and I thank them profusely. In order of appearance: Debbie Eberts, Cathy Mallonee, Kara Guillot, David Coale, Mike Lynn, Bill Weinacht, Alva Alvarez, Andres Correa, Dee Janice, Jared Eisenberg, Pat Disbennett, Rodney Sowards, the late Ricardo Garza, and Robert Tobey. I also want to thank the appeals team, who came in after the verdict: Marla Broaddus, Hon. Craig Enoch, and Joe Hood. Thanks also to our jury consultants, Alison Richardson and Jason Bloom, and to Stewart Hoge and Leland de la Garza for their general advice and support.

I want to thank the dedicated staff of the 143rd Judicial District Court. First, the presiding judge, Hon. Michael Swanson, who was the most attentive trial judge before whom I have ever tried a case; Cathy Adams, retired court coordinator; and Breck Record, the court reporter who supervised a team of reporters providing excellent service during the trial, turning around each day's transcripts overnight. It is not easy for our overworked staff and judiciary in Texas to take on a case of this size.

Thank you to my husband, John, and my sons, Scott and Joe, who have always been there for me and have supported me and understood when I could not always be there for them. I always was with you in spirit, even when I could not be physically present. I thank my parents, Craig and Nina Stallwitz, and my siblings, Cathy Mallonee (and her husband Phil, who did not protest when I brought Cathy to live in Dallas and Pecos for nine months), Cheryl Pudwill, and David Stallwitz.

Thank you to a few of my colleagues and mentors: Ann Marie Painter, a confidant and fellow girl warrior since the 1990s; Mike Powell, who introduced me to Pickens and taught me everything I know about oil and gas law; Hon. David Godbey, who gave me my first "stand up" role; Robert Beatty, Certified Smart Person; and Jerry Clements, the woman head of Locke Lord, who famously said more women need to "get out here on the skinny branches with the rest of us." Amen.

Finally, thanks to Loren, my co-author, without whom this book would not have been possible. It was my story, but I would never have been able to produce this work without him.

LOREN

This book wouldn't have been possible without the dedication of my co-author. Lots of people say they want to do a book, but few have the determination and tenacity to see it through. The minute I saw the first few pages Chrysta wrote, I knew we had a good story, and I knew it needed to be told through her eyes. Other than her stubborn propensity for putting two spaces after every period, she has been a joy to work with.

Gail Connor Roche once again worked her editorial magic in getting the manuscript in shape. She has been protecting me from my own bad habits for more than twenty years, and I value her skills and her friendship.

Charles Glasser lent his careful legal eye to the manuscript, and Tamara Dever and Monica Thomas gave the entire project a look that was both bold and compelling.

I also want to thank the folks at Texas A&M University Press, especially Jay Dew, Kyle Littlefield, and Wynona McCormick, for their willingness to think outside the box and help get this book into readers' hands.

Last but never least, I must thank my wife Laura, who has tolerated this crazy dream of authorship—and now publishing—with patience, support, and good humor.

A NOTE ON SOURCES

All descriptions of the legal proceedings in this book are based on public records in the case of *Mesa Petroleum Partners LP v. Baytech LLC et al.,* Cause number 15-04-20996-CVR in the 143rd District Court in Reeves County, Texas.

Sources and additional comments for other subjects are as follows:

Chapter 2

(1)   T. Boone Pickens, *The First Billion is the Hardest*, (New York: Crown, 2008), 11.

(2)   "He's Half Wildcatter, Half Big Businessman," *BusinessWeek*, November 24, 1964.

(3)   T. Boone Pickens, interview with Loren Steffy, February 2016.

(4)   Pickens, *First Billion*, 23.

(5)   Pickens, *First Billion*, 25.

(6)   Daniel Yergin, *The Prize: The Epic Quest for Oil, Money and Power* (New York: Simon & Schuster, 1991), 742.

(7)   Connie Bruck, *The Predators' Ball*, (New York: Penguin, 1988), 11.

(8)   "How T. Boone Pickens Changed Corporate Finance in America," *The Economist*, September 21, 2019, 81.

(9)   Milken remains a controversial figure, and his activities were frequently under the scrutiny of the U.S. Securities and Exchange Commission. In 1989, a federal grand jury indicted him on 98 counts of racketeering and fraud (none of the charges related to Pickens' deals.) In 1990, Milken pleaded guilty to six counts of securities and tax violations, paid $200 million in fines and $400 million in restitution to investors. He was barred for life from further involvement in the securities industry. He served 22 months in prison. President Donald Trump pardoned him in February 2020.

(10) Pickens, *First Billion*, 37.

(11) Pickens, *First Billion*, 36.

(12) Michael Lewis, "Wall Street Helped Spur Internet Revolution," Bloomberg News in the *South Florida Sun Sentinel*, August 3, 1999, https://www.sun-sentinel.com/news/fl-xpm-1999-08-03-9908020668-story.html.

(13) Pickens, Steffy interview.

Chapter 4

(1)   He also named a town after her. Her niece, the socialite Electra Waggoner Biggs, inspired the names for a plane, the Lockheed L-188 Electra, and a car, the Buick Electra.

Chapter 6

(1)   U.S. Securities and Exchange Commission, "Oil and Gas Modernization," https://www.sec.gov/info/smallbus/secg/oilgasreporting-secg.htm.

Chapter 8

(1)   John M. Swanson, Ballotpedia, https://ballotpedia.org/John_M._Swanson.

Chapter 13

(1)   T. Boone Pickens, Jr., *Boone* (Boston: Houghton Mifflin Company, 1987), 276.

Chapter 20

(1)   The details of the settlement talks are confidential.

Chapter 26

(1)   The final terms remain confidential.

INDEX

A

Abbott, Greg, 93, 205
Accenture, 23
Alvarez, Alva, 108–11, 113–14,
   120, 133, 137–38, 141
Amarillo, Texas, 23, 28, 91, 180
Amazon, 30
AMI (area of mutual interest
   agreement), 89–90
Andrews Kurth, 58
Arthur Andersen Consulting, 23,
   41
Astaire, Fred, 114

B

Bakken Shale, 221
Balmorhea, Texas, 240
Barnett Shale, 48
Bassett, Ron, 86, 110, 167, 188,
   190, 281, 283
Batchelder, David, 31
Baytech, 53, 55–58, 60–61, 63–67,
   70–72, 74, 79, 81, 82, 86, 88, 94,
   140–42, 156, 183–84, 195, 223,
   246–49, 276. *See also specific*
   individuals
Bean, Judge Roy, 107

Beech Aircraft, 37
Best Western Swiss Chalet, 3–5,
   10, 103, 105, 111, 117, 186, 206,
   240
Bezos, Jeff, 30
Big Bend National Park, 99–102,
   241
Booneisms, 49, 207, 293
BP Capital, 20, 32, 73, 196, 197,
   281–82, 290
BP Energy Partners, 290
Bracken, Geoff, 74, 76–78, 87,
   156–57, 176, 178, 199–201,
   231–33, 260–61, 268, 277, 280
Bridges, Jeff, 251
Brooks, Garth, 279
Broyles, Frank, 286
Brunswick Group, 47–48
Buffett, Warren, 279
Burleson, Texas, 53
Bush, George W., 19, 85
Business Roundtable, 292

C

Campbell, Sandy, 48–52, 54–55,
   57, 59, 60, 63, 84, 117, 198–99,
   244

Castañeda, Chrysta: at Arthur
  Andersen Consulting, 23, 41;
  childhood of, 37–38; closing
  argument of, 261–68; college
  education of, 23, 38–40;
  congressional campaign of,
  45–47; at EDS, 40–41; in law
  school, 41–42; legal career of,
  42–45, 48–49; opening argument
  of, 145–52; personality of, 44;
  politics and, 186–91; at PR firm,
  47–48, 50; as runner, 99, 101–2;
  as skeet shooter, 21; Texas
  Railroad Commission campaign
  of, 283, 289–93. *See also* The
  Castañeda Firm
The Castañeda Firm: founding of,
  50; staff of, 61, 83, 87–89
Chesapeake Energy, 48–49
Chevron, 27
Cities Service Co., 26–27
Clinton, Hillary, 166, 186–87,
  189–93
Coale, David, 87–89, 120, 148, 227
Colt well, 66–67, 88–89, 144, 147,
  150, 178, 181–83, 194, 220–21,
  231–34, 246
ConocoPhillips, 41
Correa, Andres, 137–44, 152, 209–
  10, 228, 252, 254, 258
Costner, Kevin, 123
Crosby, Bing, 20

D

Daisy Bradford #3, 56
Dallas, Texas, 40, 91, 286
Dallas Cowboys, 286
Dead Man Statute, 99
Delaware Basin, 8, 57, 66, 88, 174,
  182
Delaware Basin Resources (DBR),
  80–82, 86, 94, 144, 149, 202–3,
  216, 217, 246, 249, 273–74, 276.
  See also specific individuals
Delta Air Lines, 40

Diamond Shamrock, 28
Dole, Bob, 33

E

Eagle Ford Shale, 221
Eberts, Debbie, 62, 74, 83, 87, 89,
  140, 165, 191–92, 209, 227, 240,
  275–76, 285
Electronic Data Systems (EDS),
  40–41
Exhibit 53, 146–47, 168, 177, 183,
  213–15, 231, 233–34, 246
ExxonMobil, 292–93

F

Fortenberry, Tim, 47
Fort Worth, Texas, 40, 44, 46, 56
Foster, Jodie, 154

G

Gage Hotel, 102
Garden City, Kansas, 24
Garrison, Walt, 279
Garza, Ricardo, 88, 121, 125–27,
  150, 177, 178, 188, 203–4, 212–
  22, 235–40, 250–51, 276–77, 287
General Dynamics, 40
Geymuller, Sally, 49–50, 162, 285
Ghawar Field, 4
Godbey, David, 42
Gore, Wayman, 236–39, 256, 260
Grant, Dick, 77, 200, 281
Gray, Zane, 102
Guillot, Kara, 89, 240
Gulf Oil, 14, 27, 28, 30

H

Halbouty, Michel, 24
Hall, Russell K., 216–19
Hardin Simmons lease, 147
Harvard University, 38, 39, 42, 47,
  109
Hawker Beechcraft, 37
Hedrick, Mike, 63–67, 81, 140,
  142, 143, 162, 209, 256

Hodges, Rick, 74
Holdenville, Oklahoma, 17, 22
Hollimon, Stuart, 58, 74, 131, 160,
  237, 242–43, 259–60
Houston, Texas, 36
Hugoton Field, 24
Hugoton Production Company,
  24–27

I

Icahn, Carl, 279

J

Janice, Dee, 111, 275
J. Cleo Thompson, 53–56, 60–61,
  63–67, 69–72, 74, 79, 82, 86, 88,
  94, 121, 139, 140–43, 156, 184,
  195–200, 208, 230, 246, 249,
  273–74, 276, 280–81. *See also*
  specific individuals
Jersey Lilly saloon, 107
Jones, Ed "Too Tall," 279
Jones, Jerry, 286–87
Jones Day Reavis & Pogue, 62

K

Kansas State, 38, 39–40, 119
Kerry, John, 33, 286
Kirk, Ron, 279

L

La Escalera sections, 147, 178, 231,
  233–34, 246
Landry, Tom, 286
Lewis, Michael, 30–31
Lloyd lease, 147
Lyda well, 56, 57, 64–66, 81–82,
  88, 141, 147, 155, 162, 174, 177,
  183, 198, 209, 220, 231–32, 247
Lynn, Barbara, 275
Lynn, Mike, 10, 12–14, 87, 110,
  113, 120, 137–39, 153, 158–59,
  161–65, 168, 184, 189, 192, 206,
  223, 224, 227, 230, 242, 243,
  245, 252, 254, 255–57, 260–61,
  269, 273, 275
Lynn Pinker Cox & Hurst, 13

M

Mallonee, Cathy, 88–89, 106, 117,
  191, 221, 233, 235, 240, 250,
  254
Marathon, Texas, 99–102, 104
Massachusetts Institute of
  Technology, 39
McCain, John, 33
McConn, Tim, 74, 77, 78, 85, 154–
  56, 193–99, 218, 258–59, 280
Mentone, Texas, 92
Mesa Petroleum, 24–29, 31, 36, 41
Mesa Petroleum Partners, 8, 10,
  23, 52, 54–60, 64–67, 70–72,
  74, 81–82, 121, 140–43, 147–48,
  162–63, 183, 195, 198–200,
  209, 223, 246–49, 262–63, 273–
  74. *See also specific individuals*
Mesa Power Solutions, 290
Mesa Vista Ranch, 11, 17–22, 25,
  33–34, 91, 213, 285
Midland, Texas, 62, 97–98, 292
Midland Basin, 174
Milford, Cliff, 64–67, 69–72, 74,
  82, 98, 124, 143, 208, 223–24,
  230, 235, 257, 260
Milken, Michael, 27–28
Molonson, William, 18
Monahans, Texas, 92, 93, 97
Montgomery, Rick, 55, 57–59,
  62–63, 74, 82, 123, 159, 162,
  168, 205–7, 243–48, 277

N

National Petroleum Council, 292
Northwest Airlines, 40–41
Notre Dame, 38

O

Obama, Barack, 11
Occidental Petroleum Corp., 27
Odessa, Texas, 292

Oklahoma State (Oklahoma
A&M), 19, 22, 111, 180, 279–80

P

Painter, Ann Marie, 85–86
Parks, Bob, 93
Peck, Gregory, 251
Pecos, Texas, 3–4, 52–53, 92–93,
103–5, 107–9, 117, 122, 149,
153
Pecos River, 107
Pence, Mike, 86
Pennzoil, 185
Permian Basin, 4, 5, 8, 32, 36, 62,
63, 149, 150, 174, 216, 218, 290,
293. *See also* Delaware Basin;
Midland Basin
Pesci, Joe, 182, 234
Peterman, Frank, 210–11, 280–81
Petroleum Exploration Inc. (PEI),
24
Phillips Petroleum, 18, 23, 28, 180,
257
Pickens, T. Boone: air travel
by, 91; appearance of, 11;
autobiography of, 23, 26, 180;
birth of, 18, 180; as celebrity,
5, 110–11, 117, 145; childhood
of, 17–18, 22, 180; children of,
16, 34; college education of,
22, 180; as corporate raider,
21, 24–29, 34; courtroom
behavior of, 160–61; cross-
examination of, 193–201; death
of, 34, 284–87; deposition
of, 73, 74–79, 85, 111, 161;
as environmentalist, 291–92;
expressions (Booneisms) of, 49,
207, 293; geological knowledge
of, 11–12, 121–22, 124, 179–80;
health issues of, 18–19, 74,
146, 240, 275, 277, 281–84;
legal system and, 35, 79, 84;
mathematical ability of, 25–26;
mistakes of, 76–77; natural gas

and, 31–33, 36, 77; net worth
of, 179, 184, 197, 200; ninetieth
birthday of, 279–80; oil and,
35–36; personality of, 6–7, 12,
13, 21–22, 78, 91, 153, 160–61,
166–67, 284, 287; philanthropy
of, 35, 49, 184–85; at Phillips
Petroleum, 23, 180, 257;
physical fitness of, 11; politics
and, 33, 166, 188–90, 205, 283,
286; prepping, 111–15; publicity
and, 49, 112; shareholder
activism and, 28, 29–30, 292;
testimony of, 126–27, 172–85;
wives of, 20, 32, 85–86, 280;
women and, 84–86; work ethic
of, 103
Pickens Plan, 33, 49, 188, 291
Pioneer Natural Resources, 32
Putin, Vladimir, 88

R

Rainwater, Richard, 31
Raytheon, 37
Reagan, Nancy, 20
Reagan, Ronald, 20
Record, Breck, 92
Red Bull case: basis for lawsuit, 55,
58, 60–68; closing arguments in,
249–69; damage claims in, 202–
5, 212–22, 224–28, 236–39, 258,
267–68, 274; defense witnesses
in, 229–48; depositions for,
69–82; expert witnesses in,
120–22, 124–27, 203, 212–22,
224–26, 228; first day of trial
for, 116–23; guidances in, 124–
27, 214–15; judgment entered
in, 276; jury instructions for,
268; jury selection for, 108–11,
128–35; mock trial for, 136–37;
opening arguments in, 137–52,
154–57; prepping Pickens for,
111–15; pretrial hearings of,
97–100, 104, 119; settlement